EXPECTATIONS
ABOUT GOD
AND MESSIAH

PATRICK PRILL

Yeshua
Publishing

NEW PROVIDENCE, NJ

CONTENTS

1

Why Did God Call Abram?

About 4,000 years ago, a man named Abram and his family traveled from their home in Ur of the Chaldees to settle in the land of Canaan. We don't know exactly what prompted their decision to leave the well-watered delta region of the Tigris and Euphrates Rivers. Some think that it was to escape invading Western Semitic tribes.[1] But we do know that the sojourners didn't reach the Mediterranean or the fertile valleys and arid hills of Canaan. Instead, they settled halfway there in the city of Haran.

Haran was a prosperous city located about 600 miles northwest of Ur in modern-day Turkey. It was situated on a caravan route that connected Asia to Mediterranean ports and to Africa. The city had some cultural similarities to Ur and shared a common religion. Like the people of Ur, the residents of Haran worshipped the moon god, Sin. Perhaps it was weariness from their journey, the attractive economic prospects that Haran presented, cultural familiarity, or the moderate climate that caused the travelers to settle in Haran. But stay they did.

Abram seems to have thrived amidst the trade of this commercial city. He lived in Haran for several years with his wife, his father, and his nephew until he was old and wealthy. Then, at the age of seventy-five, his life changed forever.

It was then that the LORD God spoke to Abram. The Hebrew Scriptures record:

The LORD said to Abram,

"Go forth from your native land and from your father's house to the land I will show you. I will make of you a great nation, and I will bless you; I will make your name great, and you shall be a blessing. I will bless those who bless you and curse him that curses you; and all the families of the earth shall bless themselves through you."

Abram went forth as the LORD had commanded him, and Lot went with him. Abram was seventy-five years old when he left Haran. Abram took his wife Sarai and his brother's son Lot, and all the wealth that they had amassed, and the persons that they had acquired in Haran; and they set out for the land of Canaan. When they arrived in the land of Canaan, Abram passed through the land as far as the site of Shechem, at the terebinth of Moreh. The Canaanites were in the land.

The LORD appeared to Abram and said, "I will assign this land to your offspring."

And he built an altar there to the LORD who had appeared to him. From there he moved on to the hill country east of Bethel and pitched his tent, with Bethel on the west and Ai on the east; and built there an altar to the LORD and invoked the LORD by name.

—Genesis 12:1-8 (JPS)

Singled Out By God

Abram was evidently chosen by God from among all of the other people on earth. He was singled out and told to follow God to a land that God would yet show him. (The land turned out to be Canaan.) The Scriptures don't record the details of how Abram responded to God. We can only imagine. But, we do know that he did leave his comfortable life in Haran to follow God.

Why did God select Abram and establish a special relationship with him? Was there something unique about Abram? Was he a brilliant man? Was he ethically or morally superior to the people of his day? Had Abram achieved some special credentials that made God take notice of him? Of all the people alive at the time, why did God call out this one man named Abram?

These are good questions. However, there's one that's even more basic: *Why did God call anyone at all?*

WHY DID GOD CALL ANYONE?

Fortunately, we don't have to speculate long about why God called someone to follow Him. The Scriptures shed significant light on the question and Genesis and Exodus appear to provide the answer.

We find the first clue in the conversation that God had with Abram when He first called him. God said to Abram:

> *I will make of you a great nation, and I will bless you; I will make your name great, and you shall be a blessing. I will bless those who bless you and curse him that curses you; and all the families of the earth shall bless themselves through you.*

> —Genesis 12:2-3 (JPS)

God picked someone to bless so that he would, in turn, be a blessing to all of the people on earth. However, in order for Abram, or anyone else, to be a blessing to others, it was necessary for them to learn to *"keep the way of the LORD."*[2]

This is the second clue. Twenty-four years after He first called out Abram (and changed Abram's name to Abraham), God said:

> *Shall I hide from Abraham what I am about to do, since Abraham is to become a great and populous nation and*

all the earth are to bless themselves by him? For I have singled him out, that he may instruct his children and his posterity to keep the way of the LORD by doing what is just and right, in order that the LORD may bring about for Abraham what He has promised.

—Genesis 18:17-19 (JPS)

God singled out a person to learn and to then teach their descendants how to do what is *"just and right."* Keeping the *"way of the LORD"* was a predecessor to being a blessing to all of the people on earth.

Just how did God plan to use this person as a blessing and what kind of blessing did He want to provide to others through him? This didn't become fully evident until about 450 years later. It was then that Abram's descendants were preparing to enter Canaan, the land that God had promised to them:

Thus you shall say to the house of Jacob and declare to the children of Israel: 'You have seen what I did to the Egyptians, how I bore you on eagles' wings and brought you to Me. Now then, if you will obey Me faithfully and keep My covenant, you shall be My treasured possession among all the peoples. Indeed, all the earth is Mine, but you shall be to Me a kingdom of priests and a holy nation.

—Exodus 19:4-6 (JPS)

According to the Scriptures, God singled out a man to create a nation of priests. These priests were to follow and worship God and were to be holy (set apart) from all other peoples. He called out a man to become a nation of people who would follow Him and whom He would use as a light to teach others to follow Him. God wanted His creation to know Him—to know of His greatness, His Holiness, and of His mercy— through His relationship with this man and His nation of priests.

WHO WAS ABRAM (ABRAHAM)?

On face value, Abram seems to have been an unlikely choice to become the father of a nation of priests. His background appears to have been without particular distinction. According to the Torah, Abram was from the Chaldean city of Ur (in present day southern Iraq). He was a ninth generation descendant of Shem the son of Noah, the son of Terah (a man who worshipped false gods),[4] and was married to a beautiful but barren woman named Sarai. Abram and Sarai set out with Abram's father and nephew for the land of Canaan but settled halfway there to the north in the city of Haran. We don't know how long he lived in Haran or what he did for a living, but he did become wealthy there.[5] That's about all we know about his early days and nothing of note is recorded in the Scriptures about what Abram did while he was in Chaldea.

So here you have the son of a man who worships false gods, who is married to a woman who can't have children, and who doesn't even live in the "promised land." How is his offspring going to be a nation of priests to the LORD God? He doesn't seem to have been a likely choice.

WHY DIDN'T GOD CALL MELCHIZEDEK?

Surely there were others more qualified to become the father of a nation of priests than Abram. If it was God's desire to establish a holy nation of priests in the land of Canaan why didn't He choose someone else? For example, why didn't God call King Melchizedek?

Melchizedek was evidently a great man in Abram's day and seems to have been a more logical person for God to select. Not only was Melchizedek already living in the promised land of Canaan, he was actually the King of Salem (Jerusalem), and, more significantly, he was already the priest of the Most High God. Even Abram brought tithes for God to Melchizedek and obtained Melchizedek's blessing. If Melchizedek already possessed a position of authority as king and a position of service as a priest, why didn't God choose him?[6] On face value, he seems to have been more qualified for the job than Abram.

So much for apparent qualifications.

SO, WHY DID GOD CALL ABRAM?

We do know that God didn't select Abram because of his family credentials—except that he was a descendant of Shem,[7] but by that time so were possibly thousands of other people. It's also very likely that he wasn't selected based upon his own qualifications, because others seemed far more qualified. His selection wasn't even based upon his subsequent performance. Abram fell short on several occasions after God called him, by twice calling his wife his sister[8] and by consenting to Sarah's request that he impregnate her handmaid Hagar.[9] So, why did God select him?

It seems that God intentionally selected Abram, a man without family credentials, an undistinguished man, to show that His calling isn't based upon merit. He selected Abram, a man who faltered by trying to have a family with His wife's servant, to show that His calling and covenant aren't purely based upon performance. God called Abram, a man with a barren wife to show that his promises aren't based upon our ability—they are based upon His power and desire to fulfill them. God called out Abram, established a covenant with him, changed his name to Abraham, and called him His friend[10] to show that He wants to have a close relationship with His creation.

Abraham's calling seems to have been based upon the undeserved, unmerited favor of God. Abraham then responded as any person should if confronted by such an offer from the Creator of the Universe—he believed God, entrusted his life to Him and followed Him.

WHAT ABOUT EVERYONE ELSE?

Did God set up an exclusive relationship with Abraham alone? Is this covenant relationship open only to his descendants or is it also open to others?

God evidently extended an open invitation to *anyone* who wanted to worship and serve Him. For example, God sent the reluctant prophet Jonah to lead the pagan Assyrian city of Ninevah in repentance,[11] Nebuchadnezar the king of Babylon came to believe that the God of the prophet Daniel is God,[12] and Cyrus the king of Persia believed enough to order the rebuilding of the Temple.[13] And, to make the point crystal clear, the prophet Isaiah wrote:

> *'As for the foreigners who attach themselves to the LORD, to minister to Him, and to love the name of the LORD and to be His servants—all who keep the sabbath and do not profane it, and who hold fast to My covenant—I will bring them to My sacred mount and let them rejoice in My house of prayer. Their burnt offerings and sacrifices shall be welcome on my altar: for My House shall be called a house of prayer for all peoples.'*
>
> *Thus declares the LORD GOD, who gathers the disbursed of Israel: 'I will gather still more to those already gathered.'*
>
> —Isaiah 56:6-8 (JPS)

The Psalms also reiterate the point:

> *May God be gracious to us and bless us; may He show us favor, that Your way be known on earth, Your deliverance among all nations.*
>
> *Peoples will praise You, O God; all peoples will praise You. Nations will exult and shout for joy, for You rule the peoples with equity, You guide the nations of the earth. The peoples will praise You, O God; all peoples will praise You.*
>
> *May the earth yield its produce; may God, our God, bless us. May God bless us, and be revered to the ends of the earth.*
>
> —Psalms 67:2-8 (JPS)

God blessed Abraham and his descendants to be a blessing so that all the people on the earth would come to know and worship God.

CONCLUSIONS

So what does all of this mean? Well, it seems that there are at least three significant conclusions that may be reached:

* God's call of a chosen people wasn't based upon qualifications, performance, or ability. It was based upon God's unmerited favor and God's desire for His creation to know Him. We are no more deserving of this relationship than was Abraham.

* God called Abraham and made a covenant with him and his descendants to be a nation of priests and a light to the Gentiles. We, like Abraham and the Prophets, are to worship and serve God and to be a light guiding others to God.

* God extended the call to have a relationship with Him to people everywhere, to you and to everyone else. His covenant relationship is open to everyone.

Who Was That Man?

From the creation of mankind, God has been intimately involved in the lives of people. The Scriptures record that God is compassionate and hears the prayers of those in need.[1] They recount incident after incident where God has intervened in the lives of ordinary people. He heard prayers and intervened to rescue people from oppression. He enabled the barren to have children. He raised the dead. He sent rain and withheld it. He sent prophets to deliver His counsel and to provide wisdom. He protected those who chose to walk with Him from their enemies. He even called out a group of people to be His permanent possession—His nation of priests. God has always been involved in the lives of people.

But for many people, their encounters with God went far beyond having their prayers heard and answered. For people like Adam, Eve, Noah, Abraham, Isaac, Moses, and the prophets, their encounters were likely beyond even their wildest dreams.[2] They actually heard, spoke with, and saw the God of the Universe.

All of these people's experiences were astounding. But one encounter was especially amazing. It happened to Abraham.

The LORD Appeared To Abraham

Abraham was a man who encountered the LORD God many times during his life. And, while all of these encounters were incredible, one of them especially stands out from the rest. It happened near Hebron when Abraham was ninety-nine years old:

The LORD appeared to him [Abraham] by the tere-
binths of Mamre; he was sitting at the entrance of the
tent as the day grew hot. Looking up, he saw three men
standing near him. As soon as he saw them, he ran from
the entrance of the tent to greet them and, bowing to the
ground, he said, 'My lords, if it please you, do not go on
past your servant. Let a little water be brought; bathe
your feet and recline under the tree. And let me fetch a
morsel of bread that you may refresh yourselves; then go
on—seeing that you have come your servant's way.' They
replied, 'Do as you have said.'

—Genesis 18:1-5 (JPS)

Abraham then ran into the tent, told Sarah (Sarai) to make some cakes, and had a servant-boy prepare a calf to eat. He watched as the three visitors ate. After the men had eaten, they asked Abraham where Sarah was. Abraham replied that she was in the tent. Then an interesting conversation ensued between one of the three men and Abraham:

Then one said, 'I will return to you next year, and your
wife Sarah shall have a son!' Sarah was listening at the
entrance of the tent, which was behind him. Now
Abraham and Sarah were old, advanced in years; Sarah
had stopped having the periods of women. And Sarah
laughed to herself, saying, 'Now that I am withered, am
I to have enjoyment—with my husband so old?' Then
the LORD said to Abraham, 'Why did Sarah laugh, say-
ing, 'Shall I in truth bear a child, old as I am? Is anything
too wonderous for the LORD? I will return to you at the
time next year, and Sarah shall have a son.' Sarah lied
saying, 'I did not laugh, 'for she was frightened. But He
replied, 'You did laugh.'

—Genesis 18:9-15 (JPS)

The three men that Abraham was with then set out from there and looked toward the city of Sodom. Abraham walked along with them to see them off. Then the LORD asked:

> *'Shall I hide from Abraham what I am about to do, since Abraham is to become a great and populous nation and all the nations of the earth are to bless themselves by him? For I have singled him out, that he may instruct his children and his posterity to keep the way of the LORD by doing what is just and right, in order that the LORD may bring about for Abraham what He has promised him.'*
>
> *Then the LORD said,*
>
> *'The outrage of Sodom and Gomorrah is so great, and their sin so grave! I will go down to see whether they have acted altogether according to the outcry that has reached Me; if not, I will take note.'*

—Genesis 18:17-21 (JPS)

Two of the three men then left and went to Sodom *"while Abraham remained standing before the LORD."*[3] Abraham then interceded on his nephew Lot's behalf, pleading with God to spare the righteous in the city of Sodom, since his nephew Lot and Lot's family lived there. After the conversation, the LORD departed and that evening the two men, *who were really angels*, arrived in Sodom.[4]

SO, WHAT'S SO UNUSUAL?

The thing that is so astounding about this account of events is that God appeared to Abraham as a man, or at least as an angel in the form of a man!

The LORD appeared to Abraham, allowed His feet to be washed, ate food, reclined in the tent, walked with Abraham toward Sodom, and spoke with Abraham face to face...as a man! The two angels who were with the LORD did likewise and then departed to rescue Lot and his family from Sodom prior to its destruction. The three of them, the LORD God and two angels, appeared to Abraham as men!

Could Abraham merely have been confused about the person's true identity? Not likely. God had already appeared to him at least five times before this incident occurred. God first appeared to Abraham at Haran when he was seventy-five years of age and told Abraham to leave and follow Him to a new land—the land of Canaan.[5] God appeared to him again at Shechem and promised the land of Canaan to his descendants.[6] The LORD spoke to Abraham after his nephew Lot had departed and again promised the land to his descendants.[7] The word of the LORD came to Abraham in a vision and God made a covenant with Abraham to grant him descendants and to give them the land from the River of Egypt to the Euphrates.[8] And, when Abraham was ninety-nine, God again appeared to him and confirmed his covenant and commanded Abraham to be circumcised as a sign of the covenant.[9] So, by the time the three men came to Abraham's tent, Abraham *knew* what it was to be in the presence of Almighty God. Abraham was not confused.

WHY DID GOD DO THIS?

Why would God appear to Abraham as a man? This is almost unimaginable and the Torah doesn't specifically explain why God did it.

What we do know is that God chose to love Abraham.[10] God, through the prophets, even called Abraham His friend.[11] God's favor for Abraham was so great that He chose to repeatedly reveal himself to Abraham and to be intimately involved in Abraham's life. Evidently, since no man can see the LORD's face in all its glory and live,[12] the LORD appeared to Abraham in a form which he could see, that of a man.

Abraham knew that he was entertaining God; the LORD didn't hide His identity. The LORD told Abraham and Sarah that they were going to have a child and He even revealed to Abraham that He was about to destroy Sodom! Abraham upon learning this, with a bit of fear and trembling, repeatedly appealed to God's mercy for his nephew Lot and any other righteous people who may have been in Sodom.[13] *Abraham knew that this man was God.*

God *must* have wanted Abraham to know Him personally. If He didn't, surely He wouldn't have appeared to Abraham in such a personal way.

AND GOD HAS APPEARED TO OTHERS

Abraham wasn't the only person to whom God has revealed himself. According to the Scriptures, the LORD has appeared to many other people. He appeared to Moses as an angel in the burning bush[14] and to the nation of Israel as a consuming fire on Mount Sinai.[15] All of the people of Israel saw the blazing fire and heard God's voice as He declared to them His Ten Commandments.[16] The LORD regularly spoke with Moses out of a pillar of cloud at the entrance to the Tent of Meeting[17] and even allowed Moses and the elders of the nation to see Him:

> *Then Moses and Aaron, Nadab, and Abihu, and seventy elders of Israel ascended; and they saw the God of Israel; under His feet there was the likeness of a pavement of sapphire, like the very sky for purity. Yet He did not raise His hand against the leaders of the Israelites; they beheld God, and ate and drank.*
>
> *—Exodus 24:9-11 (JPS)*

But they weren't allowed to see God's face in all its glory. Even Moses wasn't allowed to actually see God's face:

> *And the LORD said to Moses,*
>
> *'I will also do this thing that you have asked; for you have truly gained my favor and I have singled you out by name.' He [Moses] said, 'Oh let me behold Your Presence!' And He answered, 'I will make all My goodness pass before you, and I will proclaim before you the name LORD, and the grace that I grant and the compassion that I show. But,' He said, 'you cannot see My face, for man may not see Me and live.' And the LORD said, 'See, there is a place near Me. Station yourself on*

*the rock and, as My Presence passes by, I will put you in
a cleft of the rock and shield you with My hand until I
have passed by. Then I will take My hand away and you
will see My back; but My face must not be seen.'*

—Exodus 33:17-23 (JPS)

But God didn't stop appearing to people at Mt. Sinai. During the
ensuing centuries many people saw God. The prophets Isaiah, Ezekiel,
and Daniel all saw God.[18] Why? Because the God of Abraham, Isaac
and Jacob is a God who wants His creation to know Him!

OMNIPRESENT AND PERSONALLY PRESENT

Perhaps one of the most awesome things about God is that He is both
omnipresent and personally present. He is all present everywhere, all of the
time. Yet He is also personally present in the life of every person on earth.
He not only knows the details of our lives, He cares about them and us.
God is not an impersonal force. He is loving, compassionate, and involved
in the lives of people. He made us to love us and to be loved in return.[19]

CONCLUSIONS

What conclusions can be reached from Abraham's experience and the
experiences of the many other people that the Scriptures record as having
seen God? There are several points that can be made. Among them are:

* ✳ The LORD God is not only able to handle running the Universe,
  He can do it while being personally involved in the lives of people like Abraham, and you.

* ✳ God not only presides over the Universe, He shows up in it! For
  Abraham, He appeared as a man.

* ✳ God chose to love and to reveal Himself to Abraham and the
  entire nation of Israel. The Scriptures say that He also chose to
  reveal Himself to many others. God wants to be known and loved
  by His creation, including you.

3

WHATEVER HAPPENED
TO THE SACRIFICE?

For thousands of years the sacrificial system was at the core of worshipping the LORD God of Israel. The Torah, the Law of God, not only required that sacrifices be brought before the LORD to make atonement for sin, it also required that every Jewish man appear before the LORD three times every year—and it required that they not show up empty-handed!

> Three times a year—on the Feast of Unleavened Bread, on the Feast of Weeks, and on the Feast of Booths—all your males shall appear before the LORD your God in the place that He will choose. They shall not appear before the LORD empty-handed, but each with his own gift, according to the blessing that the LORD your God has bestowed upon you.
>
> —Deuteronomy 16:16-17 (JPS)

The place that God chose was the Temple in Jerusalem. For 1,020 years, from the time that Solomon built the first Temple until the Romans destroyed the last Temple in 70 CE, this was the central place of worship for all of Israel.[1]

Jews from all over the world came to Jerusalem to worship God. During major feasts and solemn occasions the population of Jerusalem swelled with worshippers. Josephus, a 1st century Jewish historian, esti-mated that during the Passover celebration, the population of Jerusalem ballooned to 2,700,200 people.[2] That was about 34% of the Jews in the world all gathered together in one city on a single day to worship God![3] Josephus also calculated that, on that single day, 256,500 lambs were sacrificed. So it's clearly not an overstatement to say that the sacrificial system and the Temple in Jerusalem were viewed to be fundamental to worshipping the LORD God of Israel.

But now there is no Temple in Jerusalem and there have been no sac-rifices for over 1,930 years. Does this mean that sacrifices and offerings to God are no longer important? And, if that's the case, were they ever truly important? To answer these questions let's start at the beginning, the very beginning.

HOW DID THE SACRIFICIAL SYSTEM GET STARTED?

Some theorize that, when God revealed himself to mankind, He merely transferred their pagan forms of worship to Himself to slowly wean them away from pagan practices. They say that God allowed peo-ple to make sacrifices to Him until they became enlightened enough to see that they weren't required.[4] But, while it's easy to see how this con-clusion could be reached, that's not what the Scriptures actually teach.

IN THE BEGINNING...

The Hebrew Scriptures imply that the sacrificial system actually started at *the beginning*—it appears that God instituted it at the time of Adam and Eve. The Scriptures record that before God ejected Adam and Eve from the Garden of Eden, He killed an animal and used it to make clothing to cover them.[5] An animal was essentially *sacrificed* to provide them with a covering of clothes.

However, Cain and Abel, Adam and Eve's children, are actually the first people recorded in the Scriptures to have brought sacrifices to the LORD. Both of them offered sacrifices. Cain brought *"an offering to the LORD from the fruit of the soil; and Abel, for his part, brought the choicest of the firstlings of his flock."* And, as you may recall, God paid heed to Abel and the animal sacrifice, but not to Cain.[6]

Noah

The next sacrifice mentioned in the Scriptures was offered by Noah just after the flood. After the waters had subsided and the ark landed on the mountains of Ararat, Noah built an altar to the LORD and *"taking of every clean animal and every clean bird, he offered burnt offerings on the altar;"* and the LORD was pleased with the odor of the sacrifice.[7]

Since the account of Noah doesn't record that God told Noah to offer these sacrifices, it seems reasonable to conclude that, even by Noah's day, sacrifices were a common expression of worship toward God.

Abraham

Abraham is the first person that the Scriptures record was specifically instructed by God to offer sacrifices to Him. This happened on the day that God made a covenant with Abraham to give the Promised Land to his descendants. God told Abram (as he was called at the time) to bring a sacrifice of: *"a three-year-old heifer; a three-year-old she-goat, a three-year-old ram, a turtledove, and a young bird."* Abraham obeyed by cutting the sacrifices in two pieces (except for the bird) and then watched as God provided the fire, which passed between them.[8]

Years later, God again told Abraham to bring a sacrifice. This time God tested Abraham's faith by telling him to offer his son, Isaac, as a burnt offering in the land of Moriah. Abraham passed the test and God spared Isaac and even provided a ram as a substitute sacrifice.[9]

The Passover

The Passover sacrifice is probably the most well-known sacrifice recorded in the Scriptures. This was the sacrifice that God told Moses and the children of Israel to prepare on the night before they were freed from slavery in Egypt. According to the Scriptures, God specified that each family was to offer a yearling male lamb without blemish. They were told to roast and eat the meat of the lamb and to put the lamb's blood on the doorposts of their houses.[10] It wasn't enough to be the descendant of Abraham, Isaac, and Jacob; the blood of the sacrificed lamb had to be on the doorposts of each house for the death angel to pass over and the first-born in their house to be spared. Their deeds and position in the community couldn't avert death; only the blood of the sacrifice could save them.

THE COVENANT WITH ISRAEL IN THE WILDERNESS

After God led Moses and the people of Israel out of Egypt, the blood of a sacrifice was used to seal the covenant that He made them:

> *Early in the morning, he set up an altar at the foot of the mountain, with twelve pillars for the twelve tribes of Israel. He designated some young men among the Israelites, and they offered burnt offerings and sacrificed bulls as offerings of well-being to the LORD. Moses took one part of the blood and put it in basins, and the other part of the blood he dashed against the altar. Then he took the record of the covenant and read it aloud to the people. And they, said, 'All that the LORD has spoken we will faithfully do!' Moses took the blood and dashed it on the people and said, 'This is the blood of the covenant that the LORD now makes with you concerning all these commands.'*

> —Exodus 24:4-8 (JPS)

So, by the time the Law was given to Israel, the practice of sacrifice was already a fundamental part of worshipping God.

The Law (the Torah) further established the importance of the sacrifice. In it God described the specific sacrifices that were to be presented to Him; how the Ark of the Pact (covenant), altar, instruments of worship and Tabernacle were to be constructed;[11] who were to serve as priests; how the priests and instruments used in worship were to be consecrated;[12] and how sacrifices were to be presented to Him.[13] God was incredibly detailed in His instructions. It seems obvious that God was very particular about how His people were to worship Him.

WHAT SACRIFICES WERE REQUIRED BY THE TORAH?

In the Torah, God described the specific types of sacrifices and offerings that were to be presented before Him and even how they were to be offered. There were grain offerings, animal sacrifices, and various other types of offerings. All of this is recorded in Leviticus and elsewhere in the Scriptures in great detail. However, to simplify things, it seems that there were several basic types of sacrifices.

SACRIFICES OF CONTINUAL WORSHIP

Daily, Weekly, and Monthly Offerings were to be presented to God by the priests in the Tabernacle. (The Temple hadn't been built yet.) The daily morning and evening sacrifice included a burnt offering of a lamb, a grain offering, and a fermented drink offering. Each week on the Sabbath, an additional burnt offering of two lambs, a grain offering and a drink offering were to be given. Then on the first day of each lunar month, still more sacrifices were to be given in addition to the daily and weekly sacrifices. All of these offerings appear to be intended primarily as continual acts of worship before God. Only the monthly sacrifice included an offering for sin.[14]

SACRIFICES OF THANKSGIVING AND FELLOWSHIP

Peace Offerings, or sacrifices of *"well-being,"* were given to God as voluntary acts of worship. These sacrifices were to be a male or female animal without blemish. The person offering the sacrifice was supposed to lay his hand on the animal's head and kill it at the entrance to the Tabernacle. The priests were then to sprinkle the blood of the sacrifice on the altar and burn the fat, kidneys and covering of the liver as an offering to God. The offeror could eat the remainder of the sacrificed animal and the priests were also entitled to a portion.[15]

The Wave Offerings were gifts to support the priests and the work of the Temple. For example, when the Tabernacle was being constructed, Moses took up an offering of jewelry to make the candlesticks and other articles of worship used by the priests. When these things were given to the priests, they were waved in the air before God and then put to use. This is why they are called wave offerings.[16]

SACRIFICES TO ATONE FOR SIN

The Sin Offering was required if an individual or even the nation had sinned unintentionally against God. It was to be made with a specified animal without defect (or other required sacrifice). The offeror was supposed to lay his hand on the head of the animal. It was then killed before the LORD. The priest dipped his finger in the blood of the sacrifice and sprinkled it seven times before the LORD in front of the curtain of the sanctuary. The priest also put some of the blood on the horns of the altar of incense and poured the rest out at the base of the altar. The fat and kidneys of the sacrifice were burned on the altar but the rest was burned outside the camp. The result of the sacrifice was atonement for the offeror. He was forgiven by God.[17]

It is interesting to note that the sacrifice ranged from a bull, if the priest had sinned, to two doves, if the sinning party was poor. If the person was unable even to afford two doves, a tenth of an ephah of fine flour without oil or incense was accepted to make atonement.[18] You didn't have to be rich to be forgiven.

The Trespass Offering was made by someone who had realized that they unintentionally violated one of the LORD's ordinances. It differed from the *sin offering* in that the *trespass offering* was focused on making restitution for individual sin offenses. The offering was a ram without blemish. In addition, the wrong committed was to be valued and 20% added. This was paid to the priest or the person wronged so that restitution would be made for the wrong.[19] Like the sin offering, the result was that the offender was forgiven:

> ...*the priest shall make expiation on his behalf for the error that he committed unwittingly, and he shall be forgiven.*
>
> —Leviticus 5:18 (JPS)

The Burnt Offering was also offered as a sacrifice for sin. It was to be a male of the flock without blemish. The offeror was to lay his hand on the head of the animal, *"that it may be acceptable in his behalf."* The animal was then killed and cut into pieces. The priests then sprinkled the blood on the altar, washed the sacrifice, and then burned all of it on the altar. The sacrifice was accepted to make atonement for the offeror.[20]

SACRIFICES ON HOLY DAYS

The Law of God required the observance of many sacred assemblies. The observance of these assemblies, such as the Feast of Weeks (Shavuot), the Feast of Trumpets (Rosh Hashanah), the Feast of Booths (Sukkot), Passover (Pasach), and the Feast of First Fruits, also required that sacrifices and offerings be presented before God at the Temple.[21] Each of these appointed feasts had a different meaning in the life of the nation of Israel and at each feast, specific burnt offerings, wave offerings, grain offerings, or sin offerings were required. While all of these assemblies were of major significance, one of them was especially important in light of the meaning of Israel's sacrificial system of worship. It was the Day of Atonement.

The Day Of Atonement, Yom Kippur, was instituted by God to ensure that atonement had been made for the sins of all of the people of Israel. It basically was a catchall sacrifice to ensure that the sins of the entire nation had been covered. That's why it's called Yom Kippur—it means *the Day of Covering.* It was to be observed by Israel each year *"for all time."*

The priest began with a Sin Offering to atone for his own sins and that of his household. Then two male goats were brought in. The first was sacrificed and the priest used his finger to sprinkle some of its blood on the cover of the Ark of the Covenant (inside of which were the actual stone tablets of the *Ten Commandments*). The blood of the first goat and the blood of the Sin Offering were then used to purge the Tabernacle and the altar of uncleanness.[22] The priest then laid his hands on the head of the second goat and confessed *"over it all the iniquities and transgressions of the Israelites, whatever their sins, putting them on the head of the goat..."*[23] The second goat was then set free, symbolizing the carrying away their iniquities.

TITHES

The tithes (tenths) required by the Scriptures weren't a sacrifice in the narrow sense of the term; they were offerings required by God to support the priests. The people of Israel were required to give one tenth of their incomes each year to provide for the needs of the priests. This included one tenth of their crop production, one tenth of their new calves and lambs—one tenth of everything produced. Since the Levites (the priests) weren't allocated land in Canaan like the other tribes of Israel, the tithes were their primary means of support. Tithes were the priests' wages for serving God.[24]

COMMON QUESTIONS ABOUT THE SACRIFICIAL SYSTEM

There are many questions that could be asked about the sacrificial system. However, rather than attempt to cover every detail associated with each sacrifice and how sacrifices were to be offered, let's look at some of the bigger questions:

- *What was the purpose of the sacrifice?*

  The purpose of the sacrifice and the type of sacrifice were always related. If a person was guilty of sin, they were to present a sin offering or a trespass offering. These sacrifices atoned for the offeror's sin. The grain offering, the peace offering, the wave offerings and the tithe however, weren't associated with atonement for sin; they were offered to honor God and to provide for the priests and the needs of the Temple.

- *Would any sacrifice do?*

  According to the Torah, no, not just any sacrifice would do. God was explicit about excluding honey and yeast from specific sacrifices. In addition, only blood sacrifices were accepted to make atonement for sin, except where the offeror was too poor to afford a blood sacrifice. In this case, fine flour without incense or oil was accepted. Each sacrifice had meaning. God mandated that He be worshipped in the manner that He desired.

- *Did it matter where the sacrifice was offered?*

  Actually, yes it did. At first, the sacrifices were to be brought only to the Tent of Meeting. It was replaced by the Tabernacle, which was then later replaced by the Temple in Jerusalem. These were the approved places of sacrifice.

Say to them further: If anyone of the house of Israel or of the strangers who reside among them offers a burnt offering or a sacrifice, and does not bring it to the entrance of the Tent of Meeting to offer it to the LORD, that person shall be cut off from his people.

—Leviticus 17:8-9 (JPS)

- **Did it matter who presented the offered sacrifice to God?**

Only the descendants of Jacob's son Levi (the Levites) were allowed to serve as priests before God in the Temple.[25] Everyone could bring sacrifices to the Temple, but only the priests could actually present them to God.

- **What was the significance of the blood?**

God used the blood of the sacrifice to represent that the cost of sin is life. He was explicit that the blood, representing life, was acceptable as an offering to make atonement for sin:

And if anyone in the house of Israel or of the strangers who reside among them partakes of any blood, I will set My face against the person who partakes of the blood, and I will cut him off from among his kin. For the life of the flesh is in the blood, and I have assigned it to you for making expiation for your lives upon the altar; it is the blood, as life, that effects expiation.

—Leviticus 17:11 (JPS)

But was offering the blood of bulls, lambs and goats of itself sufficient to attain forgiveness for the offeror? No, this doesn't appear to be the case. In the time of the prophet Isaiah, God rebuked the sacrifices of a sinful and unrepentant nation of Israel as futile and offensive to Him.[26] Sacrifices were being offered without repentance. So to God, they were offensive. God could not be paid off with sacrifices.

The cost of sin was life (as represented by blood). However, the offeror of the sacrifice had to approach God with submission and repentance for the sacrifice to be accepted. The sacrifice offered in faith and submission secured forgiveness and a covering for the guilt of sin.

BUT, WHAT COVERS OUR SIN NOW?

In 70 CE the Temple in Jerusalem was destroyed by Vespasian's Roman armies and the only thing that remains of it now is a portion of its western wall. Although Israel was reborn as a nation in 1948, the Temple has not been rebuilt and sacrifices have not been offered for over 1,930 years. This means that for almost two thousand years, the requirements in the Law for sacrifice have not been observed by Rabbinic Judaism. So, if it was the sacrificial system that secured a covering (kippur) for sins, without the Temple and the sacrifices, what covers our sins now?

1st century rabbi Yochanan ben Zakkai rationalized that acts of loving-kindness were the means of attaining God's forgiveness in the absence of the Temple and the sacrifice.[27] Commentators in the Talmud contended that studying the Torah is an even greater act than sacrifice.[28] But, while acts of loving-kindness and studying the Torah are wonderful, is that really what covers our sins?

WHAT THEN COVERS OUR SINS?

About 2,600 years ago, there was also a span of time when the Temple had been destroyed. It began in 587 BCE. It was then that King Nebuchadnezzar of Babylon invaded Israel, destroyed the Temple, and carried captives off to Babylon. From then until about 537 BCE, there were no sacrifices, and the rebuilding of the Temple wasn't completed until about 516 BCE. During this seventy-year period without the temple, what covered their sins; what do the Scriptures say?

The Prophet Micah had foretold that this destruction would happen over 100 years earlier. He prophesied God's judgment upon Samaria and Judah, that Israel would be dispossessed of its land, and that the Temple Mount would become *a shrine in the woods.*[29] But he also said that God would take Israel back and that God would cover up Israel's sins:

Who is a God like You,
Forgiving iniquity
And remitting transgression;
Who has not maintained His wrath forever
Against the remnant of His own people,
Because He loves graciousness!
He will take us back in love;
He will cover up our iniquities,
You will hurl all our sins
Into the depths of the sea.
You will keep faith with Jacob,
Loyalty to Abraham,
As you promised on oath to our fathers
In days gone by.

—Micah 7:18-20 (JPS)

The Psalms reiterate that it is God Himself who redeems Israel from sin:

If you keep account of sins, O LORD,
Lord, who will survive?
Yours is the power to forgive
So that you may be held in awe.

O Israel, wait for the LORD;
For with the LORD is steadfast love
And great power to redeem.
It is He who will redeem Israel from all their iniquities.

—Psalms 130:3-4 and 7-8 (JPS)

In ancient times, the priest went into the Temple to sprinkle the blood of the sacrifice on the Ark of the Covenant (which contained the Law of God which they had violated). It was the priest who applied the blood to cover the sins of Israel. But we, like Israel in 587 BCE, have no Temple and can offer no sacrifice. We only have forgiveness if God

Himself covers our sin. It is now only His covering that secures our atonement and redeems us from our sin.

CONCLUSIONS

There are many conclusions that can be reached from all of this. But there are at least four that are also major themes, which resound throughout the Scriptures. According to the Scriptures:

* ✳ We are all accountable to God for our sin as individuals and as a nation.

* ✳ The cost of sin is life...as represented by the sacrifice. Good deeds were indeed good, but they could not cover (atone for) sin; only the sacrifice covered sin. The sacrificial system was a daily reminder of this.

* ✳ The sacrifice did cover sins, but without repentance and trust in God, the sacrifice had no effect. The sacrifice was supposed to be offered in repentance.

* ✳ At another time when there were no sacrifices, the Prophet Micah said that God Himself would cover up Israel's sins. Like then, our forgiveness is dependent upon His provision of a covering for our sin. He alone is our redeemer.

A New Deal With God?

From the creation of man, God has indeed been intimately involved in the lives of people. He has not merely peered into His creation to amuse Himself with the trials and struggles of mankind; He has been lovingly involved in the minute details of peoples lives, their fears, their joy, their pain and their victories. God made mankind so that He could have fellowship with mankind. He made us to love us and to be loved by us in return.

Like a father, God has expectations of His "children." He, being God, defines these expectations and the nature of His relationship with the people He created. These relationships are called "covenants" in the Scriptures. They are essentially the "deal" that God has laid out for mankind and for specific people. These covenant relationships reveal a God that is interested in more than his children's happiness and comfort. He is interested in their character, their holiness, and their love for each other.

In League With Adam

God spelled out a great deal (covenant relationship) for the first man, Adam. God basically said, I want you to live with Me and to multiply and fill the earth with people. I'm giving you dominion over the whole earth and your only job is to till and care for this incredible garden and to name all the animals. And I'm only going to have one rule; don't eat from the fruit of the tree of the knowledge of good and evil.[1] Now that's a great deal!

And yet, Adam and his wife violated the covenant by eating the only fruit forbidden them. *So God changed the deal.* The new deal was that they were still to fill the earth with people and to have dominion, but they would have to raise their own food the hard way and that Eve would have pain in child birth and would be ruled over by her husband. But, the harshest part of the new arrangement was that Adam and Eve and their descendants would ultimately die.[2]

This covenant arrangement lasted for generations. It lasted until Adam and Eve's descendants abounded not only in number but also in wickedness. The world's population was a lawless mess. So God stepped in.

A NEW DEAL WITH NOAH

God established a new covenant with a righteous man named Noah. Noah's job was to build a huge ship, fill it with animals and food, and then at the appointed time to take his family and get into it. Noah did and God rescued them from the flood that He used to destroy the lawless population of the earth.[3]

As part of the new deal that God made with Noah's family, mankind was to be fruitful and fill the earth with people, to be accountable and punish the taking of human life, and to be allowed to eat animals for food. In addition, God promised never again to destroy the earth by flood. This deal was similar to Adam's but men were now explicitly accountable to each other for their actions.[4]

Generations again passed and the population of the earth again grew in number and in wickedness. People claimed to worship God, but which god?

A COVENANT WITH ABRAM

God called out a man named Abram from Chaldea to create a nation of priests to serve Him and to be a light to the rest of the world.

When God told Abram to leave Haran, He told him that He would make Abram into a great nation and that all the world would be blessed through him. He also said that He would give the land of the Canaanites to Abram's offspring.[5] Some time later, the LORD reconfirmed these promises and, after Abram prepared sacrifices, God made a covenant with Abram to give the land of Canaan to his descendants.[6]

The ultimate covenant with Abram, however, came when Abram was ninety-nine years old.

> *...the LORD appeared to Abram and said to him, 'I am El Shaddai. Walk in My ways and be blameless. I will establish My covenant between Me and you, and I will make you exceedingly numerous.' Abram threw himself on his face; and God spoke to him further, 'As for Me, this is My covenant with you: You shall be the father of a multitude of nations. And you shall no longer be called Abram, but your name shall be Abraham, for I make you the father of a multitude of nations. I will make you exceedingly fertile, and make nations of you; and kings shall come forth from you. I will maintain My covenant between Me and you, and your offspring to come, as an everlasting covenant through the ages, to be God to you and to your offspring to come. I assign the land you sojourn in to you and to your offspring to come, all the land of Canaan, as an everlasting holding. I will be their God.'*
>
> —Genesis 17:1-9 (JPS)

The mark of the covenant with God was also given; the circumcision of every male above the age of eight days.[7]

The descendants of Abraham did indeed become multitudes. After many generations and four hundred years of slavery in Egypt, they were delivered by God and led through the desert back to the promised land of Canaan by the Prophet Moses.

THE COVENANT WITH ISRAEL AND MOSES

Shortly after entering the wilderness of Sinai, God called Moses up to the mountain and instituted yet another covenant. He instructed Moses:

> *'Thus shall you say to the house of Jacob and declare to the children of Israel 'You have seen what I did to the Egyptians, how I bore you on eagles' wings and brought you to Me. Now then, if you will obey Me faithfully and keep My covenant, you shall be My treasured possession among all the peoples. Indeed, all the earth is Mine, but you shall be to Me a kingdom of priests and a holy nation.' These are the words that you shall speak to the children of Israel.'*

—Exodus 19:3-6 (JPS)

Moses did and *"All the people answered as one, saying, 'All that the Lord has spoken we will do.'"*[8]

So God gave Israel His laws. The covenant established Israel as a people chosen by God (and the Levites as priests). However, the responsibility that came with this incredible covenant was to obey the LORD's laws and commands. In addition, as long as the people of Israel obeyed God, they received prosperity and blessings. But when they turned from God's laws, they received calamity, defeat, poverty, and death.[9]

Upon entering the promised land of Canaan, Israel learned that the LORD was indeed faithful to His covenants. And, as He said He would, when the people turned away from Him, God allowed oppressive enemies to overtake them. Then, when they listened to the judges, who God used to turn the people back to Him, they again experienced peace and prosperity.

Unfortunately, the nation of Israel, wasn't content to have God as its king. It wanted to be like the kingdoms around it and to have a human monarch. In spite of God's warnings, Israel rejected God's kingship for that of a man.[10] So God granted them a king. The first King, Saul, was great in appearance and stature but was presumptuous and disobeyed God. Because of this, God rejected him, and instead selected a young shepherd boy named David.

THE DEAL WITH KING DAVID

David was a young man who loved God. God made him king and made a covenant with him, saying: *"Your house and your kingship shall ever be secure before you; your throne shall be established forever."*[11]

Unfortunately King David's grandson, Rehoboam, lacked his grandfather's wisdom. His oppressive policies caused the nation to be divided. The northern kingdom of Israel turned from God and was ultimately defeated by the Assyrians. David's descendants continued to reign over the southern kingdom of Judah. But over time, Judah's sin caused God to allow their defeat as well, just as He had promised to Moses in the Sinai.

THE NEW COVENANT TO COME

The LORD God used the Prophet Jeremiah to prophesy this impending defeat and captivity of Judah (Southern Israel) at the hands of the Babylonians during the years prior to its occurrence in 587 BCE. The LORD also used Jeremiah to describe days that were yet coming. In chapter 30 of Jeremiah, God described the restoration of Israel in the promised land and the re-establishment of the throne of David.

A NEW COVENANT

It was following this promise of restoration that the LORD used Jeremiah to describe a time when He will make yet another covenant with the House of Israel:

> *See, a time is coming—declares the LORD—when I will make a new covenant with the House of Israel and the House of Judah. It will not be like the covenant I made with their fathers, when I took them by the hand to lead them out of the land of Egypt, a covenant which they broke, so that I rejected them—declares the LORD. But such is the covenant I will make with the House of Israel after these days—declares the LORD: I will put My Teaching into their inmost being and inscribe it upon their hearts. Then I will be their God, and they shall be my people. No longer will they need to teach one another and say to one another, 'Heed the LORD'; for all of*

them, from the least of them to the greatest, shall heed Me—declares the LORD. For I will forgive their iniquities, And remember their sins no more.

Thus said the LORD, Who established the sun for light by day, The laws of moon and stars for light by night, Who stirs up the sea into roaring waves, Whose name is LORD of Hosts: If these laws should ever be annulled by Me— declares the LORD—Only then would the offspring of Israel cease to be a nation before Me for all time.

—Jeremiah 31:31-35 (JPS)

A new covenant is promised. It isn't like the covenant that God confirmed through Moses. Instead of inscribing the Teaching of the LORD on paper or stone tablets, God will inscribe it on our hearts. God will not nullify His word; instead, so that we may obey it, He will enable us by placing it in our hearts.

The prophet Ezekiel, who was a contemporary of Jeremiah's, also spoke of a new covenant to come:

...thus said the Lord GOD: I am going to take the Israelite people from among the nations they have gone to, and gather them from every quarter, and bring them to their own land. I will make them a single nation in the land, on the hills of Israel, and one king shall be king of them all. Never again shall they be two nations, and never again shall they be divided into two kingdoms. Nor shall they ever again defile themselves by their fetishes and their abhorrent things, and by their own transgressions. I will save them in all their settlements where they sinned, and I will cleanse them. They shall be my people and I shall be their God. My servant David shall be king over them; there shall be one shepherd for all of them. They shall follow My rules and faithfully

*obey My laws. Thus they shall remain in the land which
I gave to My servant Jacob and in which your fathers
dwelt; they and their children and their children's children shall dwell there forever, with My servant David as
their prince for all time. I will make a covenant of friendship with them—it shall be an everlasting covenant with
them—I will establish them and multiply them, and I
will place My Sanctuary among them forever. My
Presence shall rest over them; I will be their God and
they shall be My people. And when My Sanctuary abides
among them forever, the nations shall know that I the
LORD do sanctify Israel.*

—Ezekiel 37:21-28 (JPS)

In this new covenant, Israel would be restored as a nation in
Palestine with a descendant of David as their King, the Temple would
be restored, and God's Presence would rest over them. This is an awesome prophecy!

HAS THE NEW COVENANT COME YET?

Has this covenant come to pass yet? Did the LORD establish it in the
6th century BCE when He restored the nation of Israel after its captivity
in Babylon?

It's obvious from reading the Prophet Malachi that 100 years after
Israel's return from Babylon (about 425 BCE), the priests had broken
God's covenant with Levi[12] and the people of Israel were profaning
God's altar and living in lawlessness. So, the Teaching of the LORD
apparently still had not yet been written in their hearts. And, while the
Temple (Sanctuary) was rebuilt upon their return, it was later destroyed
by the Romans in the 1st century CE.

However, like Jeremiah and Ezekiel, Malachi also wrote of a
covenant to come:

*Behold, I am sending My messenger to clear the way before
Me, and the Lord whom you seek shall come to His Temple*

suddenly. As for the angel [messenger] of the covenant that
you desire, he is already coming. But who can endure the
day of his coming, and who can hold out when he appears?
For he is like a smelter's fire and like a fuller's lye. He shall
act like a smelter and purger of silver; and he shall purify the
descendants of Levi and refine them like gold and silver, so
that they shall present offerings in righteousness.

—Malachi 3:1-3 (JPS)

Malachi prophesied that the messenger of a covenant will be sent by God to prepare the way for God. Then the Lord will come to His Temple quickly.

THE NEW COVENANT AND MESSIAH

It is interesting to note that Ezekiel, Malachi, and Jeremiah all wrote of a coming new covenant and that they all also wrote about Messiah in the context of the new covenant. From their prophecies, it appears that the coming of Messiah and the coming of the new covenant are related events.

Rabbis have long viewed the *"Lord whom, you seek"* described in Malachi 3:1-3 (the verses above) to be speaking of Messiah.[13] If this is the case, the coming of Messiah and the coming new covenant are interrelated.

Ezekiel prophesied of a covenant of friendship between Israel and God at the time when a descendant of King David (evidently Messiah) again rules Israel:

Then I will appoint a single shepherd over them to tend
them — My servant David. He shall tend them, he shall be
a shepherd to them. I the LORD will be their God, and
My servant David shall be a ruler among them — I the
LORD have spoken. And I will grant them a covenant of
friendship. I will banish vicious beasts from their land,
and they shall live secure in the wasteland, they shall
even sleep in the woodland. I will make these and the
environs of My hill a blessing: I will send down rain in
its season, rains that bring blessing. ...They shall know

*that I the LORD their God am with them and they, the
House of Israel, are My people—declares the Lord God.
For you, My flock, flock that I tend, are men; and I, your
Shepherd, am your God—declares the Lord God.*

—Ezekiel 34:23-26 and 34:30-31 (JPS)

Jeremiah also speaks of Messiah in the context of the restoration and
the new covenant. Two chapters after he introduced the new covenant, he
reiterated God's commitment to fulfill the covenant that He made with
David to have his offspring (again believed to be Messiah) rule in Israel:

*See the days are coming—declares the LORD when I
will fulfill the promise that I made concerning the House
of Israel and the House of Judah. In those days and at
that time, I will raise up a true branch of David's line,
and he shall do what is just and right in the land. In
those days Judah shall be delivered and Israel shall dwell
secure. And this is what he shall be called: "The LORD
is our Vindicator." For thus said the LORD: There shall
never be an end to men of David's line who sit upon the
throne of the House of Israel. Nor shall there ever be an
end to the line of levitical priests before Me, of those who
present burnt offerings and turn the meal offering to
smoke and perform sacrifices.*

*The word of the LORD came to Jeremiah: Thus said the
LORD: If you could break My covenant with the day
and My covenant with the night, so that day and night
should not come at their proper time, only then could
My covenant with My servant David be broken—...*

—Jeremiah 33:15-21 (JPS)

It appears that Jeremiah, Ezekiel and Malachi all wrote about the same
New Covenant to come. It also appears that this *New Covenant* is in effect

at the time of Messiah's coming. And, based upon the date of Malachi's writing (around 430 BCE), it's obvious that the *New Covenant* wasn't in effect during the restoration of Israel at the time of the prophets Ezra and Nehemiah. So, when will the *New Covenant* come? The Scriptures don't explicitly say, but it appears that it will come when Messiah comes.

CONCLUSIONS

So, what is the point?

* God is God. *He* sets the basis for our relationship with him and makes changes in the relationship, as He deems appropriate.

* God's *New Covenant* builds upon the previous covenants he made with Adam, Noah, Abraham, Moses, and David:
  – God's presence and Sanctuary will be with Israel forever
  – He will multiply Israel
  – He will establish Israel in Palestine (Canaan)
  – He will be Israel's God
  – David and his descendants will be king forever

* God's *New Covenant* with Israel is even better than the covenant He made through Moses. He will write His Teaching in our hearts (we will know His word) and we will heed God. Evidently, since we can't live up to His word on our own, He will enable us.

* It isn't clear from the Scriptures when the *New Covenant* will become effective, but it appears that it is linked to the coming of Messiah.

5

A MESSIAH FOR ISRAEL?

There has been renewed interest in the subject of the Messiah with the 1994 death of Hassidic Grand Rabbi Menachem Mendel Schneerson. Many of his followers had hoped him to be the Messiah. Many of them still believe that he is the Messiah and that he will yet rise from the dead to lead Israel. So, how can we know whether the Rebbe, or anyone else for that matter, really is the Messiah? How will we know the real Messiah when he comes?

Moses ben Maimon (Maimonides), a 12th century Jewish philosopher, responded to this question in the Mishneh Torah by saying:

> If a king will arise from the House of David who is learned in the Torah and observant of the mitzvoth, as prescribed by the written law and the oral law, as David, his ancestor was, and will compel all of Israel to walk in [the way of the Torah] and reinforce the breaches [in its observance]; and fight the wars of God, we may, with assurance, consider him the Messiah.
>
> If he succeeds in the above, builds the Temple in its place, and gathers the dispersed of Israel, he is definitely the Messiah.[1]

But still, based upon this statement alone we wouldn't know for sure and many people could still be misled. That's why God told us through the prophets who we should be looking for—the *only* basis for proving that someone is the Messiah is from the Holy Scriptures.

HOW DO YOU KNOW WHICH SCRIPTURES TALK ABOUT MESSIAH?

Determining which Scriptures are speaking of Messiah seems a daunting task. It seems unlikely that mankind could ever grasp the true depth of meaning of the prophecy in the Scriptures. However, some Scriptures seem to clearly speak of a Messianic king to come. In the majority of these cases, it's very clear that the person being spoken of is no ordinary man, based upon the circumstances described alone. In other cases, where it's less obvious, we can turn to the historical interpretations of the many rabbis who have wrestled with these questions. Rabbis have recorded a great deal over the centuries in the Mishnah and Talmud (the oral law), the Midrashim (rabbinical commentary), and other rabbinical writings. And, though they often differ in their interpretation of specific Scriptures, there tends to be general agreement in their view of which Scriptures speak of Messiah.

Of course, even a rabbi could be wrong. So ultimately, we should search the Scriptures for ourselves and ask God to give us understanding. He wouldn't have described the Messiah if He didn't want us to know him.

SO WHAT DO WE KNOW ABOUT MESSIAH FROM THE SCRIPTURES?

The Scriptures tell a great deal about Messiah. They definitely tell us enough to know that not just anyone could fit the description.

HE'S FROM BETHLEHEM OF EPHRATH

The prophet Micah speaks of a time when the nations of the world go up to the House of God for His instruction; a time when war has ended forever and when God judges over the nations:[2]

> *In that day I will assemble the lame [sheep] and will gather the outcast and those I have treated harshly; and*

I will turn the lame into a remnant and the expelled into a populous nation. And the LORD will reign over them on Mount Zion now and for evermore.

And you, o Migdal-eder, outpost of Fair Zion, it shall come to you: the former monarchy shall return—the kingship of Fair Jerusalem.

—Micah 4:6-8 (JPS)

Micah continues by responding to Israel's lament over having no king:

And to you, o Bethlehem of Ephrath, least among the clans of Judah, from you one shall come forth to rule Israel for Me—one whose origin is from old, from ancient times.

—Micah 5:1 (JPS)[a]

The king who is going to reign when God ushers in everlasting peace is a man who has ancient origins and who is from the town of Bethlehem. Both of Micah's statements agree as Migdal-eder is near Bethlehem.[3] Obviously, this is no ordinary king.

He Is A Descendant Of King David

God promised King David that *"your house and your kingship shall ever be secure before you; your throne shall be established forever."*[4] Isaiah spoke of the child who would be born to fulfill this prophecy. He spoke of a brilliant light dawning upon Israel and of the yoke of bondage being broken.[5] Then he prophesied:

For a child has been born to us, a son has been given us. And authority has settled on his shoulders. He has been named 'The Mighty God is planning grace; The Eternal Father, a peaceable ruler'—"In token of abundant

[a] The 6th century Babylonian Talmud (Yoma 10A and Sanhedrin 98B) states the belief among Rabbis that Micah 5:1-2 is speaking of the Messiah.

*authority and of peace without limit upon David's
throne and kingdom, that it may be firmly established in
justice and equity now and evermore. The zeal of the
LORD of Hosts shall bring this to pass.*

—Isaiah 9:5-6 (JPS)[b]

The king who is to reign *"in abundant authority"* and *"unlimited
peace"* is a descendant of king David. The prophet Jeremiah confirmed
this.[6] So, the Messiah isn't just some Jewish man who claims to be a
leader and who makes peace treaties—if he isn't a direct descendant of
David, he isn't the Messiah!

HE WILL BE PRECEDED BY THE PROPHET ELIJAH

Before the Messiah comes onto the world stage he is to be preceded
by a messenger who will prepare the way before him.[7] The prophet
Malachi identifies the messenger as the prophet Elijah:

*Lo, I will send the prophet Elijah to you before the com-
ing of the awesome, fearful day of the LORD. He shall
reconcile parents with children and children with parents, so that when I come, I do not strike the whole land
with utter destruction.*

—Malachi 3:23 (JPS)[c]

You may remember that the prophet Elijah suddenly appeared in
about 875 BCE before Ahab, the king of Israel. Ahab had set up the worship of the pagan god Baal in Israel and was murdering the prophets of

---

[b] The Babylonian Talmud (Sanhedrin 94A, Shabbath 55A, and Sanhedrin 98B) references the belief that Isaiah 9:5-6 is speaking of Messiah. Other Scripture references are
also cited in Sanhedrin 98B in support of the belief that Messiah will be King David's
descendent.

[c] The Babylonian Talmud (Erubin 43A-B and Shabbath 118A) references the belief
that Elijah will precede Messiah. To this day a place is set and a cup of wine is poured
for Elijah at the Passover Seder because Elijah is believed to precede and announce the
Messiah's coming.

God. Elijah's message to him was basically: clean up your act or else! God used Elijah to confront a wicked king and to seek to turn a nation back to Himself. It sounds as though the mission of Elijah will be similar the second time around.

Whether this Scripture refers to the literal reappearance of Elijah or one who has the same message as Elijah, the Messiah will likely be preceded by a messenger proclaiming, "repent and turn back to God!"

HE WILL BE A HUMBLE PERSON

Contrary to what our expectations may be, the Messiah will evidently be a humble man. The prophet Zechariah described him as lowly and riding on a donkey; not on a regal stallion.

> *Rejoice greatly, Fair Zion; raise a shout, Fair Jerusalem! Lo, your king is coming to you. He is victorious, triumphant, yet humble, riding on an ass, on a donkey foaled by a she-ass. He shall banish chariots from Ephraim and horses from Jerusalem; the warrior's bow shall be banished. He shall call on the nations to surrender, and his rule shall extend from sea to sea and from ocean to land's end.'*

—Zechariah 9:9-10 (JPS)[d]

Again, this is no ordinary king. This king is going to rule the world from Jerusalem! But he is going to ride into Jerusalem on a donkey.

HE COMES AT A TIME WHEN THERE IS A TEMPLE

As mentioned, the prophet Micah said that the Messiah would reign at a time when the nations of the world go up to the House of God to seek His instruction.   And the prophet Malachi said that the Messiah would come to His Temple suddenly:

> *Behold, I am sending My messenger to clear the way before Me, and the LORD whom you seek shall come to*

[d] The Babylonian Talmud (Sanhedrin 98A, 98B, and 99A), the 4th century Genesis Rabba (98:9), the 13th century Zohar (2:238A) and many other sources state that Zechariah is speaking of Messiah.

His Temple suddenly. As for the angel [messenger] *of the covenant that you desire, he is already coming.*

—Malachi 3:1(JPS)[e]

So, it appears that the Messiah will appear during a time when there is a Temple in Jerusalem. Some rabbis actually contend that Messiah will rebuild the Temple,[8] though there is no clear reference in the Scriptures to that effect.

In any case, since there hasn't been a Temple since 70 CE, it's doubtful that anyone in the last 1,930 years could have been the Messiah.

HE ESTABLISHES A KINGDOM OF JUSTICE, REVERENCE AND PEACE

Messiah will be awesome! Not only will he deliver Judah; He will reestablish the throne of king David, usher in *"peace with out limit"* and rule over the world from Jerusalem! The prophet Isaiah says that the spirit of the LORD shall alight on this descendent of Jesse (David's father) and describes his reign as marked by justice, reverence for the LORD God, and miraculous peace:

> *But a shoot shall grow out of the stump of Jesse, a twig shall sprout from his stock. The spirit of the LORD shall alight on him: a spirit of wisdom and insight, a spirit of counsel and valor, a spirit of devotion and reverence for the LORD. He shall sense the truth by his reverence for the LORD: He shall not judge by what his eyes behold, nor decide by what his ears perceive. Thus he shall judge the poor with equity and decide with justice for the lowly of the land. He shall strike down a land with the rod of his mouth and slay the wicked with the breath of his lips. Justice shall be the girdle of his loins, and faithfulness the*

---

[e] There are some tough questions imbedded in this passage. For example, how can the Temple belong to the Messiah, since it is God's Temple? Rav Yisrael Meir Hokohen (the Chofetz Chaim) states that this "Master whom you seek" referenced in Malachi 3:1 is Messiah. In addition, 12th century philosopher, Moses ben Maimon (Maimonides or Rambam) concurs (Yad haHazaqa, Shoftim, Hilkhot Melachim 11-12).

girdle of his waist. The wolf shall dwell with the lamb, the leopard lie down with the kid; the calf, the beast of prey, and the fatling together, with a little boy to herd them. The cow and the bear shall graze, their young shall lie down together; and the lion, like the ox, shall eat straw. A babe shall play over a viper's hole, and an infant pass his hand over an adder's den. In all of My sacred mount nothing evil or vile shall be done; for the land shall be filled with devotion to the LORD as water covers the sea. In that day, the stock of Jesse that has remained standing shall become a standard to peoples—nations shall seek his counsel and his abode shall be honored.

—Isaiah 11:1-10 (JPS)[f]

Isaiah continues by saying, in that day, God will regather His dispersed people back in Israel.[9]

At last, a king who is led by the spirit of God; who judges righteously and upholds the cause of the poor and lowly; who rules with power; and who brings peace like the world hasn't known since the Garden of Eden! This is definitely no ordinary man.

HE HAS AN EVERLASTING KINGDOM

The prophet Daniel said that after four great kingdoms arise out of the earth, the *"holy ones of the Most High will receive the kingdom, and will possess the kingdom forever—forever and ever."* He also said that this kingdom is headed by someone who is given *"dominion, glory and kingship"* by the *"Ancient of Days,"* and that *"all peoples and nations of every language must serve him."*[g] But most significant is that his kingship lasts forever.[10]

---

[f] Maimonides believed that the ruler described in Isaiah chapter 11 is the Messiah (Yad haHazaqa, Shoftim, Hilkhot Melachim 11-12), The Babylonian Talmud (Sanhedrin 93B) and 10th century Rabbi Sa'adiah ben Joseph agree.

[g] The Babylonian Talmud (Sanhedrin 98A), the Chofetz Chaim, the 13th century Numbers Rabba (13:14), and the 7th-10th century Pirque Mashiah, Bet ha Midrash (3:70) all state the belief that this king is the Messiah.

HE WILL BEAR THE SINS OF THE WORLD

The prophet Isaiah spoke of a servant of the LORD, which rabbis for thousands of years have believed to be the Messiah. This Messiah, however, is not described as king of Israel; he is described as a servant of God:

> *The LORD will bare His holy arm in the sight of all the nations, and the very ends of earth shall see the victory of our God. Turn, turn away, touch naught unclean as you depart from there; keep pure, as you go forth from there, you who bear the vessels of the LORD! For you will not depart in haste, nor will you leave in flight; for the LORD is marching before you, the God of Israel is your rear guard.*

> *Indeed, My servant shall prosper, be exalted and raised to great heights. Just as the many were appalled at him— so marred was his appearance, unlike that of man, his form beyond human semblance—just so he startled many nations. Kings shall be silenced because of him, for they shall see what has not been told them, shall behold what they never have heard.*

> *Who can believe what we have heard? Upon whom has the arm of the LORD been revealed? For he has grown, by His favor, like a tree crown, like a tree trunk out of arid ground. He had no form or beauty, that we should look at him: no charm, that we should find him pleasing. He was despised, shunned by men, a man of suffering, familiar with disease. As one who hid his face from us, he was despised, we held him of no account. Yet it was our sickness that he was bearing, our suffering that he endured. We accounted him plagued, smitten and afflicted by God; but he was wounded because of our sins, crushed because*

of our iniquities. He bore the chastisement that made us whole, and by his bruises we were healed. We all went astray like sheep, each going his own way; and the LORD visited upon him the guilt of all of us.

He was maltreated, yet he was submissive, he did not open his mouth; like a sheep being led to the slaughter, like a ewe, dumb before those who shear her, he did not open his mouth. By oppressive judgment he was taken away, who could describe his abode? For he was cut off from the land of the living through the sin of my people, who deserved the punishment. And his grave was set among the wicked, and with the rich in his death—though he had done no injustice and had spoken no falsehood. But the LORD chose to crush him by disease, that, if he made himself an offering for guilt, he might see offspring and have long life, and that through him the LORD's purpose might prosper. Out of his anguish he shall see it. He shall enjoy it to the full through his devotion.

My righteous servant makes the many righteous, it is their punishment that he bears; assuredly, I will give him the many as his portion, he shall receive the multitude as his spoil. For he exposed himself to death and was numbered among the sinners, whereas be bore the guilt of the many and made intercession for sinners.

—Isaiah 52:10-53:12 (JPS)[h]

This suffering Messiah is crushed and killed by the LORD God. He bears the punishment for the sin of the many and makes them righteous, though he himself had *"done no injustice."* This is made even more clear

[h] The Babylonian Talmud (Sanhedrin 98A) and the 11th century Midrash Konen, Bet ha Midrash (2:29-30) relate that this "servant" is Messiah. The Talmud (Sukkah 52A) also relates that the Messiah will be killed, citing Zechariah 12:10.

by looking at the verse which says he will *"startle many nations."* The word translated "startled" is nazah. It appears about twenty-four times in the Scriptures and can also be translated "sprinkle," which generally relates to ceremonial cleansing in the Temple.[11] God will cleanse us and make us righteous through the punishment that Messiah bears.

The Messiah is taken away by oppressive judgment, maltreated, killed and buried. (The prophet Zechariah confirms this.)[12] Yet God enables him to *"see offspring and have long life."* And God gives him *"the multitude as his Spoil"* and causes him to *"be exalted and raised to great heights."*

This is obviously a perplexing passage of Scripture.

THEN ISRAEL WILL BE SCATTERED

The prophet Zechariah said that, after the shepherd of Israel is struck down, Israel will be scattered:

> *O sword! Rouse yourself against My shepherd, the man*
> *in charge of My flock—says the LORD of Hosts. Strike*
> *down the shepherd and let the flock scatter, and I will*
> *also turn My hand against all the shepherd boys.*
>
> —Zechariah 13:7 (JPS)

Israel was taken into captivity and scattered by the Assyrians and Babylonians and then later by the Romans from 70 CE through 135 CE. After being dispersed for 1,800 years, Israel became a nation once again in 1948. So after all this, will Israel be scattered yet again?

WHAT IS HIS NAME?

The Messiah is obviously pretty incredible. Not just because of what he does—usher in peace on earth (no small task)—but because of what he is called. Isaiah said *"He has been named 'The Mighty God is planning grace; The Eternal Father a peaceable ruler.'"* Actually, *"a peaceable ruler"* in Hebrew is Sar Shalom, which can also be translated 'Prince of Peace.' Jeremiah adds another name:

> *See a time is coming declares the LORD—when I will*
> *raise up a true branch of David's line. He shall reign as*

king and shall prosper, and he shall do what is just and right in the land. In his days Judah shall be delivered and Israel shall dwell secure. And this is the name by which he shall be called: 'The LORD is our Vindicator.'

—Jeremiah 23:5-6 (JPS)[i]

So the Messiah is called by several names: The Mighty God is planning grace, the Eternal Father, the Prince of Peace, and the LORD is our Vindicator. It is reasonable to assume that all of the names have meaning. They are probably either descriptive of who the Messiah is or what God will do through him.

IS THERE MORE THAN ONE MESSIAH?

There are rabbis who believe that there is to be more than one Messiah. The primary reason they believe this is because it's difficult to reconcile the pictures of the Messiah painted by the prophets. You have the prophets Micah, Isaiah, Malachi, Zechariah, and Jeremiah depicting the Messiah as the great ruler who ushers in world peace. Yet, Isaiah also depicted the Messiah as a servant who suffers for our sins and is killed so that we can be made righteous. Zechariah likewise seems to imply that Messiah will be killed and the prophet Daniel said that Messiah will *"disappear"* or be cut off.

The two-messiah concept—one the Messiah son of David and the other the 'Messiah son of Joseph'—emerged during the second Temple period and is recorded in the Talmud.[13] It seeks to explain the seemingly two pictures of the Messiah and to reconcile two views concerning redemption. (One view is the tradition that Israel's redemption will come when Israel repents, the other is that redemption will come at a fixed point in time which is determined by God as stated by the prophet Daniel.)[14] Is this two Messiah theory correct? Is there to be more than one Messiah? There appear to be three options:

---

[i] The Babylonian Talmud (Baba Bathra 75B) and the 5th century Midrash (Lamentations Rabba 1:51, ad Lam. 1:16) make reference to the Messiah in connection with Jeremiah 23:5-6. The Lamentations Rabba translated verse 6 as: "And this is the name whereby he shall be called: The Lord is our righteousness."

1. There is one Messiah who does all that is prophesied. This would imply that he dies and rises from the dead. (This is exactly what some Hassidic Jews believe will happen in the case of Rabbi Schneerson.)

2. There are two Messiahs. One of them dies and one does not.[15]

3. There are many Messiahs.

The biggest problem with the multiple Messiah theories is that they don't come from the Scriptures. The only Messiah or anointed king to come mentioned by name is called the son of David, the descendant of Jesse, the descendant of Judah.[16] This lineage is consistent with one person because King David was both Jesse's son and a descendant of Judah. But there is no 'Messiah son of Joseph' mentioned *anywhere* in the Scriptures and there are no explicit references to two or many Messiahs *anywhere* in the Scriptures.

The Scriptures actually appear to support the one resurrected Messiah view.

- The prophet Isaiah said the suffering Messiah is killed, but, afterward is exalted by God, sees offspring and is given the multitude as his spoil. Both views of Messiah are described in the same passage of Scripture and appear to be speaking of only one person.[17]

- The prophet Daniel said that the Messiah will be cut-off[18] but that his kingship lasts forever.[19]

BUT WHEN WILL THE MESSIAH COME?

There appears to be only one Scripture reference that fixes the time of the Messiah's coming. But it's very difficult to understand. The angel Gabriel was the messenger and the prophet Daniel recorded it:

> *Seventy weeks have been decreed for your people and your holy city until the measure of transgression is filled and that of sin complete, until iniquity is expiated, and eternal righteousness ushered in; and prophetic vision*

ratified, and the Holy of Holies anointed. You must know and understand: From the issuance of the word to restore and rebuild Jerusalem until the [time of the] anointed leader is seven weeks; and for sixty-two weeks it will be rebuilt, square and moat, but in a time of distress. And after those sixty-two weeks, the anointed one will disappear and vanish. The army of a leader who is to come will destroy the city and the sanctuary, but its end will come through a flood. Desolation is decreed until the end of war. During one week he will make a firm covenant with many. For half a week he will put a stop to the sacrifice and the meal offering. At the corner [of the altar] will be an appalling abomination until the decreed destruction will be poured down upon the appalling thing.

—Daniel 9.24-27 (JPS)

There are *at least* two possible starting points for this prophecy. Both are historically well documented. The first is 538 BCE when King Cyrus of Persia gave the command to return to Palestine and rebuild the Temple.[20] The other possible starting point is 445 BCE. That's when Nehemiah gave the order to rebuild Jerusalem.[21]

While the date from which to start may appear to be a dilemma, the real challenge is in understanding what is meant by the term *"weeks."* If it was literally seventy weeks and we use the first possible starting date, then the Messiah came and went at the time of Ezra before the Temple was even rebuilt (which conflicts with Malachi's prophecy). Many rabbis have said that the *"seventy weeks"* are weeks of years.[22] If this is the case, are they 365 day (solar) years or 354 day (lunar) years as used in the Jewish calendar? If they were lunar years (and an extra month were not inserted in seven out of every nineteen years as is actually the case) and the second starting date is used, the Messiah would *"disappear"* about 483 lunar years after the decree…about 469 solar years, that is about the year 24 CE. Obviously, playing with dates can be incredibly frustrating.

This passage creates *many* questions:

- What is the true starting date of the prophecy?

- What measure of time does the term *"weeks"* represent?

- If the Messiah is to disappear, is this his death?

- If the Messiah is to reign forever, how does all of this fit?

- And finally, what does *"iniquity is expiated, and eternal right-eousness ushered in"* mean?

While we may not have all of the answers to these questions, when Messiah comes all of this will fit the actual historical events and the time references will make sense.

CONCLUSIONS

There are three simple points of conclusion:

- There really is a Messiah. This is a core tenet of Judaism.

- The Scriptures actually tell us whom to look for. They say that Messiah will:

    Be born in Bethlehem...in Israel. He will be a descendant of King David and will be preceded by the prophet Elijah. The Messiah will be so humble as to ride into Jerusalem on a donkey, but he will rule the world from Jerusalem and will establish a kingdom of justice, reverence and peace. He will be called the Prince of Peace and the Mighty God is planning grace. He will suffer and die for the sins of the world to make us righteous, but afterward he will have long life and be exalted. After he is struck down, Israel will be scattered. And, finally, Messiah will come at a time when there is a Temple in Jerusalem.

- We should read the Scriptures ourselves, all of them: the Law, the Prophets, and the Writings (the Torah, Nevi'im, and Kethuvim). We need to base our expectations and conclusions upon the Scriptures lest impostors fool us or we miss the real thing. We'll be amazed at what we learn!

Is Messiah The Son Of God?

Is Messiah the Son of God? This is not an easy question. But it's a question that is crucial to having an understanding of who Messiah is and why he is coming. To view Messiah as someone that he is not is a theologically dangerous thing. At the extreme, if our expectations of him do not line up with who he really is, we could miss him when he does come. We could miss Messiah's coming, because what we are looking for may not be consistent with who he is.

Since the question of whether Messiah is the son of God is a challenging one, let's try to simplify it by first answering a more basic question as a predecessor: *Is it Scripturally possible for anyone to be considered the son of God?* Fortunately, the answer is easy—yes. And to prove it, let's start with a man with whom we are all familiar, who actually was called the "son of God."

"You Are My Son"

> *Why do nations assemble, and peoples plot vain things; kings of the earth take their stand, and regents intrigue together against the LORD and against His anointed? 'Let us break the cords of their yoke, shake off their ropes from us!' He who is enthroned in heaven laughs; the Lord mocks at them. Then He speaks to them in anger,*

terrifying them in His rage, 'But I have installed My king on Zion, My holy mountain!' Let me tell of the decree: the LORD said to me, 'You are My son, I have fathered you this day. Ask it of Me, and I will make the nations your domain; your estate, the limits of the earth. You can smash them with an iron mace, shatter them like potter's ware.'

—Psalms 2:4-9 (JPS)

In these verses and elsewhere in the Psalms, God declared King David to be His son.[1] But, David wasn't alone. Solomon and the entire nation of Israel were also called the children of God![2]

So, it really isn't much of a stretch to call Messiah the Son of God. Messiah is a Jew, the descendant of David and Solomon, and the anointed King of Israel. If God called David, Solomon, and the nation of Israel His sons, surely Messiah can also rightly be called the son of God.[a]

A 1st Century View

The view that Messiah is the son of God has been around at least since the 1st century CE. The Dead Sea Scrolls attest to this. One of the scrolls, the Qumran document referred to as 4Q246, has been translated by Joseph Fitzmyer as stating:

[He] shall be great upon the earth, [O King! All shall] make [peace], and shall serve [him. He shall be called the son of] the [G]reat [God], and by his name shall he be named. He shall be hailed the Son of God, and they shall call him Son of the Most High..., and his kingdom shall be a kingdom forever.[3]

While this text doesn't mention "Messiah" explicitly, the context of a leader who is called *"Son of the Most High"* and whose kingdom shall be *"a kingdom forever"* leaves little doubt as to who is being referenced.

---

[a] The Babylonian Talmud (Sukkah 52A) states the belief that Psalms 2:7 is also speaking of Messiah, implicitly calling him the son of God.

This may especially be true because a Scriptural parallel to such a king is in Isaiah Chapter 11, which has historically been widely believed to be speaking of Messiah.

Obviously, just finding a reference like this doesn't mean that the statement is true. The Essene sect of Judaism (or whoever wrote this) could have been wrong. But it does indicate that the belief that the Messiah is the son of God is not a new concept, nor is it a "non-Jewish" concept.

But what does it *mean* to call someone the son of God? Was the belief just that a man would be declared by God to be his son or was it that God would really *have* a son? And, in light of the Scriptures which state that there is only one God, what does it mean to say that God has a son?

THE REAL QUESTION IS: "IS THE MESSIAH GOD?"

Ultimately, when you get to the root of the matter, the real question is not, *"Is Messiah the son of God?"* The real question is: *"Is the Messiah God?"*

The Messiah is the descendant of King David. He is a man. The Scriptures are clear about this. So, how can this question be taken seriously? How could anyone suggest that Messiah is God? Those who make this contention point to the Scriptures to support their case.

GOD APPEARED AS A MAN BEFORE

Those who claim that Messiah is God first point to the Scriptures which suggest that God appeared within His creation in the form of a man before. In fact, God did appear to Abraham and others many times. On at least one of these occasions He appeared to Abraham as a man.[4] When He did so, He didn't stop being omnipresent. He didn't stop running the Universe. And, He didn't stop being God.

Their point is that if God appeared as a man before, He could do it again.

MESSIAH IS LIKE NO OTHER MAN!

Another reason they suggest that Messiah may be God is that it's obvious that He's definitely no ordinary man! He will usher in world peace and rule over the entire world from Jerusalem. Since the Tower of Babel days, no man has ever ruled the entire world, not Nebuchadnezzar, Alexander the Great, the Caesars, the Khans, Peter the Great, the Ottoman Turks, the Habsburgs, Hitler, Stalin, or Mao! No one has ruled the world. Yet, the Messiah will. He will rule in excess of six billion people! The Messiah will do the seemingly impossible. The enormity of this task alone suggests that he is like no other man.

Messiah's Name

Those who contend that Messiah is God also point to the names that Messiah is called in the Scriptures. They assert that these names are not without significance. For example, Isaiah called him: *"The mighty God is planning grace; the eternal father; a peaceable ruler"*:

> *For a child has been born to us, a son has been given us. And authority has settled on his shoulders. He has been named 'The mighty God is planning grace; the Eternal father, a peaceable ruler'—in token of abundant authority and of peace without limit upon David's throne and kingdom, that it may be firmly established in justice and in equity now and evermore. The zeal of the LORD of Hosts shall bring this to pass.*

> *—Isaiah 9:5-6 (JPS)*

Jeremiah added a name and called Messiah *"The LORD is our Vindicator"*:

> *See a time is coming declares the LORD—when I will raise up a true branch of David's line. He shall reign as king and shall prosper, and he shall do what is just and right in the land. In his days Judah shall be delivered and Israel shall dwell secure. And this is the name by which he shall be called: 'The LORD is our Vindicator'.*

> *—Jeremiah 23:5-6 (JPS)*

If we assumed that these names are descriptive of the Messiah's role or identity, we would conclude that the Messiah is part of God's plan to extend grace (unmerited favor), that the Messiah is or is from God the Eternal Father, that he is the Prince of Peace (the Sar Shalom), and that he will be the Vindicator of Israel.

Of themselves, the names don't definitively prove that Messiah is God. After all, the name *Daniel* means *God is judge*. Yet, Daniel wasn't God. However, it is because Messiah is called so many names characteristic of God and because Messiah is called "the Eternal Father" that weight is added to the contention that Messiah could be God.

Messiah's Temple

Another line of reasoning is related to the Temple. God said through Malachi that His messenger will clear the way before Him and that the Messiah will come to His Temple suddenly.

> *Behold, I am sending My messenger to clear the way before Me, and the Lord whom you seek shall come to His temple suddenly. As for the angel [Messenger] of the covenant that you desire, he is already coming. But who can endure the day of his coming, and who can hold out when he appears? For he is like smelter's fire and like fuller's lye. He shall act like a smelter and purger of silver; he shall purify the descendants of Levi and refine them like gold and silver, so that they shall present offerings in righteousness. Then the offerings of Judah and Jerusalem shall be pleasing to the LORD as in the days of yore and in the years of old.*

—Malachi 3:1-4 (JPS)

Based upon Malachi 3:23-24, the *"messenger"* is generally understood to be the prophet Elijah and *"the Lord whom you seek"* has been generally acknowledged to be the Messiah. If this is the case, then the Scriptures are saying that the Temple is the Messiah's Temple. But, we know *the Temple belongs to God.* Nowhere else in Scripture is the Temple referred to as belonging to anyone except God. It is never in Scripture called Solomon's Temple, or David's Temple, or even Israel's Temple. So why would Malachi say, as he does, that the Messiah *"shall come to His Temple?"* Many contend that it would only make sense if the Messiah actually is God.

AN EVERLASTING KINGDOM

Perhaps the most amazing thing about the Messiah's reign on the earth is that it lasts forever! Some contend that this suggests that Messiah is much more than a mere man.

The prophet Daniel described a vision from God where he saw four great kingdoms on the earth. At the time of the last kingdom, God judged the earth and took the dominion of these kingdoms away.[5] Then a new kingdom was established:

> *As I looked on, in the night vision, One like a human being came with the clouds of heaven; he reached the Ancient of Days and was presented to Him. Dominion, glory, and kingship were given to him; all peoples and nations of every language must serve him. His dominion is an everlasting dominion that shall not pass away, and his kingship, one that shall not be destroyed.*

—Daniel 7:13-14 (JPS)

This king, whom the Talmud calls the Messiah,[6] is going to have an everlasting dominion and the people of God will possess the kingdom forever.[7]

God promised King David that his house and his kingship would be secure and that his throne would be established forever.[8] Yet, David died. And David's descendants have not ruled in Judah for many hundreds of years. Messiah, who is a descendant of David, will evidently fulfill this prophecy about David's house. Messiah's kingdom will never end.

THE SACRIFICE THAT MAKES US RIGHTEOUS

The prophets Isaiah, Zechariah, and Daniel all say that the Messiah is killed.[9] Isaiah describes in great detail that the purpose of Messiah's death is to be a sacrifice for sins, to make us righteous:

> *The LORD will bare His holy arm in the sight of all the nations, and the very ends of earth shall see the victory of our God. Turn, turn away, touch naught unclean as you depart from there; keep pure, as you go forth from there, you who bear the vessels of the LORD! For you will not depart in haste, nor will you leave in flight; for the LORD is marching before you, the God of Israel is your rear guard.*

> *Indeed, My servant shall prosper, be exalted and raised to great heights. Just as the many were appalled at him—so marred was his appearance, unlike that of man, his form beyond human semblance—just so he startled many nations. Kings shall be silenced because of him, for they shall see what has not been told them, shall behold what they never have heard.*

> *Who can believe what we have heard? Upon whom has the arm of the LORD been revealed? For he has grown, by His favor, like a tree crown, like a tree trunk out of arid ground. He had no form or beauty, that we should look at him: no charm, that we should find him pleasing. He was despised, shunned by men, a man of suffering, familiar with disease. As one who hid his face from us, he was despised, we held him of no account. Yet it was our sickness that he was bearing, our suffering that he endured. We accounted him plagued, smitten and afflicted by God; but he was wounded because of our sins, crushed because of our iniquities. He bore the chastisement that made us whole, and by his bruises we were healed. We all went astray like sheep, each going his own way; and the LORD visited upon him the guilt of all of us.*

He was maltreated, yet he was submissive, he did not open his mouth; like a sheep being led to the slaughter, like a ewe, dumb before those who shear her, he did not open his mouth. By oppressive judgement he was taken away, who could describe his abode? For he was cut off from the land of the living through the sin of my people, who deserved the punishment. And his grave was set among the wicked, and with the rich in his death—though he had done no injustice and had spoken no falsehood. But the LORD chose to crush him by disease, that, if he made himself an offering for guilt, he might see offspring and have long life, and that through him the LORD's purpose might prosper. Out of his anguish he shall see it. He shall enjoy it to the full through his devotion.

My righteous servant makes the many righteous, it is their punishment that he bears; assuredly, I will give him the many as his portion, he shall receive the multitude as his spoil. For he exposed himself to death and was numbered among the sinners, whereas he bore the guilt of the many and made intercession for sinners.

—Isaiah 52:10-53:12 (JPS)

As you may recall, the Scriptures say that the sacrifice for sins must be spotless.[10] The Scriptures also say that no man is without sin.[11] Yet, Messiah is sacrificed for our sins and *does* make us righteous! A sinful man can't die as a sacrifice for his own sins much less the sins of the world. This is clear because the Scriptures say that *no man* can redeem his own life or the life of another. Only God can redeem the life of man.[12] Yet, that is what Messiah does.

Those who say that Messiah is God contend that Messiah cannot atone for mankind's sin if he is not God.

A RESURRECTED MESSIAH

Some followers of Hassidic Rabbi Menachem Mendel Schneerson believe that he will yet rise from the dead to lead Israel. As strange as it may sound, this is a concept which does, in fact, have a Scriptural root. This is exactly what Isaiah says the Messiah will do. Isaiah says that *after* Messiah offers himself as a guilt offering for sin, he is exhalted. It is *because* he gives himself as an offering for the sins of the unrighteous that he has long life and receives the multitude as his spoil. Messiah will be killed and will *then* rise from the dead.[13]

But, does this make him God? After all, God answered Elijah's prayer and raised the widow of Zarephath's son from the dead.[14] And, God answered Elisha's prayer and raised the Shunammite woman's son from the dead.[15] Yet, neither of these two people who rose from the dead were God. So, why does Messiah rising from the dead make him God?

The answer given is that it is not Messiah's resurrection alone which proves him to be God. It is what Messiah's death accomplishes (the righteousness of those for whom he dies) which proves him to be God. His physical resurrection from the dead merely validates it. Since God is an eternal spiritual being, He cannot spiritually die. So, it is reasonable that if He were to take human form and die physically as a sacrifice for our sins, that he wouldn't stay in the grave. Even in physical form God would be more powerful than death—He made death.

THE REBUTTAL ARGUMENTS

All of these preceding lines of reasoning do suggest that there is a Scriptural case supporting the contention that the Messiah could actually be God. However, there are two very obvious rebuttal arguments that can be tendered in response.

"I AM NOT MAN..."

The first argument claims that the Scriptures are definitely clear that God is not mortal. He is not man:

God is not man to be capricious, Or mortal to change His mind. Would He speak and not act, Promise and not fulfill?

—Numbers 23:19 (JPS)

I will not act on My wrath, Will not turn to destroy Ephraim. For I am God, not man, The holy One in your midst: I will not come in fury.

—Hosea 11:9 (JPS)

God is the creator, not the created. He is the all powerful (omnipotent), all present (omnipresent), all knowing (omniscient) God. He is holy and eternal, without beginning or end! But, to be a descendant of King David and King Solomon, Messiah must be *born*. This implies that Messiah has a beginning and is a powerful argument against Messiah being God.

"I AM THE LORD AND THERE IS NONE ELSE"

The second argument says that the LORD is one. To many, the concept of God having a "son" implies that there are two gods. However, Scripture is emphatic that this is not so![16] There is only one God:

I am the LORD and there is none else; Beside Me, there is no god. I engird you though you have not known Me. So that they may know, from east to west, That there is none but Me. I am the LORD and there is none else, I form light and create darkness, I make the weal and create woe—I the LORD do all these things.

—Isaiah 45:5-6 (JPS)

There is only one God. That is clear from Scripture.

FINAL REBUTTALS

These are strong rebuttal arguments. But they're not conclusive.

There are equally strong replies to both points. Let's start with the first rebuttal argument.

COULD GOD BE BORN AS A MAN?

A simple reply to the question, "Could God be born as a man," is to say that God is God and nothing is impossible for Him. Yet, God does not violate His own nature. God, who is holy, just, and pure, does not deny Himself by becoming unholy, unjust, and impure. So a better question to ask is: "Could God be born as a man without violating His own nature?"

Well, we know that God *appeared* to Abraham as a man without violating His own nature. But, for God to be *born* as a man without violating His own nature is entirely different. If life has it's beginning with conception, then the only way that Messiah could be God is if the physical laws of conception are not followed. God is eternal. He has no beginning or end. If God were born as a man, it would have to be in such a way as to not violate His eternal nature. God could not cease being God. If God had a "beginning," He would not be God.

Likewise, God cannot stop being omnipresent. He is everywhere and, since He cannot cease being Himself, the only way that He could enter His own creation as a man is if He were to do so without forfeiting His omnipresence.

COULD GOD HAVE A "SON" WHO IS HIMSELF?

If Messiah is God, as some claim, there can still only be one God. But, this would mean that God would have a "son" who is Himself? Is this possible?

As strange as this sounds, a case can be made to support it. Those who espouse this view point to the Book of Genesis where Moses calls God "*Elohim.*" *Elohim* is the plural form of the word *el*, which means God.[17] However, it is almost invariably used with *singular* verbs. Why would this *plural* word be used (over 190 times in Genesis alone) to describe the *one* true God?

In addition, Moses recorded God as saying something that is very puzzling. The context is during the creation of the universe:

And God said, 'Let us make man in our image, after our likeness.'

—Genesis 1:26 (JPS)

And the LORD God said, 'Now that the man has become like one of us, knowing good and bad, what if he should stretch out his hand and also take from the tree of life and eat and live forever!'

—Genesis 3:22 (JPS)

And, when God sent Isaiah to be a prophet to Israel He made a similar statement:

Then I heard the voice of my Lord saying, 'Whom shall I send? Who will go for us?

—Isaiah 6:8 (JPS)

Who is the *"us"* that God is referring to in these Scriptures? Philo, a 1st century Jewish philosopher, suggested that God is speaking about other beings who are His *"assistants."*[18] But, it isn't likely that He is talking to assistants or even to the angels because we know that God *alone* is the creator.[19] And, we know that He isn't referring to other *gods* because the Scriptures are so emphatic that there is only one God.[20] So who is "us?" Perhaps Messiah is part of the "us." This is one of the great mysteries of the Scriptures.

What is clear is that God created the physical universe. But, He has also appeared within it, to Abraham and the Prophets. Yet, He did not cease to be the one omnipresent God when He did so. He appeared as man, but did not cease to be God. So, perhaps He will do it again and appear as the physical human Messiah without ceasing to be the omnipresent LORD of Hosts.

Many of those who believe that God has a son contend that the "us" is Messiah.

CONCLUSIONS

There are two real conclusions here.

✳ The Messiah can rightly be called the son of God.

Since God referred to David, Solomon, and the entire nation of Israel as His sons, it's not much of a stretch to call the Messiah the son of God also.

✳ There actually is Scriptural evidence to support the contention that the Messiah is God:

A reasonable case can be made that Messiah actually is God. This case implies that God will show up within His creation as a man. Why is this plausible? The Scriptural case includes:

—God appeared as a man before.

—Messiah will do things no *mere man* has ever done: usher in eternal peace and righteousness, rule the entire world, and reign forever.

—Messiah is called names such as: the Eternal Father, the Prince of Peace, the Lord is our Vindicator, and the Mighty God is planning grace.

—God's Temple is said to belong to Messiah. This would make little sense if Messiah weren't God.

—Messiah will die as a sacrifice for our sins to make us righteous. Yet, only God is without sin and only God can make us truly righteous.

—Messiah will rise from the dead. Death cannot hold the creator of death.

—God has referred to Himself in the Scriptures in the *plural*, though He is *one*.

Based upon these arguments, it seems possible that perhaps Messiah really is God.

IS JESUS THE MESSIAH?

Is Jesus the Messiah? For most Jews this question is simply disregarded at face value. The reaction is often either one of rolled eyes and a strained response of, "No, I don't think so," or possibly, of a more terse "get a brain!" Yet, most Jews have no real understanding of the basis for which Jesus' followers claim him to be the "Jewish Messiah." But, since roughly a third of the world's population (33%) are classified as followers of Jesus and only *two tenths of one* percent (.2%) are classified as Jews,[1] one would think that all Jews would want to understand the reasoning behind the claims made by the people who follow this Jewish man named Jesus as the Jewish Messiah.

MANY WOULD-BE MESSIAHS

There have been many would-be Messiahs over the centuries. There were several claimants in the first and second centuries alone.

Herod   There was Herod the Great, who completed the restoration of the Temple in Jerusalem in 64 CE. He was, evidently, considered by some to be the Messiah (though he ordered his wife, brother-in-law, mother-in-law, two of his sons, and several close friends killed).[2]

Jesus Jesus, or Yeshua in Hebrew, was a Galilean Jew who preached and claimed to be the Messiah during 30-33 CE. He was crucified at the request of the Sanhedrin by the order of Roman governor Pontius Pilate.[3]

Theudas Flavius Josephus reported that a man named Theudas professed to be a prophet and led many people to the Jordan River in 44 CE (to be parted at his command). He and many of his followers were killed by Fadus, the Roman procurator. His head was then taken back to Jerusalem for display.[4]

Lukuas-Andreas Lukuas-Andreas is also reported to have claimed to be the Messiah. He led an ill-fated revolt against Rome in Cyrene on the north African coast in 115-117 CE.[5]

Simon Bar–Kokhba Simon Bar–Kokhba led a revolt against Rome in Palestine during 132-135 CE. Even Rabbi Akiva, considered by many to be the greatest Torah scholar of his day, was convinced that Bar–Kokhba was the Messiah and convinced thousands of others to join the revolt.[6] The revolution was squashed by the Romans and it is believed that 50% of Judea's population was killed.

Today there are yet others who are considered by their followers to be the Messiah. Yet a chief difference between them all and Jesus (Yeshua) is that they are not revered as the Jewish Messiah by close to two billion people almost 2,000 years after their deaths. This is why it's worth examining and understanding the Messianic claims made by his followers.

HOW DOES JESUS STACK-UP AGAINST PROPHECIES IN THE SCRIPTURES?

The only way to really know the Messiah when he comes is based upon the descriptions provided by God through the Prophets in the Scriptures. Based upon the Scriptures, Messiah is to be a political leader, a religious leader, and the source of spiritual redemption for Israel and the world. So the relevant question is, how did Jesus stack up against the Scriptures that say what Messiah is supposed to be and do?

Historically, Rabbis as a group have generally agreed upon which Scriptures are speaking of the Messiah. Let's examine Jesus (Yeshua) based upon some of them.

A DESCENDANT OF KING DAVID

The Scriptures say Messiah is to be a descendant of King David.[7]

Jesus' followers claimed him to be a descendant of King David. They even cite two genealogical lines from which he is supposed to have descended.[8] Interestingly, a reference in the Talmud may actually support their claims:

> *AND A HERALD PRECEDES HIM etc. This implies, only immediately before [the execution], but not previous thereto. [In contradiction to this] it was taught: On the eve of the Passover Yesu was hanged. For forty days before the execution took place, a herald went forth and cried, 'He is going forth to be stoned because he has practised sorcery and enticed Israel to apostasy. Any one who can say anything in his favour, let him come forward and plead on his behalf.' But since nothing was brought forward in his favour he was hanged on the eve of the Passover! — 'Ulla retorted: Do you suppose he was one for whom a defence could be made? Was he not a Mesith [enticer], concerning whom Scripture says, Neither shalt thou spare, neither shaft thou conceal him? With Yesu however it was different, for he was connected with the government [or royalty, i.e. influential].*
>
> —Babylonian Talmud, Sanhedrin 43a[9]

This Gemara (teaching) relates to the requirement in the Mishnah that a herald must solicit witnesses to defend an accused person before the accused can be tried and put to death. It uses the example of Jesus

(Yeshu) in relating that the need to solicit witnesses implies that it be done immediately prior to the execution, but that it need not be done further in advance of the execution. Jesus' case was different in that they solicited witnesses for forty days before the execution took place. The reason given was that Jesus was connected to the government. Another translation of the Talmud says that he was connected to the kingship.

Jesus' followers would contend that: A run of the mill 'heretic' would definitely not have been treated with such extraordinary care had he not been viewed to be someone of note, or well connected. Yet, if Jesus was well connected with the Roman leaders, they would most likely not have crucified him at the request of the subjugated Jewish government (the Sanhedrin). Likewise, had Jesus been politically well-connected within the Sanhedrin or with the High Priest, he probably wouldn't have been arrested, tried for blasphemy, and turned over to the hated Romans— unless it were considered a very grave offense. And if this were the case, they would be unlikely to advertise for forty days if Jesus weren't con-sidered to be someone of significance. Their conclusion is that Jesus' sig-nificance was based upon his genealogy rather than his connections.

> *Conclusion:* *A case could be made that Jesus may have been a descendant of king David.*

FROM BETHLEHEM OF EPHRATH

According to the prophet Micah, the Messiah is to be born in Bethlehem.[10]

Jesus' followers claim that he was born in Bethlehem, though his parents, Joseph and Mary (Miriam), were living to the north in the city of Nazareth in Galilee. They cite a decree made by Roman Emperor Caesar Augustus requiring that everyone register themselves in their city of origin as part of a census and tax. They claim that Joseph went to Bethlehem with his espoused wife Miriam, who was pregnant, during a first census made when Quirinius was the Roman governor of Syria. There, they say, Jesus was born.[11]

While Jesus' "official birth certificate" is not available, his modern day followers cite the historical accuracy of the details of the first century accounts of his birth as evidence to support early followers' claims. They contend that:

1. *Quirinius was indeed Governor of Syria at the time.*

   The first century Jewish historian, Flavius Josephus, recorded that Quirinius was a judge over the Roman province of Syria, of which Judea was a part.[12] He also recorded that Quirinius was sent into Judea to impose a tax.[13]

   Inscriptional evidence also suggests that Quirinius was actually cogovernor of Syria from about 8–6 BCE while he was in charge of the Homanadensian War in a Roman province near Syria.[14] (Others put the date at 4 BCE to 1 CE) He was then later named the Governor of Syria for what appears to be a second time in 6 CE.[15]

2. *Another Roman census required travel to one's city of origin.*

   There is evidently another recorded instance of where a Roman census required travel to a person's city of origin. It occurred in Egypt in about 104 CE.[16] Since Jewish property rights were based upon the geographic origin of each person's family,[17] it seems logical that the Romans would have chosen this approach to conducting a census and imposing tax.

3. *There was another ('second') Roman census in 6 CE.*

   A Roman census in the year 6 CE was recorded by Flavius Josephus.[18] The "first" census cited by Jesus' followers would have been earlier.

4. *A Roman census would logically have occurred shortly after 4 BCE.*

   Herod the Great, who governed Palestine, died in March or April of 4 BCE. Palestine was then split up into political tetrarchies under different officials. It would have been logical to conduct a census prior to or in conjunction with a redrawing of political boundaries. But, while a census requiring travel across political subdivisions would have taken some time to complete, it likely would not have taken place long after Herod's death.

5. Jesus' reported birth date is consistent with other recorded events.

Jesus' public 'ministry' is said to have begun when he was about thirty years old.[19] It began after that of John the Baptist, who was said to have begun his 'ministry' in the fifteenth year of the reign of Tiberias Caesar.[20] Since Tiberias Caesar's fifteenth year has been dated around 27–29 CE, Jesus would have been born in around 3 BCE—give or take a few years. This date does coincide with the other historical events cited by Jesus' followers.

So, while the detailed third-party records of Jesus' birthplace are not available, his followers' claim that Jesus was born in Bethlehem is actually historically plausible. While Jesus' parents lived in Nazareth, the political events requiring a census are plausible, the historical events and leaders mentioned are accurate, there is at least one other incidence of a Roman census requiring travel, and the dates all roughly coincide with the reported date of Jesus' birth.

> Conclusion: *It is historically plausible that Jesus could have been born in Bethlehem at the time his followers claim.*

PRECEDED BY THE PROPHET ELIJAH

The Scriptures say that Messiah will be preceded by the Prophet Elijah.[21]

Jesus was preceded by a man called John the Baptist. Jesus and his 1st century followers contended that John the Baptist was Elijah.

Jesus' followers reported John the Baptist to be the son of Zacharias, a priest.[22] He was also reported to be a distant cousin of Jesus (John's mother and Jesus' mother were related).[23] Little else is reported about him, except that he was raised and lived in the desert until he emerged as a preacher at about the age of thirty.[24] It is conjecture, but he could possibly have been a part of the Essene sect of Judaism.

Flavius Josephus, the Jewish historian, had a good deal to say about John and actually supports some of Jesus' early followers' contentions about him:

Now, some of the Jews thought that the destruction of Herod's army came from God, and that very justly, as a punishment of what he did against John, that was called the Baptist; for Herod slew him, who was a good man, and commanded the Jews to exercise virtue, both as to righteousness towards one another, and piety towards God, and so to come to baptism; for that the washing [with water] would be acceptable to him, if they made use of it, not in order to the putting away [or the remission] of some sins [only], but for the purification of the body; supposing still that the soul was thoroughly purified beforehand by righteousness. Now, when [many] others came in crowds about him, for they were greatly moved [or pleased] by hearing his words, Herod, who feared lest the great influence John had over the people might be put into his power and inclination to raise a rebellion (for they seemed ready to do anything he should advise), thought it best, by putting him to death, to prevent any mischief he might cause, and not bring himself into difficulties, by sparing a man who might make him repent of it when it should be too late. Accordingly he was sent a prisoner, out of Herod's suspicious temper, to Macherus, the castle I before mentioned and was there put to death. Now the Jews had an opinion that the destruction of this army was sent as a punishment upon Herod, and a mark of God's displeasure against him."

—Josephus, *The Antiquities of The Jews*, (18.5.2)[25]

Josephus described John the Baptist as a good man and influential preacher who preached that the people should yield to God and behave righteously toward one another. He recorded that John the Baptist was killed by Herod the Tetrarch because he feared John's great influence over the people. John was probably in his early thirties when he died.

At minimum, given his message of repentance, the respect he earned from the Jewish people, and his large number of followers, John the Baptist could rightly have been called a prophet-like figure.

So was John the Baptist, Elijah? According to Jesus' followers, John the Baptist didn't claim to be Elijah.[26] They said that he did, however, claim to be the prophet spoken of by Isaiah:

> *I am the voice of one crying in the wilderness, Make straight the way of the Lord, as said the prophet, Isaiah.*

—John 1:23 (NIV®)

Based upon the Scripture quoted, he claimed to be the prophet who precedes the actual appearance of the LORD God on earth. This claim would be every bit as dramatic as claiming to be Elijah. He was quoting from Isaiah chapter 40:

> *Comfort, oh comfort My people, Says your God. Speak tenderly to Jerusalem, And declare to her that her term of service is over, that her iniquity is expiated; for she has received at the hand of the LORD double for all her sins.*
>
> *A voice rings out: 'Clear the desert a road for the LORD! Level in the wilderness a highway for our God! Let every valley be raised, every hill and mount made low. Let the rugged ground become level and the ridges become plain. The Presence of the LORD shall appear, ∣nd all flesh, as one, shall behold—for the LORD Himself has spoken.*

—Isaiah 40:1-5 (JPS)

But, while John the Baptist came short of actually claiming to be Elijah, Jesus went so far as to specifically state that John the Baptist was in fact Elijah.[27]

John the Baptist's influence over the people was so great that Herod had him killed. Yet, John the Baptist is reported to have told his "disciples" to follow Jesus rather than himself.[28] Jesus' disciples claimed that it was because of John the Baptist that they first followed Jesus. They said that John the Baptist had called Jesus the Messiah[29] and the *"son of God."*[30] He is also reported to have called Jesus *"the lamb of God who takes away the sin of the world,"* (evidently referencing Isaiah 53).[31] Peter, Andrew, and probably James and John and others among Jesus' first disciples were originally followers of John the Baptist.

> Conclusion: *A case could be made that John the Baptist was a prophet and that his message and lifestyle were similar to Elijah's. Many of Jesus' first disciples followed Jesus because of John the Baptist*

A HUMBLE MAN

Zechariah prophesied that Messiah would be a humble man who rides into Jerusalem on a donkey, but that he would also rule over the entire world.[32]

Like Zechariah's prophecy, Jesus is recorded as having ridden into Jerusalem on a donkey.[33] This, however, could have been an event easily staged by anyone. In addition, Jesus did not fulfill the remainder of the prophecy—he did not rule *"from sea to sea and from ocean to land's end."*[34]

> Conclusion: *Jesus could easily have fulfilled the first part of this prophecy. He has not, however, fulfilled the later.*

COMING AT A TIME WHEN THERE IS A TEMPLE

According to the prophet Malachi, Messiah is coming at a time when the Temple of God in Jerusalem is standing.[35]

This prophecy obviously rules out a lot of people as the Messiah. The Temple was destroyed by the Roman General Titus' armies in 70 CE, at the command of Emperor Vespasian. Jesus did live when the Temple was still standing and could have easily frequented the Temple grounds and taught there as recorded by his first century followers.[36]

Conclusion: *Jesus did live in Israel at a time when the Temple was still standing. He could have easily taught there as his followers claimed.*

HE WILL BEAR THE SINS OF THE WORLD

Isaiah prophesied of a servant of the LORD who was smitten by God because of our sins. This servant was to bear the punishment of Israel and to carry our guilt so that we could be made whole. He was to be our guilt offering. Isaiah said this servant of the LORD would be taken away by oppressive judgment; that he would be maltreated, beaten and bruised beyond human semblance, yet submissive; that he would be killed and buried, though he had done no injustice and hadn't lied; that it is God who would crush and kill Messiah; and that Messiah would bear our sins and make us righteous through his death. Finally, after his death, Messiah would see "offspring," would be exhalted and raised to great heights by God, would live a long life and would receive the multitude as his spoil.[37]

This is where the life of Jesus gets interesting. This prophecy is one of the principle reasons why he has so many followers.

Jesus' first century followers said that he was a wise and good man who was a teacher of the Law of God. They said that he was accused of blasphemy by the Sanhedrin but that he didn't respond in defense or fight the charges.[38] He is also recorded by his followers to have been beaten severely and turned over to the Roman Governor who had him crucified just before Passover.[39] They contended that Jesus fulfilled the prophecies of Isaiah chapters 52 and 53 that Messiah will die for the sins of Israel and will make us righteous. They claimed that *he is the Passover sacrifice* and the fulfillment of the Temple sacrificial system. They also claimed that Jesus rose from the dead three days later and that he ascended to heaven.

Third party historical records actually add credence to their claims. Jesus is recorded in the Talmud as having been condemned and executed.[40] Flavius Josephus also confirms several of these events and contentions in his *Antiquities of the Jews*. Two translations of Josephus' writings confirm that Jesus was considered to be a wise and good man, that he was thought to be the Messiah, that he was crucified by Pontus Pilate, and that his followers claimed that he rose from the dead three days later. William Whiston's 1736 translation renders Josephus' account as follows:

> Now there was about this time Jesus, a wise man, if it be lawful to call him a man, for he was a doer of wonderful works—a teacher of such men as receive the truth with pleasure. He drew over to him both many of the Jews, and many of the Gentiles. He was the Christ; and when Pilate, at the suggestion of the principal men amongst us, had condemned him to the cross, those that loved him at the first did not forsake him, for he appeared to them alive again the third day, as the divine prophets had foretold these and ten thousand other wonderful things concerning him; and the tribe of Christians, so named from him, are not extinct at this day.

—Josephus, *The Antiquities Of The Jews,* (18.3.3)[41]

A 10th century Arabic version is translated by Shlomo Pines as:

> At this time there was a wise man who was called Jesus. His conduct was good, and [he] was known to be virtuous. And many people from among the Jews and the other nations became his disciples. Pilate condemned him to be crucified and to die. But those who had become his disciples did not abandon his discipleship. They reported that he had appeared to them three days after his crucifixion and that he was alive; accordingly, he was perhaps the Messiah, concerning whom the prophets have recounted wonders.

—Josephus, *The Antiquities Of The Jews,* (18.3.3)[42]

Jesus' followers claim that he fulfilled the prophecies of Isaiah and that he did rise from the dead and, after appearing to hundreds of people over the space of forty days, that he ascended to heaven.[43]

> Conclusion: *A historically strong case can be made that Jesus was a good and wise man who died in a brutal manner very similar to that described by the Prophet Isaiah. His followers also contend that there were hundreds of people who witnessed his resurrection from the dead as prophesied by Isaiah.*

BUT, WHEN SPECIFICALLY WILL MESSIAH COME?

The only Scripture that seems to provide a time reference for the Messiah's appearance is in the book of Daniel and is difficult to understand. The Angel Gabriel is recorded as telling Daniel when Messiah would vanish:

> *Seventy weeks have been decreed for your people and your holy city until the measure of transgression is filled and that of sin complete, until iniquity is expiated, and eternal righteousness ushered in; and prophetic vision ratified and the Holy of Holies anointed. You must know and understand: From the issuance of the word to restore and rebuild Jerusalem until the [time of the] anointed leader is seven weeks; and for sixty-two weeks it will he rebuilt, square and moat, but in a time of distress. And after those sixty-two weeks, the anointed one will disappear and vanish. The army of a leader who is to come will destroy the city and the sanctuary, but its end will come through a flood. Desolation is decreed until the end of war.*

—Daniel 9: 24-26 (JPS)

This prophecy is another significant reason why Jesus gained so many followers. They contend that the dates cited by Gabriel coincide with Jesus' death. They also state that Jesus' death, as the sacrifice for mankind's sin, *"expiated"* (atoned for) our iniquity and enabled us to have *"eternal righteousness"* in fulfillment of this prophecy.

Many people contend that Daniel was referring to weeks of years rather than normal seven day weeks. This view is even footnoted twice in a popular English translation of the Babylonian Talmud.[44] If this is the case, the time span from the decree to rebuild the Temple to Messiah's disappearance would be 69 weeks of years, or 483 years.

We know that King Cyrus of Persia made the decree to rebuild the Temple in about 445 BCE. (Nebuchadnezzar had destroyed it several decades earlier.) If Messiah was to vanish 483 years later, that would make it about the year 38 CE. Since, historians generally agree that Jesus lived from about 4 BCE to about 30 CE, Jesus' death did occur in the same general time frame which would result from this interpretation of the Scriptures in Daniel.

> *Conclusion:*   *Based upon one interpretation (referenced in the Talmud) of the time frames mentioned by the prophet Daniel, Jesus' death did occur within a few years of the time when Messiah was to "disappear." The prophecy, however is difficult to understand.*

THEN ISRAEL WILL BE SCATTERED

Zechariah prophesied in the 6th century BCE, *"strike down the shepherd and let the flock scatter; and I will turn also My hand against the shepherd boys."*[45]

Jesus' followers assert that Jesus was the shepherd spoken of by Zechariah and that Israel was indeed crushed and scattered shortly after his death.

While the Roman Empire's subjugation of Israel in 63 BCE must have contributed to the Diaspora (the dispersion) of Jews outside of Israel, the *final* dispersion of Israel started a century later when Israel rebelled. The first Jewish revolt against Rome lasted about nine years (from 66 to 74 CE). When it ended, Jerusalem was in ruins, the Temple was destroyed, possibly a million Jews were dead,[46] and Rome remained in control. The second revolt came sixty years later and ended in crushing defeat. It was led by Simon Bar–Kokhba in 135 CE. When it was over, the nation of Israel was essentially wiped off of the map. It was replaced by a Roman province called Syria-Palestine. Jerusalem was renamed Aelia Capitolina and Jews and Jewish practices were banned from within it. Up to 50% of the inhabitants of Judea were dead and what remained of Jewish life shifted from Jerusalem to Galilee as thousands of Jews fled the country.[47] Israel ceased to exist as a nation for the next 1,813 years.

Jesus' followers contend that he is the "shepherd" who was struck down and that Israel was crushed and scattered after his death. Historically, the two major crushing events that scattered Israel did occur within the century after his death.

Conclusion: *The two principle events that led to the demise of Israel and the scattering of Jews throughout the world did occur in the century after Jesus' death.*

A KINGDOM OF JUSTICE, REVERENCE AND PEACE

Isaiah prophesied of a coming king who would be a descendant of Jesse (King David's father). He spoke of a conquering king who would rule the earth with justice and equity. This king would rule in a spirit of reverence for the LORD and there would be great peace. Isaiah also said that God would also regather His dispersed people to Palestine.[48]

Jesus' followers acknowledge that he was not a conquering king nor did he rule over the entire world. In addition, he did not regather Jews to Palestine. They contend, however, that he will return from heaven to fulfill these prophecies in the future. They point to the prophecies of Isaiah that Messiah will rise from the dead and be exhalted by God as evidence that Scripture supports their claim.[49]

> *Conclusion:*   *Jesus did not fulfill these prophecies. The only way that he could rule the earth is if he were to return from the dead as his followers claim that he will.*

AN EVERLASTING KINGDOM

Like Isaiah, the prophet Daniel prophesied of *"one like a human being"* who is given *"dominion, glory and kingship"* by *"the Ancient of Days"* and who is served by all peoples on earth.[50]

Again, Jesus' followers acknowledge that Jesus has not fulfilled this prophecy about Messiah. They contend that he will, however, when he returns from heaven.

> *Conclusion:*   *These prophecies have not yet been fulfilled. The only way that Jesus could rule the earth is if he were to return from the dead as his followers suggest.*

WHAT IS HIS NAME?

Messiah has been called many names by the prophets:

- The Almighty God is planning grace
- Eternal Father
- Prince of Peace[51]
- The LORD is our vindicator *(or Righteousness)*[52]

Jesus' name in Hebrew is *Yeshua*. It means *savior*. His followers contend that he is the savior of the world. They say that he was the Passover sacrifice and the fulfillment of the sacrificial system.[53] They contend that God will extend forgiveness and will account as righteous anyone who accepts Jesus as their sin offering and follows him as Messiah.[54] They further contend that God has extended His grace (unmerited favor) to the world through Jesus' sacrifice.

A name in and of itself doesn't prove a person's true identity, but

Jesus' name (Yeshua, or *savior*) does fit the role that his followers claim him to have filled.

> Conclusion: *Jesus' name, Yeshua, does fit the savior role, which his followers claim him to have filled, but it doesn't of itself prove he was Messiah.*

IS THERE MORE THAN ONE MESSIAH?

Jewish philosophers like Rabbi Sa'adiah ben Joseph (Saadya Gaon) and the Rabbis of the Talmud have wrestled with the seeming conflict between the Scriptures which say that Messiah will rule the world from Jerusalem[55] and those which say that Messiah will be killed.[56] They suggest that a possible solution is their theory that maybe there will be *two Messiahs*.[57]

Jesus' early followers and modern Christian philosophers contend that Jesus fulfilled the Scriptures related to the birth, life, and death of Messiah except for those related to Messiah's reign as King. They say that he physically rose from the dead three days after his death and ascended into heaven and that he will yet return to earth to reign as King. They contend that there are not *two* Messiahs—there is *one* who was killed and is resurrected from the dead. They point to the prophecies of Isaiah to support their claims:

> *By oppressive judgment he was taken away, Who could describe his abode? For he was cut off from the land of the living through the sin of my people, who deserved the punishment. And his grave was set among the wicked, and with the rich in his death—though he had done no injustice and had spoken no falsehood. But the LORD chose to crush him by disease, that, if he made himself an offering for guilt, he might see offspring and have long life, and that through him the LORD's purpose might prosper. Out of his anguish he shall see it. He shall enjoy it to the full through his devotion.*

My righteous servant makes the many righteous, it is their punishment he bears; assuredly, I will give him the many as his portion, he shall receive the multitude as his spoil. For he exposed himself to death and was numbered among the sinners, whereas he bore the guilt of the many and made intercession for sinners.

—Isaiah 53:8-12 (JPS)

Jesus' followers contend that Isaiah is speaking of one Messiah who is to be killed and resurrected from the dead to reign. They further contend, correctly, that nowhere in the Scriptures is there an explicit reference that there will be two Messiahs.

Conclusion: *A strong case can be made that there is only one Messiah, the descendant of King David. In addition, it is not unreasonable to conclude from Scriptures in Isaiah that Messiah will be killed and then resurrected from the dead to reign.*

FINAL CONCLUSIONS

There is actually third-party historical evidence that supports the case that Jesus fulfilled many of the prophecies in the Scriptures about the Messiah. A historically supportable case can be made that:

- he was a descendant of King David
- he was born in Bethlehem
- he was preceded by an Elijah-like prophet
- he could have entered Jerusalem humbly
- he did live at a time when the Temple was standing in Jerusalem
- he was regarded in his day as a wise and virtuous man
- he did die in a sacrificial manner which would suggest that his

intent was to bear the sins of the world

- the nation Israel was crushed and scattered after his death
- his name, Yeshua, was significant in meaning

Likewise, history confirms that he did not fulfill a key component of the prophecies about Messiah:

- he did not establish an everlasting kingdom of justice, reverence and peace on the earth

But, his 1st century followers claimed that he rose from the dead and that he will yet return to establish his kingdom on earth and fulfill these remaining prophecies. So much of the case for Jesus being the Messiah rests upon one question: *did he really rise from the dead?* The point is that if Jesus really did rise from the dead, he really could be the Messiah. But if he did not, he is merely a man well spoken of—but dead.

WHY WAS JESUS KILLED?

Jesus was regarded as a good and virtuous man during his day.[1] He was considered by many to be a great teacher of the Law of God. He was even thought to be the Messiah by a large following of people. Unlike other 'Messiah figures,' however, he was not a political revolutionary or military leader seeking to rebel against the Roman Empire nor was he seeking to undermine the then subjugated Jewish government, or the Levitical priesthood. So, why then was he killed?

FOR BLASPHEMY!

The Talmud says that Jesus was put to death for sorcery and apostasy!

> *AND A HERALD PRECEDES HIM etc. This implies, only immediately before [the execution], but not previous thereto. [In contradiction to this] it was taught: On the eve of the Passover Yeshu was hanged. For forty days before the execution took place, a herald went forth and cried, 'He is going forth to be stoned because he has practised sorcery and enticed Israel to apostasy. Any one who can say anything in his favour, let him come forward and plead on his behalf.' But since nothing was brought forward in his favour he was hanged on the eve of the Passover! — Ulla retorted: Do you suppose that he was*

one for whom a defence could be made? Was he not a Mesith [enticer], concerning whom scripture says, Neither shalt thou spare, neither shalt thou conceal him. With Yeshu however it was different, for he was connected with the government [or royalty, i.e. influential].

—Babylonian Talmud, Sanhedrin 43a2

So what could Jesus (Yeshu) have done that would so infuriate the religious leaders of Israel that they would turn him over to the hated Romans to be executed? What was his apostacy?

Jesus' Blasphemy: Who He Claimed To Be

From Jesus' words, as recorded by his disciples, his apostacy was not his teaching about the Law (Torah). He held the Law in high regard and seemed to teach along the lines of the Pharisaic sect (rabbinic Judaisim). The principle controversy about Jesus doesn't appear to have stemmed from what he taught, but from who he claimed to be.

So, what did he claim?

Anointed By God

Jesus claimed to be the one spoken of in Isaiah Chapter 61, one anointed by God.[3] At minimum, he was claiming to be a prophet:

The spirit of the Lord God is upon me, because the LORD has anointed me; He has sent me as a herald of joy to the humble, to bind up the wounded of heart, to proclaim release to the captives, liberation to the imprisoned; to proclaim a year of the LORD's favor…

—Isaiah 61:1-2 (JPS)

He is recorded as having made this claim while reading from the Prophet Isaiah in a Nazareth synagogue. He then proceeded to tell the people that they would see no miracles from him because *"no prophet is accepted in his hometown."* Evidently, this infuriated those gathered in the synagogue because they responded by trying to throw him off a cliff.[4]

But Jesus wasn't killed for claiming to be a prophet. Many others had made such claims. Jesus claimed to be much more than a prophet…

THE PROMISED MESSIAH AND THE KING OF THE JEWS

Jesus claimed to be the Messiah of Israel.[5] Though, he is recorded as not having flaunted this claim.[6] His followers' writings suggest that he was pretty low key about it until the end of his three-year 'public ministry.' As you would expect, however, when he became more open about his claimed identity, opposition grew.

On face value, it appears that claiming to be Messiah was enough for the high priest to condemn Jesus to death:

> *Then the high priest stood up before them and asked Jesus, "Are you not going to answer? What is this testimony that these men are bringing against you?" But Jesus remained silent and gave no answer. Again the high priest asked him, "Are you the Christ [or Messiah], the Son of the Blessed One?" "I am," said Jesus. "And you will see the Son of Man sitting at the right hand of the Mighty One and coming on the clouds of heaven." The high priest tore his clothes. "Why do we need any more witnesses?" he asked. "You have heard the blasphemy. What do you think?" They all condemned him as worthy of death.*

—Mark 14:60-64 (NIV®)

But were they condemning Jesus only for claiming to be Messiah? Others like Simon Bar–Kokhba in 135 CE claimed to be Messiah. But rather than condemn Bar–Kokhba, Rabbi Akiva encouraged thousands to follow him. So, while Jesus' claim to be Messiah was enormous in significance, the claim of itself may not be why he was condemned to death. After all, Jesus claimed to be much more than a human Messiah.

THE SACRIFICE FOR SINS

Jesus said that he would die for the sins of the world and then rise from the dead after three days.[7] At least that's what his disciples claimed.[8] They said that he fulfilled the prophecy of Isaiah that Messiah would die as a sacrifice to make us righteous before God.[9]

THE ONLY WAY TO GOD

Not only did Jesus claim that he was going to be the sacrifice for sin,[10] he claimed to have the right to forgive sin,[11] and to be the only way to reach God and heaven after death.

> *Jesus said to her, "I am the resurrection and the life. He who believes in me will live, even though he dies; and whoever lives and believes in me will never die. Do you believe this?"*
>
> —John 11:25-26 (NIV®)

> *Jesus answered, "I am the way and the truth and the life. No one comes to the Father except through me."*
>
> —John 14:6 (NIV®)

> *Then Jesus declared, "I am the bread of life. He who comes to me will never go hungry, and he who believes in me will never be thirsty. But as I told you, you have seen me and still you do not believe. All that the Father gives me will come to me, and whoever comes to me I will never drive away. For I have come down from heaven not to do my will but to do the will of him who sent me. And this is the will of him who sent me, that I shall lose none of all that he has given me, but raise them up at the last day. For my Father's will is that everyone who looks to the Son and believes in him shall have eternal life, and I will raise him up at the last day." At this the Jews began to grumble about him because he said, "I am the bread that came down from heaven." They said, "Is this not Jesus, the son*

of Joseph, whose father and mother we know? How can he now say, 'I came down from heaven'?"

—John 6:29-42 (NIV®)

These comments must have infuriated the Sanhedrin and the priests! But Jesus didn't stop there.

The Son of God

Jesus claimed to be the Son of God. Of itself, this sort of claim would more than raise an eyebrow, but it wouldn't necessarily justify one's death. After all, the Scriptures say that both King David and King Solomon were called the sons of God.[12] The Scriptures even say that the nation of Israel was considered to be the children of God.[13] So, what's the problem?

When Jesus said that he was the Son of God he meant much more than what is implied by the Scriptures about David or Solomon. His disciple John's record of his words makes Jesus' meaning more evident:

Once more Jesus said to them, "I am going away, and you will look for me, and you will die in your sin. Where I go, you cannot come." This made the Jews ask, "Will he kill himself? Is that why he says, 'Where I go, you cannot come'?" But he continued, "You are from below; I am from above. You are of this world; I am not of this world. I told you that you would die in your sins; if you do not believe that I am, you will indeed die in your sins." "Who are you?" they asked. "Just what I have been claiming all along," Jesus replied. ...I am telling you what I have seen in the Father's presence, and you do what you have heard from your father." "Abraham is our father," they answered. "If you were Abraham's children," said Jesus, "then you would do the things Abraham did. As it is, you are determined to kill me, a man who has told you the truth that I heard from God. Abraham did not do such things. You are doing the things your own father does." "We are not

illegitimate children," they protested. "The only Father
we have is God himself." Jesus said to them, "If God
were your Father, you would love me, for I came from
God and now am here. I have not come on my own;
but he sent me. Why is my language not clear to you?
Because you are unable to hear what I say. You belong
to your father, the devil, and you want to carry out your
father's desire. He was a murderer from the beginning,
not holding to the truth, for there is no truth in him.
When he lies, he speaks his native language, for he is a
liar and the father of lies. Yet because I tell the truth,
you do not believe me! Can any of you prove me guilty
of sin? If I am telling the truth, why don't you believe
me? He who belongs to God hears what God says. The
reason you do not hear is that you do not belong to
God." The Jews answered him, "Aren't we right in say-
ing that you are a Samaritan and demon-possessed?" "I
am not possessed by a demon," said Jesus, "but I honor
my Father and you dishonor me. I am not seeking glory
for myself; but there is one who seeks it, and he is the
judge. I tell you the truth, if anyone keeps my word, he
will never see death." At this the Jews exclaimed, "Now
we know that you are demon-possessed! Abraham died
and so did the prophets, yet you say that if anyone
keeps your word, he will never taste death. Are you
greater than our father Abraham? He died, and so did
the prophets. Who do you think you are?" Jesus
replied, "If I glorify myself, my glory means nothing.
My Father, whom you claim as your God, is the one
who glorifies me. Though you do not know him, I
know him. If I said I did not, I would be a liar like you,
but I do know him and keep his word. Your father
Abraham rejoiced at the thought of seeing my day; he

> *saw it and was glad." "You are not yet fifty years old,"*
> *the Jews said to him, "and you have seen Abraham!" "I*
> *tell you the truth," Jesus answered, "before Abraham*
> *was born, I am!" At this, they picked up stones to stone*
> *him, but Jesus hid himself, slipping away from the tem-*
> *ple grounds.*
>
> —John 8:21-59 (NIV®)

So what's the big deal? Wasn't King David called the "son of God" in the Holy Scriptures?

Yes, David was called the son of God. But there is a big difference in what was being claimed. Jesus claimed to come from heaven. He claimed to have been in God's presence. He claimed to have power over death. He claimed to have pre-existed Abraham. He claimed that he appeared to Abraham. And finally, he claimed to be the *"I am"*—as in the burning bush *"I am."*[14] Jesus wasn't just claiming to be a son of God—he was claiming to be *The* Son of God.

From the account given, the crowd understood the significance of what Jesus was saying. They wanted to stone him.

The council of Israel obviously agreed with the people. They wanted to see Jesus dead!

> *At daybreak the council of the elders of the people, both*
> *the chief priests and teachers of the law, met together,*
> *and Jesus was led before them. "If you are the Christ,"*
> *they said, "tell us." Jesus answered, "If I tell you, you will*
> *not believe me, and if I asked you, you would not answer.*
> *But from now on, the Son of Man will be seated at the*
> *right hand of the mighty God." They all asked, "Are you*
> *then the Son of God?" He replied, "You are right in say-*
> *ing I am." Then they said, "Why do we need any more*
> *testimony? We have heard it from his own lips.*
>
> —Luke 22:66-71 (NIV®)

> *As soon as the chief priests and their officials saw him,*
> *they shouted, "Crucify! Crucify!" But Pilate answered,*
> *"You take him and crucify him. As for me, I find no basis*
> *for a charge against him." The Jews insisted, "We have a*
> *law, and according to that law he must die, because he*
> *claimed to be the Son of God."*
>
> —John 19:6-7 (NIV®)

But again, Jesus didn't stop there.

GOD IN THE FLESH

Jesus didn't just claim to be The Son of God, he claimed that he and God *"are one."* He didn't claim to be a separate being from God. He claimed to be God!

> *Then came the Feast of Dedication at Jerusalem. It was*
> *winter, and Jesus was in the temple area walking in*
> *Solomon's Colonnade. The Jews gathered around him,*
> *saying, "How long will you keep us in suspense? If you*
> *are the Christ, tell us plainly." Jesus answered, "I did tell*
> *you, but you do not believe. The miracles I do in my*
> *Father's name speak for me, but you do not believe*
> *because you are not my sheep. My sheep listen to my*
> *voice; I know them, and they follow me. I give them eter-*
> *nal life, and they shall never perish; no one can snatch*
> *them out of my hand. My Father, who has given them to*
> *me, is greater than all; no one can snatch them out of my*
> *Father's hand. I and the Father are one." Again the Jews*
> *picked up stones to stone him, but Jesus said to them, "I*
> *have shown you many great miracles from the Father.*
> *For which of these do you stone me?" "We are not ston-*
> *ing you for any of these," replied the Jews, "but for blas-*
> *phemy, because you, a mere man, claim to be God."*
>
> —John 10:22-33 (NIV®)

Based upon this record of who Jesus claimed to be, the crowd understood the significance of what was being said. Once again, they were prepared to stone Jesus.

COULD JESUS' FOLLOWERS HAVE BEEN CONFUSED ABOUT WHO JESUS CLAIMED TO BE?

Some may wonder if perhaps Jesus' followers were unclear about who Jesus was claiming to be. After all, many of them were uneducated people. Yet, they were very clear about what Jesus was saying.

- The Apostle John, a fisherman by trade, was one of Jesus' first disciples. In a letter written about 60 years after Jesus' death, he claimed that Jesus was *the true God and eternal life.*[15]
- Rabbi Saul (Paul) was a scholar of the Torah. He was educated by Rabban Gamaliel the Elder (the grandson of Hillel the Elder) at Beth Hillel, one of the two great 1st century Rabbinic academies. Saul became a follower of Jesus after Jesus' death. In his letters he clearly explained that he believed Jesus to be God:

> *For I could wish that I myself were cursed and cut off from Christ for the sake of my brothers, those of my own race, the people of Israel. Theirs is the adoption as sons; theirs the divine glory, the covenants, the receiving of the law, the temple worship and the promises. Theirs are the patriarchs, and from them is traced the human ancestry of Christ, who is God over all, forever praised! Amen.*

> —Romans 9:3-5 (NIV®)

Paul also said that Jesus was in nature God:

> *Your attitude should be the same as that of Christ Jesus: Who, being in very nature God, did not consider equality with God something to be grasped, but made himself nothing, taking the very nature of a servant, being made in human likeness. And being found in appearance as a*

man, he humbled himself and became obedient to death—even death on a cross! Therefore God exalted him to the highest place and gave him the name that is above every name, that at the name of Jesus every knee should bow, in heaven and on earth and under the earth, and every tongue confess that Jesus Christ is Lord, to the glory of God the Father.

—Philippians 2:5-11(NIV®)

Paul even called Jesus the creator of the universe:

He is the image of the invisible God, the firstborn over all creation. For by him all things were created: things in heaven and on earth, visible and invisible, whether thrones or powers or rulers or authorities; all things were created by him and for him. He is before all things, and in him all things hold together. And he is the head of the body, the church; he is the beginning and the firstborn from among the dead, so that in everything he might have the supremacy. For God was pleased to have all his fullness dwell in him, and through him to reconcile to himself all things, whether things on earth or things in heaven, by making peace through his blood, shed on the cross.

—Colossians 1:15-20 (NIV®)

Jesus' followers were clear that Jesus wasn't just claiming to be a son of God. He was claiming to be God in the flesh!

So, Why Did They Kill Jesus?

Well, it's pretty obvious. The leaders of the Sanhedrin and the High Priest turned Jesus over to the Romans to be executed because of all of Jesus' claims about himself. Their conclusion was that surely anyone making such claims must be a blasphemer worthy of death. Their appeal to Pilate was: *"We have a law, and according to that law he must die, because he claimed to be the Son of God."*16

JESUS' FOLLOWERS HAVE A DIFFERENT ANSWER

Jesus' followers' answer the question of why Jesus was killed differently. They do acknowledge that Jesus made all of these claims. They also acknowledge that the priests and Sanhedrin were livid and wanted to see Jesus dead, and that they were successful in getting the Romans to execute Jesus. But, they contend that is not why Jesus was killed.

Jesus' followers maintain that Jesus is who he claimed to be—God. They say that he entered his own creation in the form of a man for the purpose of dying as a sacrifice for mankind's sin. They say that this was his plan from before the creation of the world.17 They quote him as saying that his mission was to die as a ransom for mankind so that mankind may have forgiveness and salvation:

> *...the Son of Man did not come to be served, but to serve, and to give his life as a ransom for many.*
>
> —Matthew 20:28 (NIV®)

> *...the Son of Man came to seek and to save what was lost.*
>
> —Luke 19:10 (NIV®)

> *I have spoken to you of earthly things and you do not believe; how then will you believe if I speak of heavenly things? No one has ever gone into heaven except the one who came from heaven—the Son of Man. Just as Moses lifted up the snake in the desert, so the Son of Man must be lifted up, that everyone who believes in him may have eternal life. For God so loved the world that he gave his*

one and only Son, that whoever believes in him shall not perish but have eternal life. For God did not send his Son into the world to condemn the world, but to save the world through him.

—John 3:12-17 (NIV®)

They contend, "yes, the Sanhedrin had Jesus killed—but it was God Himself who orchestrated it."

WHY DID THEY BELIEVE JESUS?

There are about 2 billion people today who claim that Jesus is both the Messiah of Israel and the spiritual savior of the world. They believe this in large part because the people who recorded the events of Jesus' life were convinced that he was. This raises at least two questions. The first is, "who were these people?" And the second is, "why on earth did they believe Jesus to be the Messiah?"

WHO WERE "THEY"?

Most people know about Jesus' twelve disciples. The original "twelve" were selected by Jesus out of his possibly hundreds of followers to be his select students. They lived with him and were instructed by him during his three year "public ministry." The stated intent was that they would, in turn, instruct others.[1] The *twelve* were:

> *These are the names of the twelve apostles: first, Simon (who is called Peter) and his brother Andrew; James son of Zebedee, and his brother John; Philip and Bartholomew; Thomas and Matthew the tax collector; James son of Alphaeus, and Thaddaeus; Simon the Zealot and Judas Iscariot, who betrayed him.*

> —Matthew 10:2-4 (NIV®)

Just exactly who were these men? We obviously have limited information. But, based upon what they wrote about each other, we do know the following:

Andrew and Peter Andrew and his brother Simon Peter were Galilean fishermen living in Bethsaida.[2] They were partners of James and John and fished the Sea of Tiberias (the Sea of Galilee).[3] Andrew (and probably Peter also) was a follower of John the Baptist. He reportedly brought Peter to see Jesus based upon John the Baptist's statement that Jesus was the son of God.[4]

John and James John and his brother James were also Galilean fishermen living in Bethsaida. They were the sons of a man named Zebedee and were called the "sons of thunder" by Jesus (perhaps because of their boldness.)[5] They were evidently not poor as they had employees and John an acquaintance of Caiaphas the high priest.[6]

Matthew Matthew was a Jewish tax collector for the Roman authorities in Capernaum, a town in Galilee. To have held this position, he was probably a Roman citizen and was probably reasonably wealthy. Undoubtedly, he would not have been popular with his countrymen. He is said to have left his profession to follow Jesus.[7]

Philip Philip was a Galilean from Bethsaida.[8] Little else about his background is known.

Thomas Thomas was probably also a Galilean. However, nothing is known about his background.

Bartholomew Bartholomew was evidently also called Nathanael.[9] He was born in Cana, a city in Galilee and is cited as having been introduced to Jesus by Philip.[10]

Thaddaeus Thaddaeus was evidently the surname of a man named Judas.[11] That's about all we know about him.

Simon   Simon was a Zealot prior to meeting Jesus. The Zealots were a group of Jewish revolutionaries who wanted to liberate Israel from Roman rule. They led the great revolt in 66 to 70 CE which resulted in utter defeat by the Romans and possibly one million dead Jews.[12]

Judas Iscariot   Nothing is known about Judas' background, except that he was from Kerioth, a town in southern Judah.[13] He was made treasurer over the funds that were at Jesus' disposal. Judas was called an embezzler by the other disciples and betrayed Jesus to the Jewish authorities, evidently for money.[14] After Jesus' death, he is said to have committed suicide.[15]

All of these men were Jews. Except for Judas Iscariot, all of them appear to have been from Galilee.[16] At least four of them were fishermen—and probably reasonably successful, as fishermen go. One was a rich tax collector. One was a revolutionary. One knew the high priest. The others were probably quite ordinary people, since nothing is mentioned of their backgrounds.

Since Jesus was raised in Nazareth, a town in Galilee, and began his teaching ministry there, it isn't surprising that his core group of disciples were also primarily from Galilee. They would probably have been looked down upon by Jews in Jerusalem as being less than pure Jews, since the Galilean population was intermixed with Assyrian immigrants over 700 years earlier.[17] Old prejudices die hard. Even though Galilee had a population of over three million people, it was not the cosmopolitan Jerusalem.[18] Jesus' followers would not have been regarded as being among the socially elite of Israel.

Of the original twelve disciples, only three appear to have been authors of the "New Testament:" Peter, John, and Matthew. They appear to have written eight of the twenty-seven "books" of the New Testament. Two books were written by two of Jesus' brothers: James and Jude. Luke, a medical doctor, interviewed the disciples to write two books. He was also an eyewitness to many of the events he recorded. Mark, a compatriot of Peter's, likely relayed Peter's account of events. And finally, Rabbi Saul (Paul) wrote the remaining fourteen books (assuming that he also wrote the book of Hebrews).

WHY DID THEY BELIEVE JESUS?

Why did these men follow Jesus? Were they all just buddies from Galilee? Did they know each other from the synagogue? Or was Jesus just a likable, charismatic guy?

Through the writings of his followers, it is evident that there were several reasons why they originally followed Jesus and why they continued to follow him after his death. The first of these reasons was simple. It was because John the Baptist told them to.

BECAUSE OF JOHN THE BAPTIST

John the Baptist was considered to be a prophet of God by large numbers of people in the first century. He was held in high esteem and had great influence over the people of Israel. It was reportedly because of him that Jesus gained his first followers. Andrew and Simon Peter were disciples of John the Baptist. It is likely that James and John were also. *They began following Jesus because of what John the Baptist said about him.* The disciple John recorded John the Baptist as saying:

> *"I baptize with water," John replied, "but among you stands one you do not know. He is the one who comes after me, the thongs of whose sandals I am not worthy to untie." This all happened at Bethany on the other side of the Jordan, where John was baptizing. The next day John saw Jesus coming toward him and said, "Look, the Lamb of God, who takes away the sin of the world! This is the one I meant when I said, 'A man who comes after me has surpassed me because he was before me.' I myself did not know him, but the reason I came baptizing with water was that he might be revealed to Israel." Then John gave this testimony: "I saw the Spirit come down from heaven as a dove and remain on him. I would not have known him, except that the one who sent me to baptize with water told me, 'The man on whom you see the Spirit come down and remain is he who will baptize with*

*the Holy Spirit.' I have seen and I testify that this is the
Son of God." The next day John was there again with
two of his disciples. When he saw Jesus passing by, he
said, "Look, the Lamb of God!" When the two disciples
heard him say this, they followed Jesus. Turning around,
Jesus saw them following and asked, "What do you
want?" They said, "Rabbi" (which means Teacher),
"where are you staying?" "Come," he replied, "and you
will see." So they went and saw where he was staying,
and spent that day with him. It was about the tenth hour.
Andrew, Simon Peter's brother, was one of the two who
heard what John had said and who had followed Jesus.
The first thing Andrew did was to find his brother Simon
and tell him, "We have found the Messiah" (that is, the
Christ). And he brought him to Jesus. Jesus looked at him
and said, "You are Simon son of John. You will be called
Cephas" (which, when translated, is Peter).*

—John 1:26-42 (NIV®)

These men started following Jesus because John the Baptist said he
was the Messiah, the Son of God. But they claim that they had this val-
idated by a higher authority than John.

BECAUSE OF WHAT THEY HEARD

The second reason cited by the original "twelve" for why they followed Jesus was because of what they said they heard.

*Jesus' disciples claimed that they heard a voice from heaven, which
proclaimed Jesus to be God's son.* Five different authors (John,
Matthew, Luke, Mark and Peter) recorded three separate occasions
when the disciples heard a voice from heaven declaring Jesus to be God's
son. The first event occurred while Jesus was being baptized by John the
Baptist in the Jordan River.[19] The second was while Jesus was praying
on a mountain with three of his disciples.[20] And, the third was while
Jesus was praying with several of his disciples in a crowd of people.[21]

While Being Baptized

As soon as Jesus was baptized, he went up out of the water. At that moment heaven was opened, and he saw the Spirit of God descending like a dove and lighting on him. And a voice from heaven said, "This is my Son, whom I love; with him I am well pleased."

—Matthew 3:16-17 (NIV®)

On The Mountain

We did not follow cleverly invented stories when we told you about the power and coming of our Lord Jesus Christ, but we were eyewitnesses of his majesty. For he received honor and glory from God the Father when the voice came to him from the Majestic Glory, saying, "This is my Son, whom I love; with him I am well pleased." We ourselves heard this voice that came from heaven when we were with him on the sacred mountain.

—2 Peter 1:16-18 (NIV®)

While He Was Praying

Whoever serves me must follow me; and where I am, my servant also will be. My Father will honor the one who serves me. "Now my heart is troubled, and what shall I say? 'Father, save me from this hour'? No, it was for this very reason I came to this hour. Father, glorify your name!" Then a voice came from heaven, "I have glorified it, and will glorify it again." The crowd that was there and heard it said it had thundered; others said an angel had spoken to him. Jesus said, "This voice was for your benefit, not mine. Now is the time for judgment on this world; now the prince of this world will be driven out.

But I, when I am lifted up from the earth, will draw all
men to myself." He said this to show the kind of death
he was going to die.

—John 12:26-33 (NIV®)

These men claimed that they actually heard God say that Jesus is His son! They contend that this is one of the reasons they followed him.

BECAUSE OF WHAT THEY SAW

The disciples said that they also came to believe that Jesus is the Messiah, the Son of God, because of the events, that they said they witnessed. They claimed that they personally witnessed events and "miracles" which were so inexplicable that they could only conclude that God was responsible.

The Miracles

Jesus' disciples said that they saw him perform many incredible miracles. They said they saw him: turn water to wine; raise the dead; feed thousands with a basket of food; heal the sick; walk on water; calm a storm; and cast out demons.

- **Turn water to wine:** Jesus' first miracle was said to have been turning water into wine at a wedding celebration at Cana in Galilee.[22]

- **Raise the dead:** Three people were said to have been raised from the dead by Jesus: Lazarus, a man from Bethany;[23] Jairus' daughter, he was a ruler of the Synagogue, probably living in Galilee;[24] and the son of a widow living in the town of Nain.[25]

- **Feed thousands:** Jesus was reported to have on one occasion fed over 5,000 people with five loaves of bread and two fish and then taken up twelve baskets of left over pieces. (His disciples claimed that eight month's wages wouldn't have purchased enough food to give everyone a bite.)[26] On another occasion they said he fed over 4,000 people with seven loaves of bread and a few small fish.[27]

- **Heal the sick:** Jesus is said to have healed the blind, the lame, the mute, paralytics, invalids, and the leprous. On many occasions specific names were cited: Bartimaeus was blind, Malchus had his ear severed, and Peter's mother-in-law had a fever. They were all reportedly healed.[28]

- **Walk on water:** John, Matthew, and Mark recorded Jesus as having walked three miles on the Sea of Galilee out to their boat one night during a storm. At first, they thought he was a ghost. [29]

- **Calm a storm:** Once, while crossing the Sea of Galilee in a boat with his disciples, Jesus is said to have commanded a storm squall to be still and it complied.[30]

- **Cast out demons:** Jesus is reported to have had authority over demonic power and that he cast out demons from those who were afflicted by them.[31]

These men claimed that these miracles really happened and that they saw them. Did Jesus really do these things? Well, it seems clear that *something* was happening. Otherwise, the Talmud wouldn't have attributed Jesus' miracles to *"sorcery"*[32] and Flavius Josephus wouldn't have recorded that Jesus *"was a doer of wonderful works."*[33] These men saw *something*. But, were they miracles?

Two thousand years after the fact, it is difficult to conclusively *prove or disprove* any historical event. However, these men said that they saw Jesus do these things. And, they uniformly cited the miracles as a reason why they followed Jesus and believed him to be the Messiah, the Son of God.

The Events In Nature Surrounding His Crucifixion

It's recorded by Jesus' followers that, while Jesus was nailed to the cross, there was a great earthquake and that the sky was darkened for three hours.[34] They said that those who observed these events were terrified and came away convinced that Jesus was the Son of God.

Jesus' present day followers are quick to point out that other sources appear to corroborate that these events actually did happen. 1st century historians Phlegon and Thallus were quoted by 3rd century church father, Julius Africanus, who contended that the historians had incorrectly attributed the darkness that occurred during Jesus' crucifixion to an eclipse of the sun:

> On the whole world there pressed a most fearful darkness; and the rocks were rent by an earthquake, and many places in Judea and other districts were thrown down. This darkness Thallus, in the third book of his History, calls, as appears to me without reason, an eclipse of the sun. For the Hebrews celebrate the passover on the 14th day according to the moon, and the passion of our Savior falls on the day before the passover; but an eclipse of the sun takes place only when the moon comes under the sun. And it cannot happen at any other time but in the interval between the first day of the new moon and the last of the old, that is, at their junction: how then should an eclipse be supposed to happen when the moon is almost diametrically opposite the sun? Let that opinion pass however; let it carry the majority with it; and let this portent of the world be deemed an eclipse of the sun, like others a portent only to the eye. Phlegon records that, in the time of Tiberius Caesar, at full moon, there was a full eclipse of the sun from the sixth hour to the ninth—manifestly that one of which we speak. But what has an eclipse in common with an earthquake, the rending rocks, and the resurrection of the dead, and so great a perturbation throughout the universe? Surely no such event as this is recorded for a long period. But it was a darkness induced by God, because the Lord happened then to suffer.[35]

In addition, Agapius, a 10th century historian, cited what appears to be Phlegon and a philosopher named Ur.s.y.w.s to support both the darkness and the earthquake.[36]

Given the evidence available, it appears likely that *something* actually did happen. And, given the timing of the darkness and/or earthquake, Jesus' followers attributed them to Jesus' crucifixion. They contended that they were a confirmation that Jesus is who he claimed to be.

His Resurrection and Ascension

It has been established historically (by Jesus' followers, the Talmud, and Flavius Josephus) that Jesus was executed by the Romans at the request of the High Priest and the Sanhedrin (the Jewish government). Roman soldiers nailed him to a wooden cross and he died. He was dead.

Yet, Jesus' disciples claimed that he physically rose from the dead and that they saw him. They actually record at least ten occasions when they claim they saw him:

The Sunday after the Crucifixion:

- Mary Magdalene and two other women (another Mary and Salome) said they saw Jesus near his empty tomb the Sunday morning after his crucifixion.[37]

- Simon Peter also reportedly saw him later that day.[38]

- Two disciples, one named Cleopas, said they spoke with him later that afternoon while traveling from Jerusalem to Emmaus, a town six miles away. They said that they walked with him and that he taught them from the Scriptures.[39]

- The two returned to Jerusalem to tell the other disciples that they had seen Jesus. While they spoke, locked behind closed doors that evening with the "eleven" and other disciples, they said that he appeared to them, ate with them, taught them, and encouraged them.[40]

Other Reported Occasions

- Thomas and a group of disciples saw him one week later.[41]

- Then James (evidently, James the brother of Jesus) saw him.[42]

- The "eleven" met Jesus on a mountain in Galilee where they received the "great commission" to evangelize the world.[43]

- Peter, Thomas, Nathanael, James and John and two other disciples said that they spoke and ate with him by the Sea of Galilee.[44]

- Over 500 people are said to have seen him on one occasion.[45]

His disciples said that these events occurred over a span of forty days.[46] Then, they say that they followed him from Jersualem toward Bethany to the Mount of Olives (just outside of Jerusalem). There, they say, they saw him ascend up into the heavens.[47]

Did these things really happen? Did Jesus rise from the dead and appear to them? They said he did. They claimed that they saw him. They said that his resurrection was why they continued to follow him after he was crucified.

BECAUSE OF WHAT JESUS SAID

Jesus has been called a great teacher and Jesus' disciples were evidently quite taken with his teaching style. He taught in public using simple parables and then explained the parables to his disciples in private. He also taught as a person who actually possessed authority, not as the scribes or rabbis of the day.[48] All of this got his followers' attention.

Jesus' basic teachings appear to be consistent with Pharisaic (Orthodox) Judaism. He taught from the Torah (the Law), the Nevi'im (the Prophets), and the Kethuvim (the Writings). He taught that the greatest Commandment in the Law was to love the LORD:

> 'Love the Lord your God with all your heart and with all your soul and with all your mind.' This is the first and greatest commandment. And the second is like it: 'Love your neighbor as yourself.' All the Law and the Prophets hang on these two commandments."

> —Matthew 22:37-40 (NIV®)

He also emphasized the importance of the Law:

> I tell you the truth, until heaven and earth disappear, not

the smallest letter, not the least stroke of a pen, will by any means disappear from the Law until everything is accomplished. Anyone who breaks one of the least of these commandments and teaches others to do the same will be called least in the kingdom of heaven, but who-ever practices and teaches these commands will be called great in the kingdom of heaven. For I tell you that unless your righteousness surpasses that of the Pharisees and the teachers of the law, you will certainly not enter the kingdom of heaven.

—Matthew 5:18-20 (NIV®)

Yet, he strongly criticized the Pharisaic leaders, calling them hyp-ocrites. They obviously weren't thrilled about this.[49]

But it was evidently not just his teaching style or his basic theology or his willingness to challenge the religious establishment that caused people to believe him. It was what he is reported to have said. He told his followers that he would be crucified (executed) and that three days later he would rise from the dead.[50] They claimed that he did and that his death as a sacrifice for sin and subsequent resurrection are the basis for salvation. This is the "gospel" which they taught.[51]

BECAUSE OF WHAT THEY EXPERIENCED

Spiritual Authority

The original twelve disciples said that when they obeyed Jesus and went out to preach and heal as he commanded, miraculous things hap-pened. They said that they were given power and authority by God to heal people and to drive out demons.

Calling the Twelve to him, he sent them out two by two and gave them authority over evil spirits. These were his instructions: "Take nothing for the journey except a staff—no bread, no bag, no money in your belts. Wear sandals but not an extra tunic. Whenever you enter a house, stay there until you leave that town. And if any place will not welcome you or listen to you, shake the dust off your feet when you leave, as a testimony against them." They went out and preached that people should repent. They drove out many demons and anointed many sick people with oil and healed them.

—Mark 6:7-13 (NIV®)

Later, another group of seventy-two followers were sent out to do the same. They reported similar results.[52]

The Holy Spirit

Jesus' disciples claimed that they experienced the fulfillment of Joel's prophecy that the Holy Spirit would be poured out upon the children of Israel. They said that it happened in Jerusalem during Shavuot, the holiday of the harvest, in the same year that Jesus was crucified.[53] (Shavuot was the second of the three major annual festivals and is also called the Feast of Pentecost.)

BECAUSE OF THE SCRIPTURES

Jesus' first followers also claimed that they believed Jesus to be the Messiah based upon the fulfillment of prophecy in the Holy Scriptures. Peter contended that they were not following fables; but that they were eyewitnesses when God proclaimed Jesus to be His Son and that their belief was based upon the Scriptures.[54]

Paul, a rabbi who became a follower of Jesus later, also went to great length in quoting from the Scriptures to present his case that Jesus is the Messiah. For example, in his letter to the church in Rome he quotes extensively from: Habakkuk, Psalms, Proverbs, Isaiah, Genesis, Exodus, Deuteronomy, Malachi, Hosea, Leviticus, 1 Kings, Jeremiah, Job, and 2 Samuel.[55] He contended that his belief in Jesus was not merely based upon his experience, but that it was based upon Jesus' fulfillment of prophecy in the Scriptures.

Jesus' followers evidently believed that the Scriptures supported Jesus being the Messiah.

WHAT ABOUT HIS ENEMY, SAUL?

Saul was a rabbi trained by Rabban Gamaliel the Elder at the rabbinic academy called the House of Hillel. He was a Pharisee and was a zealous persecutor of the followers of Jesus at the time immediately following Jesus' death. But something happened to Saul. He described the events that caused him to go from being persecutor to follower of Jesus:

> *I am a Jew, born in Tarsus of Cilicia, but brought up in this city. Under Gamaliel I was thoroughly trained in the law of our fathers and was just as zealous for God as any of you are today. I persecuted the followers of this Way to their death, arresting both men and women and throwing them into prison, as also the high priest and all the Council can testify. I even obtained letters from them to their brothers in Damascus, and went there to bring these people as prisoners to Jerusalem to be punished. "About noon as I came near Damascus, suddenly a bright light from heaven flashed around me. I fell to the ground and heard a voice say to me, 'Saul! Saul! Why do you persecute me?' "'Who are you, Lord?' I asked. "'I am Jesus of Nazareth, whom you are persecuting,' he replied. My companions saw the light, but they did not understand the voice of him who was speaking to me. "'What shall I do, Lord?' I asked. "'Get up,' the Lord said, 'and go into Damascus. There you will be told all that you have been assigned to do.' My companions led me by the hand into Damascus, because the brilliance of the light had blinded me. "A man named Ananias came to see me. He was a devout observer of the law and highly respected by all the Jews living there. He stood beside me and said, 'Brother Saul, receive your sight!' And at that very moment I was able to see him. "Then he said: 'The God of our fathers has*

*chosen you to know his will and to see the Righteous
One and to hear words from his mouth. You will be his
witness to all men of what you have seen and heard.
And now what are you waiting for? Get up, be baptized
and wash your sins away, calling on his name.' "When I
returned to Jerusalem and was praying at the temple, I
fell into a trance and saw the Lord speaking. 'Quick!' he
said to me. 'Leave Jerusalem immediately, because they
will not accept your testimony about me.' "'Lord,' I
replied, 'these men know that I went from one synagogue to another to imprison and beat those who
believe in you. And when the blood of your martyr
Stephen was shed, I stood there giving my approval and
guarding the clothes of those who were killing him.'
"Then the Lord said to me, 'Go; I will send you far
away to the Gentiles.'"*

—Acts 22:3-21 (NIV®)

Saul claimed that he saw Jesus after his death. He further claimed to
have seen visions from God confirming Jesus to be God's son. He
claimed that Jesus was Messiah, the Son of God and that he had risen
from the dead. He even went so far as to say that Jesus was *"in very
nature God"*, that Jesus is God.[56]

Saul not only became a follower of Jesus, he wrote 14 books (letters)
of the New Testament, and traveled throughout Asia Minor (Turkey),
Greece, Israel, Crete, Cyprus, Italy, Lebanon, and Syria proclaiming Jesus
to be the risen Messiah of Israel, the Son of God. He is reported to have
paid a high price for his message and for his zeal. Saul and Luke report
that Saul was beaten with rods three times, given thirty nine lashes five
times, stoned and left for dead, and imprisoned in Philippi, Caesarea,
Jerusalem and Rome.[57] He was finally arrested, taken to Rome, imprisoned, and there it is said that he was executed.[58] His final letters were
written from prison in Rome.

Saul (Paul) is the one follower of Jesus that is the most perplexing.

He was born a Roman citizen,[59] was well educated, and held a position of power and influence. Yet, he gave it all up to follow Jesus.

WHAT ABOUT HIS FAMILY?

It was reported by Jesus' disciples that his brothers did not believe him while he was alive.[60] Yet, after his death his brothers James and Jude both wrote epistles (letters) declaring themselves to be servants of Jesus the Messiah.[61] James actually became a leader of the church in Jerusalem[62] and was called an apostle of Jesus by Rabbi Saul (Paul).[63] Josephus recorded that "James, the brother of Jesus, who was called Christ" and others were accused of being "breakers of the law" and were delivered by Ananus the High priest to be stoned.[64] Josephus doesn't specify James' infraction, but Eusebius, in his 4th century *Ecclesiastical History,* relates that it was because of his belief that Jesus was the Messiah.[65]

Jesus' followers contend that you can fool a lot of people but that it's tough to fool your family.

WERE THEY ALL DELUSIONAL?

Some people have speculated that Jesus' followers were merely delusional and that they *thought* they saw Jesus after his crucifixion. They speculate that the disciples wanted to believe that Jesus was still alive so they either hallucinated or somehow saw what they wanted to see.

It isn't likely that such a diverse set of people would share the same delusion. It is difficult to believe that dozens or possibly hundreds of people had the same delusion in different places and at different times over a forty-day period. It's also pretty strange to expect your enemy to have the same delusion. It's much more likely that they were all either fooled or that they were just plain lying.

WERE THEY MISTAKEN OR FOOLED?

Jesus' followers could have been mistaken or fooled into thinking that he rose from the dead. Had this been the case, it would imply that either Jesus never really died, or that he did die and others then faked his resurrection.

OPTION ONE: JESUS NEVER REALLY DIED.

For Jesus' followers to have been mistaken about his resurrection would imply that he didn't really die. The problem with this contention is that *everyone*—the Talmud, Josephus, and Jesus' followers—all said that he died. He was executed by Roman soldiers. The likelihood of surviving a Roman execution then was probably as small as surviving execution by lethal injection today—basically, zero.

But, what if Jesus' followers paid off the Roman soldiers to make it appear that Jesus died? Or what if someone else really died in Jesus' place? These scenarios are possible, but they don't hold up well. For example, considering the contempt that the Sanhedrin had for Jesus, it is likely that they would have had witnesses there to see him die. They had paraded about the city for forty days telling everyone that they were going to have him killed. Surely someone would have been in attendance to watch. In addition, if he wasn't dead, surely they would have found him. Someone would likely have seen him and turned him in to the authorities.

OPTION TWO: JESUS DIED BUT SOMEONE ELSE FAKED HIS RESURRECTION APPEARANCES.

This contention is also pretty weak. It assumes that someone was making appearances in Jerusalem, Galilee and elsewhere acting as though he were Jesus risen from the dead. It also assumes that people were actually fooled into thinking that this person was Jesus. All of Jesus' core group of disciples would have to have been fooled. So would Jesus' family as well as his enemy, Saul.

Or, perhaps it is more likely that many or all of them were in on a very big, very well-organized deception.

WERE THEY LYING?

A WELL-ORGANIZED CONSPIRACY?

Were Jesus' followers lying about his resurrection? If so, it was a very well-organized conspiracy. It would have required getting the core eleven disciples and possibly hundreds of other followers to consent to the same lie and to stick with it successfully to their deaths (until about 90 CE). In fact, it would require multiple "waves" of followers to consent to the same lie. At minimum, it would have required four waves of conspirators:

- the original twelve *(including Matthew, Peter, and John)*
- a second wave of disciples *(including Luke and Mark)*
- his family *(including James and Jude)*, and
- his enemy, Saul

It would have been very difficult for them to have maintained the lie.

DID THEY KNOWINGLY DIE FOR A LIE?

The first disciple who was reported to have been killed was James, the brother of John. Herod Agrippa I, the Roman ruler over Galilee, had him killed. He reportedly did it to please his Jewish subjects.[66] James, the brother of Jesus was stoned to death. John was imprisoned by the Sanhedrin on at least one occasion[67] and probably flogged as well.[68] He was ultimately exiled to the Island of Patmos.[69] Peter was also reported to have been imprisoned and flogged by the Sanhedrin[70] and later crucified by the Romans during Nero's reign.[71] Evidently, Paul was also executed by the Romans. Mark was killed by a mob while evangelizing Egypt in 68 CE.[72] Thomas, the apostle who doubted Jesus' resurrection, was killed in Mylapore, India after having won thousands of converts.[73] We don't know with certainty what happened to the rest of the original disciples. However, they were intensely persecuted by both Jews and Romans. During the reign of Nero, Jesus' followers were killed en mass. They were crucified, killed by wild animals in the arena as sport, and impaled upon stakes, covered with pitch and set afire to light Roman banquet halls.[74] These people were beaten, stoned, imprisoned, and killed. Yet, they contended to their deaths that Jesus really is the Messiah and that he really did rise from the dead. Did they die for a lie, for their own lie?

Jesus' current day followers concede that, yes, people throughout history have died for causes which turned out to be lies. But they contend that, if Jesus' followers died for a lie, it would have been for something that they *knew* to be a lie. They assert that most people who die for a lie are dying for something that they believe to be true. In the case of Jesus' disciples, if they were lying about Jesus' miracles and resurrection, they knew it.

But, what if they had something to gain? Haven't people died out of greed and selfish ambition? Haven't people lied, thinking they were accomplishing some greater good? What would Jesus' followers have to gain from a lie?

WHAT DID THEY HAVE TO GAIN?

Why would Jesus' followers have lied about his resurrection? Did they stand to gain something?

This question is perplexing because Jesus' disciples gained nothing in the physical sense of the word. They did gain notoriety, which resulted in their persecution, imprisonment and death. They did not gain wealth. They claimed that early followers actually sold possessions and shared communally.[75] They did not gain power in the sense of having large numbers of personal followers. They tended to minimize their own roles as leaders.[76] And finally, they did not gain freedom from Rome. In fact, they didn't even preach rebellion. They taught that people should love their enemies and that they should obey those in authority.[77]

So, what did they gain, if they did lie? Nothing, but persecution.

WHERE WAS THE BODY?

It would have been impossible for Jesus' followers to get anyone to believe a lie about his resurrection from the dead unless they had stolen Jesus' body. It would have been very easy for the Romans or the Jewish officials to stop the Jesus movement by simply dragging his body out into the street. The Romans brought back Theudas' head to Jerusalem to quell his followers. It would have been just as easy to stop stories of Jesus' resurrection by producing his dead body. But they didn't.

Jesus' followers contended that they did not steal the body. They claimed that the priests and the Pharisees had the Roman authorities post guards at Jesus' grave to ensure that no one could steal the body. They said that these leaders knew Jesus had said he would rise from the dead in three days and that they wanted to ensure that no one would steal the body and start resurrection stories.[78] Their contention is logical. Neither the Sanhedrin nor the Romans would have wanted the people following a phantom messiah. It would have upset the established order of the day.

One thing is certain, either Jesus really did rise from the dead or the Roman guards failed miserably given that two thousand years later, about two billion people believe that Jesus is the Messiah of Israel and that he did rise.

CONCLUSIONS

Jesus' early disciples had reasons for following him. They *claimed* that they followed him because of:

- John the Baptist's proclamation that Jesus was the Son of God
- the voice they heard from heaven three times which said Jesus was God's Son
- the miracles which they saw Jesus perform
- the earthquake and darkness during Jesus' execution
- his resurrection from the dead
- Jesus' teaching and adherence to the Law
- the power which God also gave to them to perform miracles
- the outpouring of the Holy Spirit
- the prophecy of the Scriptures

Jesus' followers, family, and at least one enemy said that, based upon these reasons, they were convinced that Jesus is the Messiah. And, it's not likely that they were all delusional or that they were fooled into believing these things.

The Bottom Line... So, what is the bottom line? Well, it's pretty basic: Jesus' followers, family, and Saul were either all liars and died willingly for a lie—or, they were telling the truth and they really saw and experienced the things they claimed.

10

DID JESUS REJECT JUDAISM?

WHAT IS JUDAISM?

What is Judaism? This is a tough question to answer in a way that will satisfy the various branches of Judaism. Orthodox, Conservative, Reformed, and Hassidic Jews wouldn't all necessarily agree on the definition of Judaism. But, to answer the question of whether Jesus rejected Judaism, some basic definition of what Judaism is has to first be established. And, since the divergence of religious practice by Jesus' followers occurred during the first century, the relevant definition of Judaism to use should be a first century one.

WHO WAS A JEW?

There are two parts to the question, *what is Judaism?* The first part is to define *who was considered to be a Jew* in the first century. Lawrence H. Schiffman provides a basic definition as follows:

> *The halakhic definitions of a Jew in the pre-Christian era have been established: ancestry through the mother or conversion, including circumcision for males, immersion, acceptance of the Torah, and offering of a sacrifice. These continued to be the only possible ways to enter the Jewish people in the period in which Christianity came to the fore.*[1]

A Jew was someone who was born of a Jewish mother or someone who converted to Judaism and was circumcised, baptized, accepted the Law, and offered a sacrifice at the Temple.

BELIEFS OF FIRST CENTURY JUDAISM

The second part of the question is to understand *what first century Jews believed.* There were at least four major schools of Jewish thought in Palestine in the early first century: the Pharisees, the Saducees, the Essenes, and the Zealots.[2]

The Pharisees were the forerunners of modern Rabbinic Judaism. They believed in: the sovereignty and providence of God; living humbly and virtuously; the resurrection of man's spirit from the dead; rewards after this life for those who are virtuous and punishment in eternal prison for those who are evil; and the Temple sacrificial system.[3] In addition to teaching a strict observance the Law of Moses, the Pharisees observed the oral law as interpreted and passed down by the scribes.[4]

The Saducees were primarily from the leading families in Israel and dominated the priesthood and high priesthood in the Temple. They were in competition with the Pharisaic scribes as the interpreters of the Law of Moses.[5] Their beliefs differed from the Pharisees in that they did not believe in the resurrection from the dead nor did they practice anything beyond what the Law specifically required. They rejected the oral law but, when in positions of authority, they evidently conformed to Pharisaic practices since the majority of people embraced Pharisaic beliefs.[6] In addition, they evidently weren't united and collegial as a group, since Josephus referred to their conduct toward each other as "barbarous." [7]

The Essenes were widely known for their regard for virtue and their desire to separate themselves from the world. Their membership of roughly 4,000 was composed primarily of unmarried men who lived communally, giving all of their personal property for the common use. Their desire to live separated lives extended into basic religious practices. They didn't even go to the Temple in Jerusalem to offer sacrifices because they didn't want to expose themselves to what they perceived as the lawlessness of those who lived there.[8] They were known for their careful observance of the Law of Moses and were said to more strictly observe the Sabbath than any other Jews.[9] Like the Pharisees, they also believed in the immortality of souls and the rewards for righteousness after this life.[10]

The Zealots (also called the fourth philosophy) held to the basic beliefs of the Pharisees. Where they differed was their desire for liberty at any cost. They forcefully rebelled against their Roman occupiers and maintained that God was their only ruler and Lord.[11]

These groups differed in beliefs about several things including, the resurrection from the dead, whether to rebel against the Romans, and whether to pay taxes to Rome. But, they generally would have agreed upon a core set of beliefs. With a few exceptions, the major ones would at least have included:

1. Worship of the One True God *(The God of Abraham, Isaac and Jacob)*

2. Israel's Covenant Relationship with God
   - Israel set apart from other peoples to act as a nation of priests
   - Circumcision as a sign of the covenant
   - Acceptance of Gentile converts

3. The Law of God as the Standard of Conduct and the Standard of Worship:
   - Temple Worship and Atonement Through the Sacrificial System
   - Festivals, Feasts and Fasts to Commemorate God's Protection and Provision
   - Sabbath Observance as Part of the Covenant
   - Dietary and Health Ordinances
   - Criminal Code

- Property Rights
- The Judicial System and Cities of Refuge
- Labor Law
- Social Responsibility
- Treaties and War
- Marriage, Divorce and Sexual Relations

4. The Holy Scriptures as God's Communications with Man Through the Prophets

5. The Coming Messiah Who Would Deliver Israel

DID JESUS REJECT JUDAISM?

Using the above as a minimum definition for 1st century Judaism, did Jesus reject either his own Jewishness or the basics of Jewish theology? Let's look at each of these core beliefs versus what is recorded about Jesus' teachings.

WORSHIP OF THE ONE TRUE GOD

Jesus evidently held to the belief that the God of Abraham is the one true God. When asked what the greatest commandment is, he replied:

> 'Love the Lord your God with all your heart and with all your soul and with all your mind.' This is the first and greatest commandment. And the second is like it: 'Love your neighbor as yourself.' All the Law and the Prophets hang on these two commandments.
>
> —Matthew 22:37-40 (NIV®)

In answering, he quoted from Deuteronomy 6:5. The context of which is found in the preceding verse four, which says; "Hear, O Israel! The LORD is our God, the LORD alone."[12] From this reference and others, it seems clear that Jesus did regard the God of Abraham, Isaac, and Jacob as the one true God. However, Jesus expanded upon this belief with his claim to be the one and only *son of God who is one with the Father.*

He essentially claimed that *he is the God of Abraham, Isaac, and Jacob.*

ISRAEL'S COVENANT RELATIONSHIP

The Torah describes that God established a covenant with a man named Abraham. Abraham was set apart from the other people of the earth so that his descendants would become a nation of priests (Israel) to lead others to God. As a sign of the covenant relationship, God instituted the circumcision of every male participant in the covenant, including Gentile converts.

Jesus' disciple John records many references which Jesus made to Abraham's relationship to God. In addition, Jesus contrasted the relationship of unconverted Gentiles to God versus Israel's relationship to God to be that of dogs rather than that of children.[13] Based upon these references, Jesus was clear in his acknowledgment of the special relationship that Israel was granted by God.

THE LAW OF GOD

Jesus' followers maintain that Jesus did not reject the Law. In fact he seemed very emphatic about his belief in all of the Holy Scriptures, including the Torah:

> *Do not think that I have come to abolish the Law or the Prophets; I have not come to abolish them but to fulfill them. I tell you the truth, until heaven and earth disappear, not the smallest letter, not the least stroke of a pen, will by any means disappear from the Law until everything is accomplished. Anyone who breaks one of the least of these commandments and teaches others to do the same will be called least in the kingdom of heaven, but whoever practices and teaches these commands will be called great in the kingdom of heaven. For I tell you that unless your righteousness surpasses that of the Pharisees and the teachers of the law, you will certainly not enter the kingdom of heaven.*

—Matthew 5:17-48 (NIV®)

Jesus contended that not even a single letter will drop out of the Law until everything written in the Law and the Prophets is fulfilled.[14]

One of Jesus' major points of conflict with the religious establishment of his day was not whether *he* believed the Law, it was over what he claimed to be *their* failure to follow it. He repeatedly blasted the Pharisees (the rabbis) publicly for hypocrisy and legalism.[15] He also blasted the Saducees (the priests) for not knowing the Scriptures.[16] Jesus is recorded as lamenting: *"Has not Moses given you the law? Yet not one of you keeps the law."*[17] He warned the people of Israel:

> *The teachers of the law and the Pharisees sit in Moses' seat. So you must obey them and do everything they tell you. But do not do what they do, for they do not practice what they preach.*

> —Matthew 23: 2-3 (NIV®)

Jesus is also recorded as having blasted the Pharisees for following "oral tradition" at the expense of obeying the Law itself:

> *Then some Pharisees and teachers of the law came to Jesus from Jerusalem and asked, "Why do your disciples break the tradition of the elders? They don't wash their hands before they eat!" Jesus replied, "And why do you break the command of God for the sake of your tradition? For God said, 'Honor your father and mother' and 'Anyone who curses his father or mother must be put to death.' But you say that if a man says to his father or mother, 'Whatever help you might otherwise have received from me is a gift devoted to God,' he is not to 'honor his father' with it. Thus you nullify the word of God for the sake of your tradition. You hypocrites! Isaiah was right when he prophesied about you: "'These people honor me with their lips, but their hearts are far from me. They worship me in vain; their teachings are but rules taught by men.'"*

> —Matthew 15:1-9 (NIV®)

Jesus was reported to be a stickler for the Law. Although we don't have specific references to his teachings about all 613 commands included in the Law, his followers did provide many quotations. A sampling of his teachings includes the following;

Festivals, Feasts and Fasts   Jesus evidently did observe the sacred feasts and fasts. His followers recorded occasions when he went to Jerusalem for the Feast of Dedication (Hanukkah), the Feast of Tabernacles, and the Passover.[18] In addition, there are no recorded instances of Jesus ever teaching against any of the feasts or fasts.

Dietary and Health Ordinances   There are many ordinances in the Law which relate to a wide variety of health and diet issues. They include laws about how to deal with infectious diseases, mildew infestation, purification after childbirth, clean and unclean foods, and the list goes on.[19]

Jesus evidently complied with and taught these ordinances. For example, Jesus' disciples recorded that after healing a man of leprosy, he instructed the man to go to the Temple to offer the gift prescribed in the Law for the healing of the disease.[20]

The Sabbath   In the Law, the seventh day of the week was declared to be a day of rest. No work of any kind was to be performed. This is one area where Jesus created controversy. Jesus' disciples recorded that the Pharisees accused him of being a Sabbath breaker, citing two unlikely reasons, which they considered to be unjust interpretations of the Law.

1. *Healing on the Sabbath*

   Jesus was accused of being a Sabbath breaker several times for *healing* on the Sabbath. On various Sabbaths he is recorded as having healed: a man with a crippled hand,[21] a lady who had been crippled for eighteen years,[22] a man who had been an invalid for thirty-eight years[23], and a man who had been blind from birth.[24] After each occurrence, his followers said that he was accused by the religious leaders of breaking the Sabbath.

Jesus is said to have defended himself by referring to the Law. He responded that it is lawful to do good on the Sabbath. He reasoned as follows:

He said to them, "If any of you has a sheep and it falls into a pit on the Sabbath, will you not take hold of it and lift it out? How much more valuable is a man than a sheep! Therefore it is lawful to do good on the Sabbath."

—Matthew 12:11-12 (NIV®)

Now if a child can be circumcised on the Sabbath so that the law of Moses may not be broken, why are you angry with me for healing the whole man on the Sabbath? Stop judging by mere appearances, and make a right judgment.

—John 7:23-24 (NIV®)

2. *Eating grain on the Sabbath*

Jesus' followers were also accused by the Pharisees of breaking the Sabbath. The Pharisees had observed them eating grain as they walked through a field.[25]

Jesus is recorded as having responded to the accusation by saying that: 1) his followers were innocent of breaking the Law, and 2) he had authority over the Sabbath.

He answered, "Haven't you read what David did when he and his companions were hungry? He entered the house of God, and he and his companions ate the consecrated bread— which was not lawful for them to do, but only for the priests. Or haven't you read in the Law that on the Sabbath the priests in the temple desecrate the day and yet are innocent? I tell you that one greater than the temple is here. If you had known what these words mean, 'I desire mercy, not sacrifice,' you would not have condemned the innocent. For the Son of Man is Lord of the Sabbath."

—Matthew 12:3-8 (NIV®)

Marriage, Divorce & Sexual Conduct The Law outlined in great detail the types of sexual relations which are improper,[26] and regulations related to marriage[27] and divorce.[28] Entire chapters are devoted to these topics.

It appears that Jesus' teaching on both divorce and adultery were based upon an even stricter standard than the Law allowed. He taught very strongly against divorce and taught that mental adultery was the same as actually committing the act:

Some Pharisees came to him to test him. They asked, "Is it lawful for a man to divorce his wife for any and every reason?" "Haven't you read," he replied, "that at the beginning the Creator 'made them male and female,' and said, 'For this reason a man will leave his father and mother and be united to his wife, and the two will become one flesh'? So they are no longer two, but one. Therefore what God has joined together, let man not separate." "Why then," they asked, "did Moses command that a man give his wife a certificate of divorce and send her away?" Jesus replied, "Moses permitted you to divorce your wives because your hearts were hard. But it was not this way from the beginning. I tell you that anyone who divorces his wife, except for marital unfaithfulness, and marries another woman commits adultery."

—Matthew 19:3-9 (NIV®)

You have heard that it was said, 'Do not commit adultery.' But I tell you that anyone who looks at a woman lustfully has already committed adultery with her in his heart.

—Matthew 5:27-28 (NIV®)

His contention was that sin committed in the heart is the same as sin physically committed.

HOLY SCRIPTURES

As previously stated, Jesus was reported to be emphatic about his belief in the Holy Scriptures. His disciples recorded his frequent quotations from the Scriptures. For example, Matthew recorded Jesus as quoting from Genesis, Exodus, Leviticus, Deuteronomy, Hosea, Micah, Malachi, Isaiah, Jeremiah, Psalms, Zechariah, and Daniel. Matthew recorded about thirty-nine quotations in all.

Perhaps one of the reasons Jesus was so emphatic about the validity of the Scriptures is that he pointed to them as the basis for himself claiming to be Messiah:[29]

> He said to them, "This is what I told you while I was still with you: Everything must be fulfilled that is written about me in the Law of Moses, the Prophets and the Psalms." Then he opened their minds so they could understand the Scriptures. He told them, "This is what is written: The Christ will suffer and rise from the dead on the third day, and repentance and forgiveness of sins will be preached in his name to all nations, beginning at Jerusalem. You are witnesses of these things.
>
> —Luke 24:44-48 (NIV®)

THE COMING MESSIAH

Judaism for centuries had taught of the coming Messiah who would provide spiritual redemption and physical deliverance for Israel. By the 1st century, messianic hope and expectation was high. The harsh Roman occupation of Palestine made people long for the Messiah and freedom from oppression.

Jesus also taught about Messiah's coming. Like Isaiah, Jeremiah and Daniel, he taught that Messiah would be killed. And, like Isaiah, he said that Messiah would rise from the dead to reign. The difference was that *he said he was the Messiah* and that he was the one who would be killed and rise from the dead.[30]

So, What Did Jesus "Add" To Judaism

There were really three things that could be said were "added" by Jesus to the teachings of 1st century Judaism, although, in reality, the basic teachings were not really new at all. They were based upon three promises which God gave in the Scriptures hundreds of years before. The first was that he *personalized the Messiah*. The second was the *New Covenant* between God and man, which he taught. And, the third was his teaching about the *Spirit of God*.

A Personal Messiah & Savior Jesus personalized the teachings about Messiah by saying that he was the Messiah. The basic messianic promises of the Scriptures go back to Moses and are repeated by the prophets through Malachi. The belief in the Messiah and even the belief that the Messiah is the son of God were not new. What was *new* was that here was a man who was saying that it was him!

Another aspect of Jesus' teaching that was perceived as new was that spiritual salvation could be found through faith in this personal Messiah. John the Baptist also taught this.[31] The logic behind this obviously was that if Messiah is God, then forgiveness and spiritual salvation not only *could* be found through him, but his death as a sacrifice for the sins of mankind *would* secure it for them. He actually taught his followers that he would die as a sacrifice for their sins. Again, this wasn't really new. The Prophet Isaiah had conveyed this about Messiah over 600 years before.[32]

A New Covenant Jesus claimed that he was ushering in a *New Covenant* between Israel and God. Again, the concept of a *New Covenant* was nothing new. Malachi, Ezekiel, and Jeremiah had all prophesied that it was coming. And all three of these prophets referenced the *New Covenant* in the context of the coming Messiah.[33] But Jesus said that the *New Covenant* was now in effect and that he was the only means of access to it.

According to Jesus, this *New Covenant* was that forgiveness for sins and spiritual salvation could be found through faith in the Messiah and his atoning death as a sacrifice for sins. The covenant was the means of access to righteousness, eternal life, heaven, and to God the Father:

> *Jesus answered, "I am the way and the truth and the life. No one comes to the Father except through me.*
>
> —John 14:6 (NIV®)

> *Jesus said to her, "I am the resurrection and the life. He who believes in me will live, even though he dies; and whoever lives and believes in me will never die. Do you believe this?"*
>
> —John 11:25-26 (NIV®)

> *No one has ever gone into heaven except the one who came from heaven—the Son of Man. Just as Moses lifted up the snake in the desert, so the Son of Man must be lifted up, that everyone who believes in him may have eternal life. "For God so loved the world that he gave his one and only Son, that whoever believes in him shall not perish but have eternal life. For God did not send his Son into the world to condemn the world, but to save the world through him. Whoever believes in him is not condemned, but whoever does not believe stands condemned already because he has not believed in the name of God's one and only Son.*
>
> —John 3:13-18 (NIV®)

Unlike the covenants with Abraham and Moses, this *New Covenant* was not sealed with the blood of circumcision or the blood of sacrifices. According to Jesus, it was sealed with the blood of Messiah.

The Spirit of God   Jesus told his disciples that he would send them the Spirit of God as prophesied by the prophet Joel.[34] Joel's prophecy would likely have been well-known, since he prophesied in the 9th century BCE. He had said that God will pour out His spirit on all flesh:

> *After that, I will pour out My spirit on all flesh; your sons and daughters shall prophesy; your old men shall dream dreams, and your young men shall see visions. I will even pour out my spirit upon male and female slaves in those days.*

> —Joel 3:1-2 (JPS)

Jesus is recorded as saying that this prophecy would be fulfilled after he ascended to heaven:[35]

> *On one occasion, while he was eating with them, he gave them this command: "Do not leave Jerusalem, but wait for the gift my Father promised, which you have heard me speak about. For John baptized with water, but in a few days you will be baptized with the Holy Spirit." So when they met together, they asked him, "Lord, are you at this time going to restore the kingdom to Israel?" He said to them: "It is not for you to know the times or dates the Father has set by his own authority. But you will receive power when the Holy Spirit comes on you; and you will be my witnesses in Jerusalem, and in all Judea and Samaria, and to the ends of the earth.*

> —Acts 1:4-8 (NIV®)

Again, the prophecy that God was going to pour out His Holy Spirit was not new to Judaism. But Jesus' contention that it was about to happen would have definitely been viewed as new.

CONCLUSIONS

Based upon what his disciples recorded of his teachings, it appears that Jesus did not reject Judaism. He did not reject his own Jewishness or the basic teachings of 1st century Judaism. However, Jesus did reject some specific teachings of the Oral Law (tradition of the fathers), which he said did not line up with the Holy Scriptures. He also rejected what he perceived as legalism and hypocrisy on the part of the Pharisees and the lack of understanding of the Scriptures on the part of the Saducees.

Jesus did not reject Judaism, but the leaders of Judaism did reject Jesus. His major confrontations with the Pharisees and Saducees were not because he was rejecting the Law or the Prophets—he didn't reject them. They were because of who Jesus claimed to be. They refused to accept that he was the Messiah, the Son of God.

11

DID JESUS' FOLLOWERS REJECT JUDAISM?

If Jesus didn't reject Judaism, then what happened? How did the rift and ultimate separation between his followers and Rabbinic Judaism occur? If Jesus didn't reject Judaism, *did his followers reject it?* Were they the ones who were responsible for the separation?

Let's start with a cornerstone event that crystallized the doctrinal differences between Jesus' followers and the religious leaders of Judaism. It occurred not long after Jesus' death.

THE JERUSALEM COUNCIL CONCERNING GENTILE BELIEVERS

Within about eighteen years after Jesus' crucifixion, a disagreement emerged among his followers. The disagreement was over what Gentile believers must do to receive spiritual salvation. Judean followers had gone to Antioch, a city in Asia Minor, and had begun teaching that *"Unless you are circumcised, according to the custom taught by Moses, you cannot be saved."*[1] This brought them into conflict with Rabbi Saul (Paul), Barnabas and other followers in Antioch. So, the Antioch believers sent a delegation to Jerusalem to see the leaders of the church there to resolve the conflict.

When the meeting started, some of Jesus' followers from Jerusalem, who were Pharisees, contended that *"the Gentiles must be circumcised and required to obey the Law of Moses.*"[2] It's recorded that, after extended debate, Simon Peter then rose and said:

> *Brothers, you know that some time ago God made a*
> *choice among you that the Gentiles might hear from my*
> *lips the message of the gospel and believe. God, who*
> *knows the heart, showed that he accepted them by giv-*
> *ing the Holy Spirit to them, just as he did to us. He made*
> *no distinction between us and them, for he purified their*
> *hearts by faith. Now then, why do you try to test God by*
> *putting on the necks of the disciples a yoke that neither*
> *we nor our fathers have been able to bear? No! We*
> *believe it is through the grace of our Lord Jesus that we*
> *are saved, just as they are.*

—Acts 15:7-11 (NIV®)

James, the brother of Jesus, then addressed the group of leaders by concurring with Peter and saying:

> *It is my judgment, therefore, that we should not make it*
> *difficult for the Gentiles who are turning to God. Instead*
> *we should write to them, telling them to abstain from*
> *food polluted by idols, from sexual immorality, from the*
> *meat of strangled animals and from blood. For Moses*
> *has been preached in every city from the earliest times*
> *and is read in the synagogues on every Sabbath.*

—Acts 15:19-21(NIV®)

They agreed with James and concluded their meeting by sending messengers with Paul and Barnabas back to Antioch with both a written and a verbal message conveying the requirements proposed by James. The message was:

> *The apostles and elders, your brothers, To the Gentile*
> *believers in Antioch, Syria and Cilicia: Greetings. We have*

heard that some went out from us without our authoriza-
tion and disturbed you, troubling your minds by what they
said. So we all agreed to choose some men and send them
to you with our dear friends Barnabas and Paul— men
who have risked their lives for the name of our Lord Jesus
Christ. Therefore we are sending Judas and Silas to con-
firm by word of mouth what we are writing. It seemed
good to the Holy Spirit and to us not to burden you with
anything beyond the following requirements: You are to
abstain from food sacrificed to idols, from blood, from the
meat of strangled animals and from sexual immorality.
You will do well to avoid these things. Farewell.

—Acts 15:23-29 (NIV®)

So, was this a cop-out on the part of the leaders of Jesus' followers in Jerusalem? They would have contended, "no." The first question they were addressing was: *what is required for Gentiles to be saved?* Their answer was: the same thing as is required for Jews, faith in Jesus, the Messiah. The second question was: *In light of this, what requirements of the Law should be imposed upon Gentile believers?* Another way of asking the second question is, *what requirements must be met to allow membership in the church (synagogue)?* In answering the second question the statement is made that everyone has heard and has access to the Law taught by Moses. So this assumes the presumption that the Law is viewed as the standard of conduct. But they didn't make compliance with all 613 laws contained in the Torah a *predecessor* to admitting Gentile believers into the church. They gave them four: *"abstain from food sacrificed to idols, from blood, from the meat of strangled animals and from sexual immorality."*[3] In addition, they excluded them from the requirement to be circumcised.

Did they lower the bar for the Gentiles? And, was their reduction of the 613 laws in the Torah down to four requirements an implicit rejection of Judaism? Jesus' followers would respond "no" to both questions. The reasons for their contention will be addressed shortly.

WHAT ABOUT PAUL?

Did Rabbi Saul (Paul) reject Judaism? After all, it has been said that he created a new religion by shifting the focus of Judaism from the Law to the Messiah.[4] In fact, Paul was merely one of the many disciples of Jesus who placed their primary focus upon him as Messiah. They did so, not only because they believed him to be God, but because he was viewed as the sole means of access to the *New Covenant*.

DID PAUL REJECT JUDAISM?

Paul stated that he did believe the Law and the Prophets. He is recorded as saying *"I believe everything that agrees with the Law and that is written in the Prophets."*[5] He also stated that the Law is good and quoted from it as the basis of conduct.[6] He even said that he was not free from God's Law.[7] His point was not that the Law is not good. After all, he said that it is the Law that teaches us what is right and makes us conscious of sin.[8] His point was that no one can be "justified" before God by merely obeying the Law:

> *We who are Jews by birth and not 'Gentile sinners' know that a man is not justified by observing the law, but by faith in Jesus Christ. So we, too, have put our faith in Christ Jesus that we may be justified by faith in Christ and not by observing the law, because by observing the law no one will be justified.*

—Galatians 2:15-16 (NIV®)

He used Abraham as an example to support his contention that righteousness before God (justification) is not attained by obeying the Law. Paul quoted from Genesis, stating that Abraham's belief in God was *"credited to him as righteousness"*[9], 430 years before the Law was given. He further explained that, even when the Law was given, it didn't do way with God's covenant with Abraham or the promises that He had made to Abraham's descendants.[10]

Paul's contention essentially was that Judaism was off track. From his perspective, Israel had departed from pursuing a righteousness which comes by faith in God and instead sought to attain their own right-eousness by obeying the Law[11], something which he claimed, it was never intended to do:[12]

> *But now a righteousness from God, apart from law, has been made known, to which the Law and the Prophets testify. This righteousness from God comes through faith in Jesus Christ to all who believe. There is no difference, for all have sinned and fall short of the glory of God, and are justified freely by his grace through the redemption that came by Christ Jesus. God presented him as a sacrifice of atonement, through faith in his blood. He did this to demonstrate his justice, because in his forbearance he had left the sins committed beforehand unpunished—he did it to demonstrate his justice at the present time, so as to be just and the one who justifies those who have faith in Jesus. Where, then, is boasting? It is excluded. On what principle? On that of observing the law? No, but on that of faith. For we maintain that a man is justified by faith apart from observing the law. Is God the God of Jews only? Is he not the God of Gentiles too? Yes, of Gentiles too, since there is only one God, who will justify the circumcised by faith and the uncircumcised through that same faith. Do we, then, nullify the law by this faith? Not at all! Rather, we uphold the law.*
>
> —Romans 3:21-31 (NIV®)

Why then was the Law given to us? Paul contended it was given to make us conscious of sin and *"to lead us to Christ [Messiah] that we might be justified by faith."* [13] He stated that faith in Messiah is the end point (conclusion) of the Law.[14] Paul further reasoned, *"now that faith has come, we are no longer under the supervision of the law."*[15] He seems to have meant that for those, who are made righteous through faith in Messiah, the effect is as if the Law is canceled or abolished.[16]

Paul's basic contention was that he was not rejecting Judaism. He claimed that he had found Judaism in Messiah, God in the flesh.

"BUT JESUS' FOLLOWERS DON'T OBSERVE THE LAW"

Many would contend that Jesus' followers did reject Judaism, based upon the things that they *didn't* do. And, in fact, there are several areas where the religious practices of Jesus' 1st century followers differed from that of 1st century Judaism. The first of these differences was the practice of the sacrificial system.

SACRIFICE AND OFFERINGS

When the Temple in Jerusalem was destroyed in 70 CE, the sacrificial system mandated by God in the Law ceased. Today, there is still no Temple. There hasn't been a place to offer sacrifices to God for almost 2,000 years. *So, since the 1st century, no branch of Judaism has been able to comply with the sacrificial system prescribed by God in the Torah.*

Before the Temple was destroyed, however, Jesus' followers did appear to have observed at least part of the Law that required sacrifices and offerings to God. In one instance they are recorded as going to Jerusalem for Shavuot (Pentecost), a feast that required sacrifices.[17] But, Jesus' early followers didn't comply with the sin offering provisions of the sacrificial system. The reason they cited for not doing so was their belief that *Jesus was the sacrifice that forever ended all sacrifices for sin.*[18] They reasoned as follows:

> *When Moses had proclaimed every commandment of the law to all the people, he took the blood of calves, together with water, scarlet wool and branches of hyssop, and sprinkled the scroll and all the people. He said, "This is the blood of the covenant, which God has commanded you to keep." In the same way, he*

*sprinkled with the blood both the tabernacle and
everything used in its ceremonies. In fact, the law
requires that nearly everything be cleansed with blood,
and without the shedding of blood there is no forgiveness. It was necessary, then, for the copies of the heavenly things to be purified with these sacrifices, but the
heavenly things themselves with better sacrifices than
these. For Christ did not enter a man-made sanctuary
that was only a copy of the true one; he entered heav-
en itself, now to appear for us in God's presence. Nor
did he enter heaven to offer himself again and again,
the way the high priest enters the Most Holy Place
every year with blood that is not his own. Then Christ
would have had to suffer many times since the creation
of the world. But now he has appeared once for all at
the end of the ages to do away with sin by the sacrifice
of himself. Just as man is destined to die once, and
after that to face judgment, so Christ was sacrificed
once to take away the sins of many people; and he will
appear a second time, not to bear sin, but to bring salvation to those who are waiting for him.*

—Hebrews 9:19-28 (NIV®)

They believed that Jesus' death was a fulfillment of Isaiah's prophecy that Messiah would die to make us righteous. To them, this meant
that no further sacrifice for sin was required.

CIRCUMCISION

The Torah records God's command that circumcision be instituted as
a sign of the covenant that He made with Abraham. Abraham and all of
his male descendants above the age of eight days old were to be circumcised.[19] This command was then incorporated by God into the Law about
430 years later[20] and is still practiced by Jews and many Gentiles today.

But, at the Jerusalem Synod (council) of 50 CE, Jesus' followers concluded that Gentile believers need not be circumcised. Their instructions to the Gentile believers in Antioch excluded circumcision as a requirement for spiritual salvation and fellowship (or affiliation) with other believers.

Their reason for this omission is evident from their writings. They concluded that Jesus' blood, which was shed on the cross as he was executed (sacrificed), sealed the *New Covenant*. They said that because of this, the blood of circumcision, which sealed the covenant with Abraham, and the blood of the sacrifices, which sealed the covenant with Moses, are no longer required. Paul's contention was not that we should not obey God; it was that circumcision is now rendered meaningless in light of the *New Covenant*:

> *Was a man already circumcised when he was called? He should not become uncircumcised. Was a man uncircumcised when he was called? He should not be circumcised. Circumcision is nothing and uncircumcision is nothing. Keeping God's commands is what counts.*
>
> —1 Corinthians 7:18-19 (NIV®)

> *Those who want to make a good impression outwardly are trying to compel you to be circumcised. The only reason they do this is to avoid being persecuted for the cross of Christ. Not even those who are circumcised obey the law, yet they want you to be circumcised that they may boast about your flesh. May I never boast except in the cross of our Lord Jesus Christ, through which the world has been crucified to me, and I to the world. Neither circumcision nor uncircumcision means anything; what counts is a new creation.*
>
> —Galatians 6:12-15 (NIV®)

Paul further contended that it was Abraham's faith that caused God to declare him righteous and that this occurred long before Abraham was circumcised. He reasoned that circumcision was the "sign" of the covenant that God made with Abraham; not the basis for it:

> *We have been saying that Abraham's faith was credited to him as righteousness. Under what circumstances was it credited? Was it after he was circumcised, or before? It was not after, but before! And he received the sign of circumcision, a seal of the righteousness that he had by faith while he was still uncircumcised. So then, he is the father of all who believe but have not been circumcised, in order that righteousness might be credited to them. And he is also the father of the circumcised who not only are circumcised but who also walk in the footsteps of the faith that our father Abraham had before he was circumcised. It was not through law that Abraham and his offspring received the promise that he would be heir of the world, but through the righteousness that comes by faith.*

> —Romans 4:9-13 (NIV®)

In the view of Jesus' 1st century followers, if Jesus' blood sealed the *New Covenant*, then the sign of the old covenant had been eclipsed.[a]

DIETARY LAWS (KOSHER)

Some of Jesus' modern day followers teach adherence to the dietary laws taught in the Torah. But most don't teach or stress the importance of these commands. Why?

There are likely several reasons. First and most significantly, Jesus

---

[a] Reform Judaism in the United States also does not require circumcision for converts, only for children of Jewish parents. However, it is not for the same reason. They have essentially waived the requirement rather than view it to have been made moot by a *New Covenant*.

taught his 1st century followers that what they ate did not make them spiritually unclean; it was what was in their hearts...

> *For from within, out of men's hearts, come evil thoughts, sexual immorality, theft, murder, adultery, greed, malice, deceit, lewdness, envy, slander, arrogance and folly. All these evils come from inside and make a man 'unclean.'*

—Mark 7:21-23 (NIV®)

But it is obvious that Jesus' 1st century followers didn't disregard the dietary laws in the Torah. At the Jerusalem Synod of 50 CE, the leaders among Jesus' followers actually included conformance to three dietary restrictions in their instructions to new Gentile believers:

> *It seemed good to the Holy Spirit and to us not to burden you with anything beyond the following requirements: You are to abstain from food sacrificed to idols, from blood, from the meat of strangled ani- mals and from sexual immorality. You will do well to avoid these things.*

—Acts 15:28-29 (NIV®)

The three dietary restrictions are significant in that they are consistent with a focus upon their Messiah Jesus as the sacrifice for sin. By abstaining from eating food sacrificed to idols and from eating blood (which was offered to God as part of sin offerings), they appear to have been stressing the importance of understanding their belief that Jesus was the sacrifice for sin and that his blood was the sign of the *New Covenant*.

Paul's letter to Jesus' followers in the Greek city of Colosea in the 1st century also provides at least part of the reason for the lessened focus upon dietary restrictions. He basically contended that many of the dietary restrictions taught at the time hadn't been commanded by God at all:

Since you died with Christ to the basic principles of this world, why, as though you still belonged to it, do you submit to its rules: "Do not handle! Do not taste! Do not touch!"? These are all destined to perish with use, because they are based on human commands and teachings. Such regulations indeed have an appearance of wisdom, with their self-imposed worship, their false humility and their harsh treatment of the body, but they lack any value in restraining sensual indulgence.

—Colossians 2:20-23 (NIV®)

Thus the dietary restrictions included in the Law seem to have been viewed as good by Jesus' followers. But, they were not viewed as requirements for spiritual salvation, only faith in Jesus the Messiah was.

SABBATH

The Sabbath was both a labor law and a religious ordinance to Israel. It was a legal holiday, a day to rest and have sacred assemblies.[21] The Torah (the Law) teaches that it is to be observed from the evening of the sixth day to the evening of the seventh. No one is to work, not even to gather firewood, or to build a fire, or to bake dinner.[22] The only people who could legally fulfill their duties on the Sabbath were the priests who served in the Temple of God.

Jews were commanded to celebrate the Sabbath as a lasting covenant forever:

The Israelite people shall keep the sabbath, observing the sabbath throughout the ages as a covenant for all time: it shall be a sign for all time between Me and the people of Israel. For in six days the LORD made heaven and earth, and on the seventh day He ceased from work and was refreshed.

—Exodus 31:16-17 (JPS)

As a by-product of keeping the Sabbath, God promised to bless Israel:

> *If you refrain from trampling the sabbath, From pursuing your affairs on My holy day; If you call the sabbath "delight," The LORD's holy day "honored"; And if you honor it and go not your ways Nor look to your affairs, nor strike bargains—Then you can seek the favor of the LORD. I will set you astride the heights of the earth, And let you enjoy the heritage of your father Jacob—For the mouth of the LORD has spoken.*

—Isaiah 58:13-14 (JPS)

Most of Jesus' followers teach that the Sabbath is holy and should be observed. But, while some of Jesus' followers (such as 7th Day Adventists) celebrate the Sabbath on the 7th day of the week, most observe it on the first day of the week.

There are several reasons for the change to a first day of the week Sabbath:

- Jesus' followers said that Jesus rose from the dead on the first day of the week (Easter Sunday).[23]

- Jesus' 1st century followers had a custom of gathering and collecting an offering for the poor on the first day of the week.[24]

- Jesus' followers weren't welcome in the synagogues to participate in the normal Sabbath activities. As we will review later, in the 1st century CE, Rabban Gamaliel II forced a separation of sorts by ordering the inclusion of a curse directed at Jesus' followers in the benediction which was recited in the synagogues. Anyone who was truly a follower of Jesus would have been unable to recite this benediction.

- Because Jesus' followers gathered on Sunday, Emperor Constantine made it a day of rest in the Roman Empire.[25]

Rabbi Saul (Paul) wrote to believers in Greece to not be concerned if others judged them for not participating in the special Sabbaths and festivals. His contention essentially was that they were obscured by the salvation and forgiveness that Jesus secured for them:

> *When you were dead in your sins and in the uncir-cumcision of your sinful nature, God made you alive with Christ. He forgave us all our sins, having can-celed the written code, with its regulations, that was against us and that stood opposed to us; he took it away, nailing it to the cross. And having disarmed the powers and authorities, he made a public spectacle of them, triumphing over them by the cross. Therefore do not let anyone judge you by what you eat or drink, or with regard to a religious festival, a New Moon cel-ebration or a Sabbath day. These are a shadow of the things that were to come; the reality, however, is found in Christ.*

—Colossians 2:13-17 (NIV®)

Was this change in the day of the week appropriate? Jesus didn't command it. This is debated among some of Jesus' followers to this day.[b]

OBSERVANCE OF FEASTS AND SOLEMN OCCASIONS

Many feasts and solemn occasions were observed by 1st century Judaism. Many of them were specifically instituted by God, as record-ed in the Scriptures. Among these are Pasach (Pass Over), Yom Kippur (the Day of Atonement), and Sukkot (the Feast of Booths). Other occa-sions were the equivalent of national holidays. Some of these, such as Purim, were recorded in Scripture but were not specifically instituted by God. Still other occasions, such as Hanukah, were observed but were neither recorded in Scripture nor commanded by God.

---

[b] Today, Reform Judaism in the United States also has Sabbath services on Sunday.

Key Feasts or Fasts Observed in the 1st Century	Recorded in Scripture?	Commanded by God?
Yom Kippur	Leviticus 23:27-33	Yes
Pasach (Pass Over or Feast of Unleavened Bread)	Exodus 12:1-49	Yes
Shavuot (Pentecost)	Leviticus 23:9-21	Yes
Purim	Esther 9:18-19	No
Sukkot (Feast of Booths)	Leviticus 23:34-44	Yes
Rosh Hashanah	Leviticus 23:23-25	Yes
Hanukah	No (*1 and 2 Macabees*)	No
Tzom Gedaliah	Jeremiah 41:1-5	No

Yom Kippur is the Day of Atonement. It was the one day per year when a general "catch all" sacrifice was offered for the unatoned for sins of the nation of Israel. It was mandated in the Torah to be kept. Modern Rabbinic Judaism still observes Yom Kippur, but not in the way prescribed in the Scriptures. This isn't possible because there is no longer a Temple in Jerusalem where sacrifices can be offered.

Most of Jesus' followers do not observe Yom Kippur. This is because they believe that Jesus was the sacrifice that ended all sacrifices for sin—*forever*. Even Jesus' Messianic Jewish followers that do observe Yom Kippur share in this belief.

Pasach (Passover) is the remembrance of God's deliverance of Israel from 430 years of slavery in Egypt. God commanded in the Torah that Pasach be observed by Israel forever.[26]

Many of Jesus' Jewish followers still observe the traditional Pasach seder. But for the majority of Jesus' followers the seder took on a new meaning. It was at the seder immediately preceding Jesus' death that he shared his "last supper" with his disciples. During the meal he said that the wine and bread represented his body and blood, which were given to secure the *New Covenant*.[27] The observance of the "Lord's supper" or "Communion" grew in frequency after Jesus' death and evidently became somewhat disassociated from the annual Pasach seder by his followers.[28]

Shavuot (or Pentecost, Feast of Weeks) was the feast of harvest. It was to be observed seven weeks (49 days) after the first harvest began. A sheaf of grain and two loaves of bread were to be brought to the Temple as an offering to God.[29]

Jesus' 1st century followers observed Shavuot. Though for them it took on a whole new meaning. They said that it was during Shavuot that the prophecies of Joel were fulfilled and the Holy Spirit of God was poured out upon those who follow Jesus as Messiah.[30] This is the meaning that Shavuot still bears for Jesus' present-day followers.[c]

Purim was celebrated to commemorate the deliverance of the Jews from planned genocide at the hands of the Persians in the 5th century BCE.[31] It was the equivalent of a national holiday, but its observance was not specifically commanded by God.[32]

Nothing was recorded about Purim by Jesus' 1st century followers. It is not known if they observed it or not.

Sukkot (or Feast of Tabernacles, Feast of Booths) was a seven-day harvest feast. Jewish men were to present themselves and give burnt offerings and grain offerings to the LORD at the Temple. In addition, their families were to live in Booths during the seven days in remembrance of their forefathers' deliverance from Egypt.[33] It was also during this feast that the Law was to be read to the entire nation of Israel once every seven years.[34]

---

[c] It is worth noting that the Scriptural observance of Shavuot has been deviated from by Rabbinic Judaism since the destruction of the Temple. It is now observed as a commemoration of the revelation of the Law on Mt. Sinai. (Michael Strassfeld, *The Jewish Holidays, A Guide and Commentary*, © 1985 by Michael Strassfeld, Harper & Row Publishers, New York, page 71)

It is recorded that Jesus went to Jerusalem for the Feast of Tabernacles,[35] but nothing is recorded about his disciples' observance of the feast after his death. However, since the destruction of the temple in 70 CE, it has not been possible for anyone to observe Sukkot in the way commanded in the Torah.

Rosh Hasannah (the Feast of Trumpets) was, according to the Scriptures, supposed to be a *"sacred occasion commemorated with loud blasts."*[36] It was celebrated as a sabbath and by bringing an offering to the LORD at the Temple.

Nothing about Rosh Hasannah was recorded by Jesus' 1st century followers.[d]

Hanukah was an eight day festival which celebrated the purification and rededication of the Temple in 164 BCE after it had been desecration by the Syrians three years earlier.[37] Since the canon of Hebrew Scripture ends with the prophet Malachi in the late 5th century BCE, Hanukah was not recorded in Scripture nor was its observance commanded by God.

Jesus is recorded as having gone to the Temple during Hanukah, but nothing is recorded about his followers' observance of the festival after his death.

Tzom Gedaliah is a minor fast day in observance of the assassination of Gedaliah, a Governor of Judah. Gedaliah had been appointed to office by King Nebuchadnezzar of Babylon after the Babylonians defeated Judah in the 6th century BCE. While Scriptures record that he was assassinated and that some went to the Temple to offer sacrifices, observance of a day of fasting wasn't commanded by God.[38]

---

[d] By about the 1st century, Rosh Hasannah had come to be regarded as the New Year celebration (even though it was celebrated on the 1st day of Tishri - the 7th month of the Hebrew calendar). It also came to be viewed as an annual day of judgment on mankind. (George Foot Moore, *Judaism,* © 1927 by the President and Fellows of Harvard College, Hendrickson Publishers, Inc. page 62)

[e] Few Jews today observe this day of fasting. (Michael Strassfeld, *The Jewish Holidays, A Guide and Commentary,* © 1985 by Michael Strassfeld, Harper & Row Publishers, New York, page 103)

This fast day is not mentioned in the writings of Jesus' early follow-ers nor is it observed by his followers today.[e]

WHAT ABOUT ORAL TRADITION (THE TALMUD)?

While the Talmud was not in existence during the 1st century, the oral law of the Pharisaic sect of Judaism was and ultimately became a core part of the Talmud.

WHAT IS THE TALMUD?

There are actually two *Talmuds*. The most widely referenced is the Babylonian Talmud. The other is the Jerusalem Talmud. Talmud means "study" and that is what they are. They are compilations of rabbinic teachings that were recorded over the centuries by rabbis in Jerusalem and in Babylonia. The Talmud has as it's core the *Mishnah,* which in simplistic terms is a code of Jewish law. It appeared in the 3rd century CE and is a structured presentation of the many laws contained in the Torah (the Law). Over the centuries, commentary discussing the Mishnah was added and then written discussion of the commentaries was added. The result was the Talmud.[39]

WHY DON'T JESUS' FOLLOWERS STUDY IT?

It is understandable that the Talmuds were not generally accepted by Jesus' early followers:

- Jesus' followers focused upon the *"New Testament"* teachings of Jesus' apostles, which were written in the 1st century CE.

- By the time the Talmuds were actually being compiled, a sig-nificant portion of Jesus' followers were Latin, Greek, Syriac, Armenian, and Coptic speaking, not Hebrew or Aramaic speaking.

- The focus of Jesus' teachings and those of the Talmuds differed greatly. Jesus' theology was not centered on keeping the Law as the means of attaining righteousness and forgiveness for sins, but the teachings of the Talmuds were.

- During the time when the Talmud was being compiled, Jesus' followers were not welcome in most synagogues.

- The commentators of the Talmud accused Jesus of sorcery and blasphemy, hardly the type of commentary that would be embraced by Jesus' followers.

OTHERS WHO DIDN'T ACKNOWLEDGE THE TALMUDS

It's worth noting that the Saduccean sect of Judaism in the 1st century also rejected the oral law. The Saducees were obviously *very* Jewish. They were the priests in the Temple and, with the Pharisees, were leaders in the Sanhedrin. So, even in the 1st century, rejecting the oral law wasn't synonymous with rejecting Judaism.[f]

The Talmuds were also not acknowledged by Karaite Jews. The Karaites broke away from the rest of the Jewish community in Baghdad in the 8th century. Like the Saducees of the 1st century, they rejected the Oral Law and insisted that the Torah be followed literally. Some of the things included in the Oral Law which were not observed by Karaites were:

- The use of phylacteries (which are used by Orthodox Jews to tie Scriptures to their foreheads and arms)

- The prohibition of eating milk and meat together, and

- Observance of Hanukkah

There are about 10,000 Karaites today. Most live in Israel.[40]

AND JESUS' FOLLOWERS TEACH NEW DOCTRINE

Not only do many of Jesus' present-day followers not keep some of the practices of 1st century Judaism, some of them teach *new* doctrines as well. Do these new doctrines amount to a rejection of Judaism?

Before this question can be addressed, it's important to recognize that not all of Jesus' followers are in agreement on every point of

---

[f] Today, Reform Judaism, which constitutes about 30% of Judaism in the United States, views the Talmud to be merely religious literature, no more or less. Orthodox and Conservative Judaism still look to the Talmud as being Jewish Law.

COMPOSITION OF JESUS' FOLLOWERS

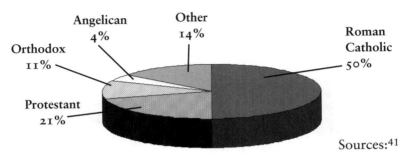

Angelican
4%

Other
14%

Orthodox
11%

Roman
Catholic
50%

Protestant
21%

Sources:[41]

doctrine or religious practice. In the same way that Orthodox, Conservative and Reformed Jews are far from being in perfect agreement, Jesus' followers have differing views on many points of doctrine. Because of this, a quick overview of how Jesus' followers are generally classified is in order.

WHO ARE JESUS' FOLLOWERS TODAY?

Of the approximately 6.1 billion people alive today, about 2 billion are classified as Jesus' followers.[42] That's a lot of people. And, just as there are various Jewish denominations, such as Orthodox, Conservative, Reformed, and Karaite, there are many denominations among Jesus' followers.

The four largest groups of people who claim to be followers of Jesus are Roman Catholic, Protestant, Anglican (Episcopal), and Eastern and Oriental Orthodox Christians. Within these groups, there are even more groups; there are hundreds of them.

There are also several "other" groups that are classified as being followers of Jesus. Many of these are independent groups and some are "marginal" groups. Within the marginal category are classified groups such as the Mormons and Jehovah's Witnesses. They have Jesus as part of their theology, but their beliefs about Jesus are inconsistent with the "mainline" groups and are rejected by them as heretical.

NEW DOCTRINES: IS THIS JUDAISM?

Some denominations of Jesus' followers teach doctrines that are viewed as new and non-Jewish by many Jews. Of the doctrines taught that were not a part of 1st century Judaism, the most significant include:

- The *New Testament* as Scripture
- Veneration of Mary
- Veneration of Saints
- The Lord's Supper
- The Trinity

Are they a divergence from 1st century Judaism?

THE SCRIPTURES

Jesus' followers differ from 1st century Judaism in their definition of what is Holy Scripture. The canon of Hebrew Scriptures has been firmly established at least since the first century BCE. It consists of thirty-nine "books" and is divided into three groups of writings: The Law, The Prophets, and The Writings *(The Torah, The Nevi'im,* and *The Kethuvim).*

"Old Testament" Jesus' followers as a group also believe the Hebrew Scriptures to be inspired by God. They regard all of the traditional Hebrew Scriptures to be the Holy Scripture. They call them the *"Old Testament."* The belief that these writings are Holy Scripture is obviously consistent with Judaism.

Apocrypha The *Apocrypha* is a group of books and writings that were written after the time of the Prophet Ezra (the last prophet of the Hebrew Scriptures). They were included in a 285-246 BCE. Greek translation of the Hebrew Scriptures called the Septuagint. In the late 4th and early 5th century CE, the Roman translator, Jerome, also included several of these writings in his translation of the "Old Testament" from the Hebrew and Greek texts into Latin (the Latin Vulgate). He was evidently compelled to include them because they were a part of the Septuagint. But, he clearly stated his opinion that the Apocrypha should be considered "church books" and not "canonical books."[43] Similarly, neither the rabbis of the Talmud[44] nor Jesus' 1st century followers considered the Apocrypha to be a part of the canon of Scripture.[45]

Because the Apocrypha was included in the Latin Vulgate, some groups of Jesus' followers have come to regard it as Scripture. Primary among them are Roman Catholic and Eastern Orthodox churches. The Roman Catholic Church accepted all but three of these books as Scripture at the Council of Trent in 1548.[46] The Eastern Orthodox Church did likewise in the following century. However, the books of the Apocrypha are considered by Eastern Orthodox churches to be "part of Scripture and are read in church liturgically, but occupy something of a marginal place in the canon" to them.[47]

"New Testament"   The writings of Jesus' earliest followers are universally regarded by his present followers to be Holy Scripture. These twenty-seven "books" are called the *"New Testament."* *New Testament* means *New Covenant.*

Is the *New Testament* Jewish? If Jesus really is the Messiah, then the *New Testament* likely *is* Scripture, and Jewish. If he is not, then it is not.

VENERATION OF MARY

Jesus' early followers all agreed that Mary (Miriam) was a woman selected by God to give birth to the Messiah (Jesus). They taught that Mary was a virgin when the Holy Spirit of God caused her to be pregnant. They taught that God used her to enter this world as a man. But, that's about all that Jesus' 1st century followers had to say about her.

Nothing is found in the writings of Jesus' earliest followers to suggest any other role or significance for Mary than to have been chosen by God to be born into this world as a man. Although this is obviously not a trivial statement. However, the notion of Mary veneration or praying to Mary did not exist in the writings of 1st through early 4th century followers. It wasn't mentioned in Hippolytus' *Church Order* which was a 3rd century Mass.[48] Nor was it mentioned in the statement of beliefs (the *Nicene Creed*) or in the canons (rulings) which resulted from the first two international councils of church Bishops that were held in Nicea in 325 CE and Constantinople in 381 CE.[49]

But, by the 2nd century, allegorical comparisons of Mary to Eve had emerged and by the late 4th century there was a recorded instance of the invocation of Mary in prayer. By the 5th century the veneration of saints and Mary appears to have been "in full bloom."[50] Many even characterize it as having reached the point of Mary worship.

Among the groups of Jesus' followers that venerate Mary are the Roman Catholic, Coptic, and Eastern Orthodox churches. The Roman Catholic Church teaches that Mary was a virgin before and after Jesus was born, even though Jesus is recorded by his disciples as having brothers and sisters.[51] Catholicism, however, does not teach that Mary is divine and insists that she is not worshipped; yet they call her the "Mother of God" and pray to her. This terminology is very confusing to non-Catholics and is a significant point of disagreement with other Christians. Catholicism has also taught that Mary played a part in the spiritual redemption of man and could be considered a co-redeemer with Jesus. Catholicism formalized two other significant teachings about Mary in the last two centuries. In 1854, the doctrine of the immaculate conception of Mary was defined, stating that Mary was born without sin. Then in 1950, Pope Pius XII formally declared that Mary's body had been carried up into heaven when she died.[52] She is now supposed to reign as queen over heaven.

Roman Catholicism has recently toned down the veneration of Mary. Vatican II, a major Roman Catholic Church council that was held from 1962 to 1965, was the first council to issue a complete statement on Mary's perceived role. The term co-redemptrix was dropped.[53] Instead, she is described as a human in need of salvation who was chosen to give birth to the Messiah. She is not the mediator, Messiah is. She does not provide spiritual salvation, Messiah does.[54]

The Eastern Orthodox Church venerates Mary in a similar way as Catholicism. They also pray to Mary and believe that she was a virgin before and after Jesus was born. They likewise believe that she was resurrected bodily after death. They differ from Catholic beliefs in that they do not believe that Mary was without original sin.[55]

Protestant churches strongly reject the idea of venerating or praying to Mary. They acknowledge that the *New Testament* does say that Mary found favor with God. But they contend (it seems, accurately) that the *New Testament* does not teach that prayers should be directed to Mary or that she should be regarded as different than any other person. They also point out that she is only mentioned once after the four gospels (Matthew, Mark, Luke, and John). This is a passing reference in the first chapter of the Acts of the Apostles. She isn't mentioned in any of Paul's letters, in Peter's general epistles, in John's general epistles, or in the epistles written by her sons James and Jude.

Is the veneration of Mary Jewish? There is nothing recorded in the Hebrew Scriptures which would suggest that it is.

Is the notion that Messiah will be born of a virgin Jewish? It's possible. Jesus' followers point to two primary Scripture references to support their belief that it is. The first is the account of the fall of Adam and Eve. In the account, God curses the serpent and says:

> *And I will put enmity between you and the woman, and between your offspring and hers; he will crush your head, and you will strike his heel.*
>
> —Genesis 3:15 (NIV®)

Jesus' followers contend that this alludes to the virgin birth of Messiah because the offspring mentioned is the woman's rather than the man's *and* the woman's.

The second reference is possibly the singularly most debated verse in all of Scripture. It is a prophecy by Isaiah:

> *Therefore the Lord himself will give you a sign: The virgin will be with child and will give birth to a son, and will call him Immanuel.*
>
> —Isaiah 7:14 (NIV®)

The word translated by Jesus' followers as "virgin" is *almah*. It means *unmarried female* or *maiden*. It is translated *maiden* in The Jewish Publication Society's translation of the Scriptures.

Jesus' followers' contend that it is not noteworthy for a maiden or young woman to have a baby. That happens every day. But, they say, that it would indeed be a *sign* if an *unmarried (virgin) female* were to have a baby. They also point out that the child's name is *Immanuel*, which means *God with us*.[56]

VENERATION OF SAINTS

Eastern Orthodox theology includes the veneration of saints and praying to saints and angels. They contend that saints and angels are in the presence of God and can influence God on man's behalf. Therefore, people should ask them to do so.[57] Protestants reject this belief.

Is praying to angels and people who have died consistent with Judaism? No, it isn't.

The Hebrew Scriptures do record many conversations between angels and man. The angel of the LORD (whom God appeared as, or at least spoke through) spoke with many people: Hagar, Abraham, Jacob, Moses, Balaam, Gideon, Manoah and his wife, and many many more.[58] But, it was really God speaking in these cases. And, Daniel had conversations with a couple of angels; one of them was named Gabriel. But, they were sent as messengers of God in *response* to Daniel's prayers to God.[59] There are no cases in the Hebrew Scriptures where man is instructed to *pray* to angels. There is a difference between conversation and *prayer*. Prayer implies worship and submission. Jesus' 1st century apostle John reiterates this by specifically recording that angels should not be worshipped.[60]

The veneration and praying to the dead is also inconsistent with Judaism, whether they be saints or not. The Torah states that we shouldn't make offerings to the dead, shave or cut ourselves for the dead, or consult the dead via mediums.[61] At one point in the Scriptures, King Saul obtained the services of a medium to contact the Prophet Samuel, who had died. He did so because God wouldn't answer his inquiries regarding the approaching enemy armies. Well,

Saul actually did contact Samuel but was then rebuked by Samuel for having done so.[62]

THE LORD'S SUPPER

The *Lord's Supper* (or Communion, as it is some times called), which is commemorated by Jesus' followers, actually had its origin in the Passover Seder. During Jesus' last Seder, he instructed his close disciples to remember him every time they gathered to eat bread and drink wine. It was to be a remembrance of Jesus' death and life-giving resurrection as they awaited his return.[63]

Catholicism, the Eastern Orthodox Church, and the Lutheran Church teach that the bread and wine consumed during the observance of the "last supper" actually becomes the body and blood of Jesus. However, many Protestants reject this doctrine and state that it is merely symbolic of the death of Jesus for the sins of man.

Is this Jewish? Since it was to be an observance to commemorate the *New Covenant*, it can only be Jewish if the *New Covenant* is real and if Jesus really is the Messiah.

THE TRINITY

Jesus' followers acknowledge that the term *"trinity"* is never mentioned in the *Hebrew Scriptures* or *New Testament* writings. Theophilus, the Bishop of Antioch in the second century, evidently initiated usage of the term and Tertullian, the Bishop of Carthage, expounded upon the theology of the trinity in the third century.[64] Jesus' followers, however, contend that the concept of the triune (threefold) nature of God appears throughout both the *Old* and *New Testaments*.

In the Hebrew Scriptures (the *Old Testament*), Jesus' followers point to Genesis where God is called by the name *Elohim*, which is a plural noun. In Genesis, God is also quoted as saying *"Let us make man in our image, after our likeness"* and *"now that the man has become like one of us, knowing good and bad..."*[65] Jesus' followers disagree with the rabbinic commentators who state that God is talking to the angels in these passages. They point to the Scriptures in Isaiah, where God is quoted as saying that He *alone* is God and that He *alone and unaided*

created everything.[66] They reason that Isaiah and Genesis are not contradictory if the one God has three natures as they contend. Their case
follows this logic:

The Spirit of God   They first point to the many references to God's
Spirit in the Hebrew Scriptures. Jesus' followers cite them to make
several points:

God's Spirit can have "location":

- God's Spirit hovered over the waters during the Creation
  —Gen. 1:1-2
- God set his Holy Spirit among the children of Israel
  —Isa. 63:11

God's Spirit can speak through people:
- The Spirit of the LORD spoke through David
  —2 Sam. 23:1-2
- God's Spirit rested on Eldad and Medad and they prophesied
  —Num. 11:29

God's Spirit can fill people:
- God filled Bezalel, son of Uri, with the Spirit of God
  —Ex. 35:30-31

God's Spirit can empower people to do God's will:
- The Spirit of the LORD came upon David in power
  —1 Sam. 16:13
- The Spirit of the LORD came upon Gideon
  —Judges 6:34

God's Spirit has emotion:
- God's Holy Spirit can be grieved
  —Isa. 63:10

God's Spirit gives wisdom and understanding:
- The Spirit of the LORD will rest on the King to come (Messiah)
  —Isa. 11:1-3

God's Spirit interacts with man:

- God's Spirit contends with man
  —Gen. 6:3

Someday God will give everyone His Holy Spirit:

- God's Spirit will be poured out to all people
  —Joel 2:28-29

Their ultimate point is that a primary role of God's Holy Spirit seems to be in directing and assisting people to obey God.

God on the Throne   Jesus' followers point out that the Hebrew Scriptures also depict a reigning God. They cite the example of Ezekiel who saw a vision of God above a throne of sapphire in heaven.[67] Daniel had a similar vision of the Ancient of Days sitting on his throne in heaven to judge as multitudes stood before Him.[68] When the elders of Israel accompanied Moses to Mt. Sinai to see God, they also saw Him with what appeared to be a pavement of sapphire under His feet.[69]

They say that these visions and appearances of God characterize His reigning presence. This seems to be different from His Holy Spirit, which interacts with man's spirit. His reigning presence is a focused single-location revelation of the presence of God as the Sovereign Ruler of the Universe. A similar incident is when God hid Moses in a cleft of a rock and had His glory pass before Moses. It was an awesome visual revelation of God's infinite majesty and glory, so awesome that Moses' face glowed from God's brilliance.[70]

God revealed His infinite glory and majesty to these people in a finite way. He revealed Himself as the Sovereign of the Universe. Yet, the Scriptures say that even the heavens cannot contain God. He is bigger than the heavens.[71] Thus, Jesus' followers reason that the revelation of God in a finite way does not limit the infinity of God. This logic is fundamental to the next point, their view that Messiah is God.

One Like a Son of Man   Daniel's vision of the Ancient of Days sitting in judgment also included "one like a son of man, coming with the clouds of heaven":

As I looked on in the night vision, One like a human being came with the clouds of heaven; He reached the Ancient of Days and was presented to Him. Dominion, glory, and kingship were given to him; All peoples and nations of every language must serve him. His dominion is an everlasting dominion that shall not pass away, and his kingship, one that shall not be destroyed.

—Daniel 7:13-14 (JPS)

Jesus' followers translate this passage as follows:

In my vision at night I looked, and there before me was one like a son of man, coming with the clouds of heaven. He approached the Ancient of Days and was led into his presence. He was given authority, glory and sovereign power; all peoples, nations and men of every language worshiped him. His dominion is an everlasting dominion that will not pass away, and his kingdom is one that will never be destroyed.

—Daniel 7:13-14 (NIV®)

Jesus' followers point out that there is something very significant about this *"one like a son of man."* He is given *"authority, glory and sovereign power"* by the Ancient of Days. He is given *"an everlasting dominion that will not pass away."* And then something amazing happens, *"all peoples, nations and men of every language worshiped him."* They translate the word *pelach* to be *"worshiped"* rather than *"serve."*

They further reason that Messiah must be God because of what Messiah does when he comes. He will die as a sacrifice to make us righteous. He will redeem us from our sin although the Hebrew Scriptures say continually that God is our redeemer and that He alone can forgive sins.[72]

Who is this *"one like a son of man"* whom they say God allows to be worshiped? The Talmud says that Daniel Chapter 7 is speaking of Messiah.[73] Jesus' followers also contend that it is Messiah and that it is Jesus.

They also point to the prophet Job, who said that God will testify upon the earth:

> *But I know that my Vindicator lives; In the end He will testify on earth — This after my skin will have peeled off. But I would behold God while still in my flesh, I myself, not another, would behold him; Would see with my own eyes: my heart pines within me.*

> —Job 19:25-27 (JPS)

The Three in One?   Jesus' followers point to the prophet Zechariah to support their contentions about the triune nature of God. The Scripture reference that they cite appears to include God as the Holy Spirit, God as the Son of God, and God as God the Father all in the same verses:

> *On that day I will set out to destroy all the nations that attack Jerusalem. And I will pour out on the house of David and the inhabitants of Jerusalem a spirit of grace and supplication. They will look on me, the one they have pierced, and they will mourn for him as one mourns for an only child, and grieve bitterly for him as one grieves for a firstborn son.*

> —Zechariah 12:9-10 (NIV®)

The translation of this verse in the Jewish Publication Society's 1985 version of the TANAKH differs from the New International Version translation. However, Rabbi Leeser's 1856 translation is remarkably similar.[74]

*But I will pour over the house of David, and over the
inhabitants of Jerusalem, the spirit of grace and of sup-
plications: and they will look up toward me (for every
one) whom they thrust through, and they will lament for
him, as one lamenteth for an only son, and weep bitterly
for him, as one weepeth for the first-born.*

—Zechariah 12:9-10 (Leeser)

One noted Christian author summarizes the teaching about the trinity as follows:

One of the most misunderstood ideas in the Bible con-
cerns the teaching about the Trinity. Although Christians
say that they believe in one God, they are constantly
accused of polytheism (worshipping at least three gods).

The Scriptures do *not* teach that there are three Gods;
neither do they teach that God wears three different
masks while acting out the drama of history. What the
Bible does teach is stated in the doctrine of the Trinity as:
there is *one* God who has revealed Himself in three persons, the Father, the Son and the Holy Spirit, and these
three persons are the one God.

Although this is difficult to comprehend, it is neverthe-
less what the Bible tells us, and is the closest the finite
mind can come to explaining the infinite mystery of the
infinite God, when considering the biblical statements
about God's being.[75]

Is the doctrine of the trinity Jewish? It does appear that a Scriptural
case can be made that it is.

CONCLUSIONS

Did Jesus' followers reject Judaism? Jesus' 1st century followers would definitely contend that they did not. They would contend that Rabbinic Judaism missed the boat by rejecting Jesus as the Messiah. They would further contend that the *New Covenant* didn't eliminate the previous covenants, it eclipsed them. They would say that the *New Covenant* is the fulfillment of the Law and God's promise through the Prophets.

It is also interesting to consider whether Jesus' 1st century followers would approve of some current day followers' beliefs. They likely would not agree with several of the divergences.

But, even Jesus' current day followers (at least most of them) would likely say that they have not rejected the Judaism of the Hebrew Scriptures. They, like their 1st century counterparts, point to their *New Covenant* through their Messiah Jesus as the fulfillment of the Law and the prophets not the rejection of them.

How Did The Branch Become Separated From The Tree?

So, how did Jesus' followers come to be viewed as a separate branch from the tree of Judaism? And, what happened to the other branches that are now extinct: the Saducees, the Essenes and the Zealots?

Even if Jesus' followers didn't reject Judaism, it's obvious that Rabbinic Judaism rejected both them and their Messiah. While Jesus was alive, the Sanhedrin viewed him as a blasphemer because of the claims he made about himself. They viewed his followers with similar disdain and, refusing to worship with them, put them out of the Synagogues.[1] Then they arrested Jesus. Since they couldn't impose the death sentence without Roman consent, they got the Romans to execute him. But Jesus' followers weren't dissuaded about their Messiah, even after his death.

Persecution of Jesus' Followers (33 to 68 ce)

Persecution by the Sanhedrin (33 to 64 ce)

Almost immediately after Jesus' execution, his followers began proclaiming that he had risen from the dead. To stop the spread of this message, the Sanhedrin had several of Jesus' disciples arrested. They had them flogged and imprisoned and warned them to stop preaching about Jesus' resurrection. Peter and John were among those arrested.[2] The persecution further intensified as Stephen was stoned to death and

Rabbi Saul (Paul) obtained permission to arrest and imprison Jesus' followers as far away as Damascus.[3] King Herod, the Roman ruler over Judea, then got into the act and had James (the brother of John) killed and, seeing that it pleased the Jews, had Peter arrested again.[4] Even Jesus' brother, James, who had become the Bishop of the church in Jerusalem, was stoned to death by the Jews.[5]

These persecutions were a continued rejection of Jesus' followers and their Messiah. The two major sects of Judaism, the *Pharisees* and the *Saducees,* sought to stamp out this upstart sect. Though Jesus' followers still consisted primarily of Jews and were acknowledged as Jews, they weren't welcome in the Synagogues in the province of Judea and were considered to have gone astray.

PERSECUTION BY THE ROMANS (64 TO 68 CE)

Much of the persecution of the Jews by the Romans wasn't directed at any specific branch of Judaism. The Roman Empire wasn't always discriminating in its exertion of authority over subjugated peoples. For example, the persecutions under Caligula and Domitian don't appear to have differentiated between sects of Judaism and the persecution under Trajan was only moderately lessened for Jesus' followers.[6] But, several persecutions were specifically directed at Jesus' followers. The first occurred under Emperor Nero in the middle of the 1st century.

It has been said that Nero set the great fire which burned Rome in 64 CE, but it was definitely Jesus' followers who were given the blame and bore the wrath of the Empire:[7]

> The first wave of Roman persecution lasted from shortly after the fire until Nero's death in 68. With barbaric bloodthirstiness, he had Christians [Jesus' followers] crucified and set afire. Their bodies lined the Roman roads, providing torchlight. Christians dressed in animal skins were mauled by dogs in the arena. According to tradition, both Peter and Paul became martyrs in Nero's Persecution; Paul was beheaded, and Peter was crucified upside-down.[8]

In light of this kind of persecution, it would be understandable for members of other branches of Judaism to want to avoid being confused for one of Jesus' followers. So, the distance that existed between them grew. The religious rejection that had previously existed now expanded to include rejection for the purpose of self-preservation.

THE JEWISH REVOLT AGAINST ROME (66 TO 74 CE)

By the mid first century, the Sanhedrin had a bigger problem to deal with than a new sect of Judaism. They had an impending revolt on their hands!

It seems that the local Roman procurator, Florus, had unjustly sided with Gentiles in a dispute in Caesarea. And though he accepted a bribe from the Jewish population, he didn't provide them justice. This angered and insulted the local Jews. But their disdain for him was further intensified when he raided the treasury of the Temple in Jerusalem. They acted out their anger when two Jews took up a mock collection for the procurator in public as a demonstration. Florus wasn't amused; he was enraged! He sent in troops who then randomly arrested and crucified the people of Jerusalem.[9]

Things almost calmed down when a representative was sent in by the Legate of Syria to investigate. But Eleazar, the captain of the Temple, then committed the first deliberate act of rebellion; he put a stop to the daily sacrifice for the Emperor in the Temple. This was a blatant denial of the Roman Emperor's authority. Florus, evidently, also had no interest in preventing a revolt, and a revolt is what he got. In 66 CE, after 127 years of subservience to the Romans, the Jews rebelled. Jewish rebels captured the Roman fortress of Antonia near Jerusalem and killed all of the Roman forces there. Then they took the fortress of Masada and marched on to liberate Jerusalem. They even ambushed the withdrawing Roman Twelfth Legion and inflicted heavy losses.[10]

Jesus' followers, however, didn't join in the revolt. They had been instructed by their leaders to submit to the rulers and authorities that were over them.[11] So, they left Jerusalem and went to Pella.[12] In doing so, they escaped the siege of Jerusalem and the famine and slaughter that ensued. Over 2.7 million people had gathered together in the city to celebrate the Feast of Unleavened Bread (Pasach) that year. When the Roman armies returned and surrounded the city, they were trapped. By the end of the siege (70 CE) and the war in 74 CE, 1.1 million Jews were dead and 97,000 were taken captive as slaves.[13]

At the end of the war, only two sects of Judaism survived: the *Pharisees* and *Jesus' followers*. The priests, who had dominated the *Saducean* sect, were executed by the Romans and their source of political power, the Temple, was destroyed.[14] The *Zealots*, who were among the leaders of the revolt, were all but annihilated by the Roman legions, or they committed suicide at Masada. The reclusive *Essenes* vanished. The *Pharisees*, however, emerged defeated, but dominant among the sects of Judaism. By escaping from the siege and surrendering to the Romans, Rabbi Yohannan ben Zakkai secured survival for the Pharisees and Rabbinic Judaism.[15] *Jesus' followers*, probably numbering in the tens of thousands, also survived by taking refuge in Pella.

THE BENEDICTION AGAINST THE MINIM (84 TO 130 CE)

About ten years after the Jewish rebellion against the Romans was crushed, Rabban Gamaliel II became the president of the Rabbinic academy at Jabne which Yohannan had preserved. He also held the title of Nasi (Prince) and was considered to be the Patriarch of the Jews by the Romans.[16] He was the most important religious and political leader of defeated Israel. He was also important because of his lineage. He was the grandson of Rabban Gamaliel the Elder and the great great grandson of Hillel, who founded the prominent rabbinic academy, the *House of Hillel*.

It was Rabban Gamaliel II who instituted a benediction against heretics (the birkat ha-minim) which was to be recited in the Synagogues. This benediction was directed specifically at Jesus' followers to exclude them from worship in the Synagogues:

> For the apostates may there be no hope unless they
> return to your Torah. As for the noserim and the minim,

may they perish immediately. Speedily may they be erased from the Book of Life and may they not be registered among the righteous. Blessed are you, O Lord, Who subdues the wicked.[17]

The first intent of the benediction was to exclude Jesus' *Hebrew* followers from participation in the Synagogue service. They were referred to as the "minim." The benediction was also directed at the "noserim," which are widely acknowledged to be Jesus' *Gentile* followers. They may have been referenced in the original benediction or added to it as they became more numerous, possibly between 150 and 350 CE.[18]

Obviously, anyone who was a Hebrew follower of Jesus would have a major problem with concluding every Synagogue service by asking God for the immediate death and eternal damnation of themselves and their friends. As intended, this drove many of them from the Synagogues.

HOW DID RABBINIC JUDAISM VIEW JESUS' GENTILE FOLLOWERS?

It's important to remember who was considered to be a Jew in the 1st century. This is especially important because of the large numbers of Gentiles who were becoming followers of Jesus. The 1st century definition of who was considered to be a Jew included:

- Ancestry through the mother or conversion, including:
- Circumcision of males
- Immersion (*tevilah*)
- Acceptance of the Torah
- Offering a sacrifice[19]

Gentile believers weren't considered to be Jews if they hadn't met these criteria.

Acceptance of the Torah as the standard of right and wrong and being baptized wouldn't have been considered to be obstacles by Gentile followers of Jesus. These were taught by Jesus' disciples. But, acceptance of the Torah as *a means* of attaining reconciliation to God would have been a problem for them. As was circumcision and the offering of sacrifices for sin, although the requirement for a sacrifice was discontinued after the destruction of the temple. They viewed these requirements of the law to have been met or made obsolete by the *New Covenant*.[20] And, without circumcision they weren't viewed to be Jewish by Rabbinic Judaism. This made them unwelcome in the Synagogues and in the homes of Rabbinic Jews.

Jesus' followers who were of Hebrew descent were still considered to be Jews, just heretical ones, because of their belief in Jesus as the Messiah. But Jesus' Gentile followers weren't even viewed as heretics. They were totally rejected by Rabbinic Judaism.

THE SIMON BAR-KOKHBA REVOLT (130 TO 135 C.E.)

The ultimate theological and political split between Jesus' followers and the rest of Judaism came early in the 2nd century. It was then that Jesus' followers (who had come to be called Christians) came to be *viewed as a separate religion*. Not only were large numbers of Gentiles becoming Jesus' followers, but, once again, Jesus' Hebrew followers refused to participate in yet another revolt against Rome.

WHAT WAS THE SIMON BAR-KOKHBA REVOLT?

During the reign of Tajan as Emperor, there were major Jewish revolts in North Africa (in Egypt and Cyrene) and in Cyprus. Both were suppressed by the Romans and a few hundred thousand Jews were killed. But they were merely a prelude to the revolt to come.[21]

Hadrian succeeded Trajan as Emperor in 117 CE. His policies to Hellenize his Empire were met with alarm in Judea because they were an attack on the very core of Judaism. The two policies most cited are his decree prohibiting the practice of circumcision and the announcement of his plan to build a new city, to be called Aelia Capitolina, on the site of Jerusalem.[22] Without circumcision, the requirement of God's covenant with Abraham could not be kept. *To Rabbinic Judaism, there would be no Jews without circumcision.* And if a pagan city were constructed on the site of Jerusalem, the hope of reconstructing the Temple would be lost, so, once again, Israel rebelled.

During 130 to 135 CE, the Jews made one last desperate effort to free their nation from the Romans. The rebels captured several small towns in Judea and occupied Jerusalem. The revolt spread to Galilee in the north, the Golan, in the south, the coastal plain, and the Judean desert. The leader of the revolt was the Nasi (Prince) of the Jews, Simon Bar–Kokhba. He was thought to be the Messiah by many Jews. Even Rabbi Akiva, considered one of the great Torah scholars of the 2nd century, believed Bar–Kokhba to be King Messiah.[23] And, with that endorsement, thousands followed him.

By the end of the revolt, 50% of Judea's population was dead and Jews were out-numbered by Gentiles in what had been their own nation. Only Galilee was spared, because of their lack of participation in the revolt.[24] Aelia Capitolina was built on the site of Jerusalem. A pagan temple to Jupiter Capitolinus was built, and Jews were banned from the city. Jews could no longer pray, circumcise their children, study the Torah or observe Jewish holidays. The penalty for violating these ordinances was death.[25] Jews in large numbers left Palestine. For those who remained, the center of Jewish life shifted to Galilee.[26]

Jesus' followers didn't follow Bar–Kokhba. They refused to rebel and they refused to follow someone whom they saw as a false Messiah. They had their Messiah, Jesus. This undoubtedly caused them to be viewed as traitors. The previously strained relations became completely severed. By the conclusion of the war, the very survival of the Pharisaic sect (Rabbinic Judaism) was at stake. Even Hebrew followers of Jesus were now viewed as a threat to their theological survival. So, on the verge of extinction, Rabbinic Judaism's rejection of Jesus' followers, for all practical purposes, became complete.

RABBINIC JUDAISM SURVIVED

In fact, Rabbinic Judaism did survive. The next Emperor, Antoninus Pius, eased the restrictions on Jews and study of the Scriptures was again allowed. However, Jews were still not allowed to reenter Jerusalem (Aelia Capitolina).

Before the Bar–Kokhba revolt, there had been large Jewish communities outside of Palestine. But Jewish revolts in Egypt, North Africa, Cyprus, and Babylon left their numbers severely depleted. By the end of the Bar–Kokhba revolt only Babylon had a significant Jewish population outside of Palestine. In total, the worldwide population of Rabbinic Jews was probably about 1.5 to 2 million.

Rabbinic Academies Are Formed In Galilee

One of Rabbi Akiba's students, Rabbi Meir, who had fled Judea during Hadrian's persecution, returned and with others reestablished the Sanhedrin in Galilee. He also established a rabbinic academy there in the town of Emmaus. Other teachers also established schools and Galilee became the center of Jewish teaching.

Like many others, Rabbi Akiba had begun to actually write down the prevailing oral law. Up to this point, as the term implies, it wasn't formally recorded. Rabbi Meir continued Akiba's efforts to arrange the oral law into subjects and ultimately passed this work (the *Mishnah*) on to Rabbi Judah Hanasi (Judah the Prince). But since there were many "Mishnahs" in process, Rabbi Judah exerted his authority as Patriarch and oversaw the compilation of *one* document, which was completed near the turn of the 3rd century.[27] It has been asserted by at least one historian of the Talmud, that it was Judah the Prince who purged the *Mishnah* of the references to Jesus that would certainly have been recorded by Jesus' many Pharisee followers.[28] Whether this is the case or not, it is clear that Jesus' Hebrew followers were not included in the codification of Judaism nor were their views accepted by the academies. They were essentially written out of Judaism.

Babylon Becomes the Center of Jewish Learning

By the 4th century, the center of rabbinic scholarship had shifted to Babylon. There was still a large Jewish population that had remained in Babylon from the deportations by Nebuchadnezzar a thousand years earlier, possibly as many as a million people.[29] Two of these Babylonian

Jews, Rabbis Samuel and Abba (Rav), had gone to Palestine to study and returned to ultimately head rabbinic academies in Babylon at Sura and Nehardea.[30] This shift in the geographic center of Judaism effectively added geographic distance to the theological distance that existed between Rabbinic Judaism and Jesus' followers.

THE TALMUD IS COMPILED

During the 3rd through 6th centuries, Rabbis in Palestine and Babylon added a collection of other oral traditions and teachings *(Gemara)* about Jewish Law to the *Mishnah*. They added:

- the *Tosefta:* a supplemental collection of traditions similar to the Mishnah

- the *Mechilta, Siphra,* and *Siphre:* running rabbinic commentary and discussion

These teachings have come to be generally termed as *Baraitha,* traditions taught by rabbis from the Mishnah era and earlier, and *Amora,* post-Mishnaic era teachings.[31] The results were the Jerusalem and Babylonian Talmuds. The Jerusalem Talmud was completed by about 400 CE and the Babylonian Talmud was completed by 525 CE. The latter is viewed as the cornerstone of theological commentary within Rabbinic Judaism.

In the Talmud, Jesus was characterized as an enticer, a sorcerer, and a blasphemer. The Talmud essentially institutionalized the rejection of the previous 500 years. Rabbinic Judaism wanted no part of Jesus or his followers.

CONCLUSIONS

While many Jews followed Jesus, most of the Jewish establishment rejected Jesus. After a brief three-year public ministry, the Sanhedrin had him arrested and turned over to the Romans to be crucified. Then, they sought to stop the spread of his teachings and the rapidly spreading stories of his resurrection from the dead by imprisoning his followers. The series of events that followed only added to the distance:

- Roman persecution of Jesus' followers
- two failed Jewish revolts—one led by a would-be-Messiah
- a benediction against Jesus' followers in the Synagogues
- the rejection of Jesus' uncircumcised Gentile followers
- the survival of Pharisaic Judaism and it's control over Jewish theology
- the codification of Rabbinic Judaism by the Pharisaic academies

By the time that Rabbinic Judaism was codified in the form of the Mishnah and the Talmud, the exclusion of Jesus and his followers was already complete. The "Christian branch" of Judaism had been rejected by the tree.

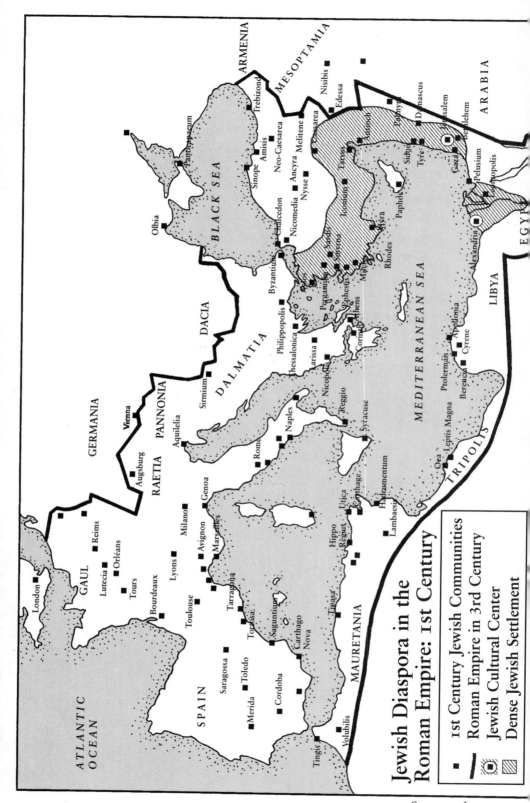

Jewish Diaspora in the
Roman Empire: 1st Century

■ 1st Century Jewish Communities
╱╲ Roman Empire in 3rd Century
◉ Jewish Cultural Center
▨ Dense Jewish Settlement

13

RABBINIC JUDAISM SURVIVED

After the Bar–Kokhba revolt in Palestine and Jewish revolts in Egypt, North Africa, and Cyprus, the Jewish population in the Roman Empire was decimated. The once large Jewish populations of Palestine and Alexandria were a fraction of their former size and the practice of the Jewish faith was so severely curtailed that the rural setting of Galilee had become the center of Jewish learning. Without the institutions of the Temple, the Sanhedrin, and the rabbinic academies of Jabne, the very survival of Rabbinic Judaism was at stake.

It was in this context that the Pharisaic branch of Judaism rallied. They re-established the Sanhedrin and rabbinic academies in Galilee and began the codification of the oral law. In doing so, they ensured the survival of Pharisaic teaching and of Rabbinic Judaism. This was now a Judaism without a nation, without a Temple, without a priesthood, and without a sacrificial system, but, it was a Judaism which had survived.

POLITICAL HISTORY

JUDAISM UNDER THE ROMAN EMPIRE

At the end of the Bar–Kokhba revolt, 50% of Judea's population had been killed. But, in spite of the decimation that had occurred, at the close of the 3rd century, Jews were still the largest population in Palestine. By the end of the 4th century, however, Jews were only a third of the total population. The followers of Jesus, which had come to be called Christians, had become dominant.

The Roman Empire Adopts Christianity

Constantine became Emperor in the Western Roman Empire in 306 CE. His *Edict of Milan* (313 CE) enacted freedom of religion within the Empire. It officially lifted the persecution that Jesus' followers had experienced and maintained the freedoms that Jews already had enjoyed in worship. But it was clear that he actively favored Christianity—and he imposed constraints upon Judaism. Jews could not own slaves, hold public office, marry Christians, or prevent a person from converting to Christianity.[2]

His successors then made Christianity the official religion of the Empire. But, they did afford Judaism a place as the only protected secondary religion. Judaism could exist, but it couldn't expand. Jewish proselytism and the building of new synagogues were prohibited.[3]

In spite of previous defeats, Jews in Palestine still held hopes of independence from Rome. So, they attempted another revolt in 351 CE. The leader of this rebellion was a man named Patricius. But, the rebellion was quickly quelled by the Romans. To prevent further insurrection, the Romans subsequently abolished the office of Patriarch in 429 CE, eliminating the last vestige of political leadership among the remaining Palestinian Jews.[4]

By 476 CE, the Western Roman Empire had been overrun by the Visigoths, Franks, and Vandals. The fiction of the Empire was maintained, however, as the Bishops of the church in Rome (the Popes) gave the title of *Emperor of the Holy Roman Empire* to various kings over the ensuing centuries. But the Roman Empire in the west was no more.

The Byzantines

In the Eastern Roman Empire (Byzantium), Christians had become the overwhelming majority of the population of Palestine by the 6th century. Under the Byzantines the practice of Judaism was still permitted, but restricted, much like it had been under the Emperors of the Western Roman Empire.

Byzantine Emperor Justinian, however, took the restrictions upon Jews even further through his *Novella 146* (553 CE), by interjecting himself into the internal affairs of Rabbinic Judaism. The Novella placed two key constraints upon Judaism by requiring that Jews use Latin or Greek translations of the Hebrew Scriptures in synagogues, rather than Hebrew, and by banning the Mishnah.[5]

Without the military might to rebel against the Byzantines themselves, the Jewish population of Palestine assisted the Persians in 613 CE as they conquered the Byzantine territories that stretched from Mesopotamia to Syria. After Jerusalem fell in the following year, the Persian King, Chosroes II, killed and deported vast numbers of Christians. He even turned the city over to Jewish leadership for three years. But the Byzantines prevailed and retook Jerusalem in 629 CE.[6] After the victory, the Byzantine emperor Heraclius killed and expelled many Jews in retaliation.

However, it was the upstart Arabs who ultimately conquered both the Persians and the weakened Byzantines in Palestine. Jerusalem was surrendered to them in 638 CE. The Byzantines then lost much of the eastern Empire to the Arabs: Palestine, Syria, North Africa, and Sicily.

In what was left of the Empire, subsequent Emperors sought to impose forced baptism of Jews; those issuing such decrees were: Leo III in 721 CE, Basil I in 873 CE, and Romanus I in 943 CE. But, while these decrees weren't seriously enforced,[7] it seems obvious that the religious and political wounds that existed between the Jews and the Byzantines did not quickly heal.

JUDAISM IN YEMEN

Converts to Judasim ruled the Himyar kingdom in Yemen from the 4th through the early 6th century. Their persecution of Christians, however, prompted the Christian Emperor of neighboring Ethiopia to invade and briefly make Yemen an Ethiopian colony. Though Jewish reign ended in 525 CE, Jews have lived in Yemen to present times.

It has only been in the last century that most Jews have left Yemen. From 1948 to 1962 about 150,000 Jews migrated from Yemen to Israel.[8]

JUDAISM UNDER THE PERSIANS

Jews had lived in Babylon in large numbers since King Nebuchadnezzar deported them from Palestine in the 7th century BCE. By the time of the Bar–Kokhba revolt, there were possibly as many as a million Jews living there.[9] After the revolt, their numbers grew as refugees from Palestine sought safety and religious freedom. By the 4th century, Babylon had become the center of Jewish religious scholarship.

From 226 CE to 642 CE, it was the Persian Sassanid dynasty, which ruled over Babylonia. They allowed Jews their own political authority within the empire and generally permitted Jews to practice their faith and to perpetuate it. Except for periods of persecution in the 3rd and 5th centuries, Jews lived in relative peace along side the pagan state religion of Zoroastrianism. It was actually during the Sassanid reign that the Babylonian Talmud was compiled by the rabbinic academies in Babylon.

Then came the Arab invasion.

JUDAISM UNDER ISLAM

Arab and Moorish Islam

Islam spread as the Arab followers of Mohammed conquered much of the Mediterranean region. By 647 CE they had conquered Mesopotamia, Palestine, Egypt, and all of Northern Africa. In 711 CE the Arabs invaded Spain and then invaded France in 720 CE. It wasn't until 732 CE that Charles Martel, the king of the Franks, stemmed the Arab advance. But, for 600 years, most of Judaism was under Arab and Moorish (Arab and Berber) Moslem control.

As "people of the book" both Christians and Jews were made subservient to Moslems, but were afforded a status above that of slaves. They were *dhimmis*—protected subjects. So long as they kept their place, and paid heavy taxes, they were generally allowed to practice their faiths. In this environment, Judaism actually rebounded.

The restrictions on Christians and Jews in the *Code of Omar* precluded them from building new synagogues and churches or repairing old ones, proselytizing, and holding public religious gatherings. They also weren't allowed to ride horses, carry weapons, or strike Muslims. And, to ensure that they could be distinguished from Muslims, they had to wear distinctive clothing and later couldn't even adopt Arabic names.[11]

While these restrictions applied to both Christians and Jews, Jews faired better than did Christians. Because Christianity was the state religion of the rival Byzantine Empire, all Christians were considered suspect. Jews, however, no longer had the political or military might to threaten the Arab conquest. In fact, Jews aided the Arabs as they overran Spain in 711. Considering their treatment by the Visigoths, this is understandable.[12]

Because of the relative freedom of religion that Jews were permitted under Islam, rabbinic academies sprung up in Spain. At the close of the 10th century, Babylon began to decline as the center of Jewish learning. Then it disappeared. In its place were centers of Jewish study in Arab-controlled Spain and Egypt.

In the 12th century a dynasty of Islamic zealots, the Almohads, emerged in North Africa. They eliminated centuries old Christian communities in North Africa and then brought their brand of Islam into Spain in 1146. They imposed forced conversions upon Jews, closed Synagogues, required Jews to wear distinctive clothing identifying them as Jews, and restricted Jewish trade. It was during this time frame that the eminent Jewish philosopher Moses ben Maimon (Maimonides) fled from Spain to Egypt.[13]

Ottoman Islam

In the 15th and 16th centuries, the Islamic Ottoman Turks expanded their empire from Asia Minor into Eastern Europe and the Middle East. They defeated the Byzantines and took their capital of Constantinople in 1453. Their conquest in Europe extended into

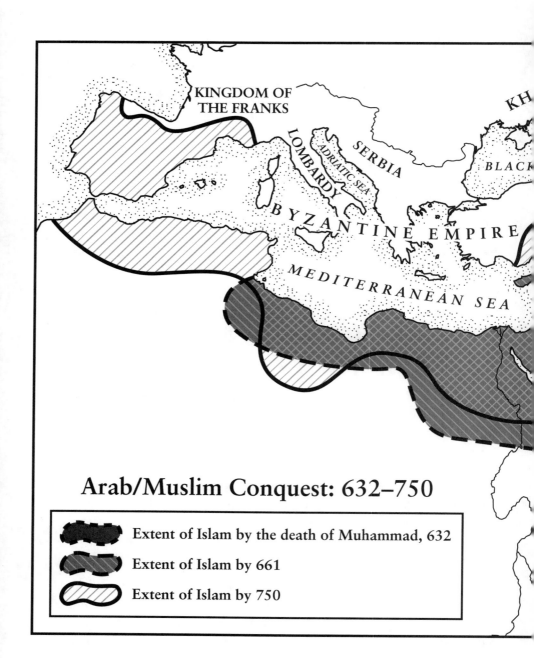

Arab/Muslim Conquest: 632–750

Extent of Islam by the death of Muhammad, 632

Extent of Islam by 661

Extent of Islam by 750

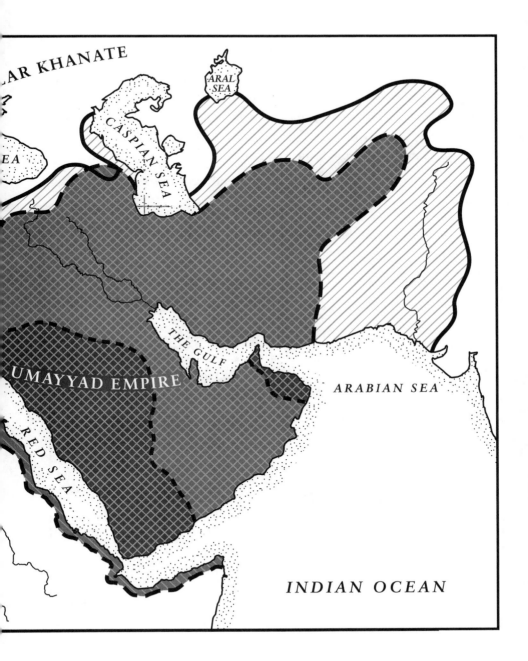

Source:[9]

Hungary, Romania, and the Balkans. They also conquered the Arab-controlled Middle East and North Africa as far west as Algeria. Once again, much of Judaism was under the control of Islam.

From the mid 15th to the mid 16th centuries, life among the Ottomans was relatively peaceful. So long as Jews paid their *dhimmi* taxes, they were allowed to govern their own affairs and the oppressive regulations imposed by Middle Eastern Islam were ignored. This environment prompted a wave of Jewish migration from Spain and Portugal to Ottoman territories.

This favorable treatment ended with the ascendancy of Murad III in the late 16th century. He threatened to kill the entire Jewish community and extorted money from them in exchange for their lives. Conditions grew even worse in the 17th century. [15]

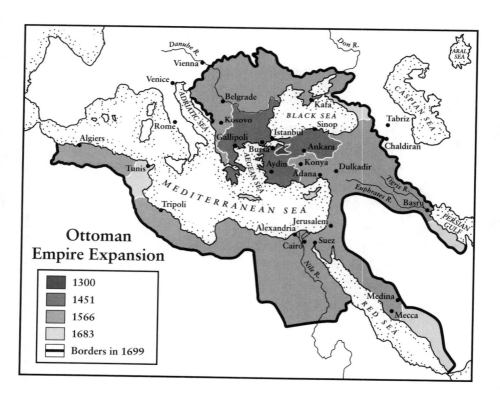

Source:[14]

JUDAISM IN KHAZARIA

From the mid 7th century until early in the 11th century, the Kingdom of Khazaria prospered as an independent nation. Located between and to the north of the Black Sea and Caspian Sea in Asia, the kingdom existed in the midst of three empires. To the west was Byzantium, to the north was the early Russian empire, and to the south was Persia (and later, the Arab Caliphate).

In about 860 CE, the throne of Khazaria became occupied by a Jew. It was then that Judaism became accepted by the ruling class of the country. By the 920s CE, Rabbinic Judaism was accepted by a significant base of the general population and coexisted with Islam, Christianity and paganism. A succession of Jewish kings occupied the throne of Khazaria at least until the turn of the 11th century.[16]

Khazaria is unique as the most significant Jewish kingdom in the world from the fall of Israel in the 1st century until modern times.

JUDAISM IN EUROPE

The Visigoths

The most overt persecution of Jews in the 1st millennium CE was under the Visigoths in Spain. King Reccared sought to force Jewish conversions to Christianity. In 616 CE, his successor, King Sisebut, ordered Jews to embrace Christianity or be banished and forfeit their property. Over 90,000 Jews, most of the Jewish population of Spain, converted. After the Muslim invasion a century later, many Jews converted back to Judaism. But, during the subsequent five centuries under Islam, many families remained in the Christian church.[17]

Charlemagne

Charlemagne (742 – 814 CE) was the grandson of Charles Martel, the Frankish King who had turned back the conquest of Islam in Western Europe. He reigned over what is now France, the Netherlands, Belgium, western and northern Germany, and northern Italy.

Charlemagne, a Christian, established a genuine religious tolerance that was to last until the crusades of the 11th century. He welcomed Jewish merchants and financial agents, had Jewish officials in his court, and established Rabbi Moses ben Kulonymus in Mainz. As Babylon declined as a center of Jewish learning, from the 10th century onward, northern France and the Rhine Valley became a center of Jewish scholarship. Rabbinic academies were formed in Mainz, Worms, and Troyes. The latter was founded by Rabbi Solomon ben Isaac (Rashi).

The tolerance granted to Jews during that era is evidenced by Rashi, who recorded the receipt of Passover gifts from Christian friends. It is also evidenced by Catholic priests who had adopted the use of synagogue melodies in their churches.[18]

The Crusades

The period of tolerance and peace enjoyed by Judaism ended with the advent of the Crusades. In the spring of 1096, Jews in the Rhineland were massacred by the advancing Crusaders, who were often unruly mobs intent upon the liberation of the Holy Land from Islam.

The Bishop of Speyer was able to stop the rioting in his town by hanging the ringleaders. The Archbishop of Cologne was also able to stop them. The Archbishop of Mainz, however, fled for his life. In the violence that ensued, many Jews were killed or committed suicide. In all over 1,000 Jews died.[19]

The first Crusade also resulted in the sacking of Jerusalem and the deaths of 30,000 of its mostly Islamic and Jewish residents. Even Armenian and Eastern Orthodox Christians fled from Jerusalem to escape the European army.[20]

The Jews of Spain

For the first hundred years after the "Christian" reconquest of Spain, Jews prospered and lived much as they had under Islam. But in 1350, conversion drives began. Jews converted in great numbers. In the kingdoms of Aragon and Castille, there were 200,000 converts. This is estimated to have been from a third to half of the Jews in Spain.

These newly converted Jews were called the *conversos* (the converted) by Christians. Unconverted Jews, however, called them *marranos* (swine). They saw them as apostates.[21]

European Persecutions

The 12th through the 16th centuries in Europe were marked by increased persecution of Jews. Some of the more significant events during this period were:

> 1144—Norwich blood libel (England)
> 1190—Massacre of Jews in York (England)
> 1290—Jews were expelled from England
> 1348-50—Black death massacres
> 1360—Jews were expelled from France
> 1394—Jews were expelled from France again
> 1492—Jews were expelled from Sicily
> 1541—Jews were expelled from Naples

Roman Catholicism

Until the 15th century, the official position of the Church of Rome to Judaism was generally one of tolerance and even protection. Doctrinal differences would have precluded the Church from promoting the views of Rabbinic Judaism. But, the church doesn't appear to have acted as oppressor.

Though it was restricted, Rabbinic Judaism was the only other 'religion' that had been recognized and protected by the Roman Empire. Jewish assemblies were allowed and synagogues were not to be disturbed. The view of Catholicism appears to have been that this was the right balance. The general policy of the Roman Church, until the 12th century, was that which was communicated by Pope Gregory I (590-604 CE). He wrote: "Just as license must not be granted to the Jews to presume to do in their synagogues more than the law permits them, so they should not suffer curtailment in that which has been conceded to them."[22] In 1120 CE, a papal bull *(Constitutio pro Judaeis)* issued by Calixtus II, extended Gregory I's position. It condemned forced baptism, assaults on Jews or their property, and the desecration, of synagogues and Jewish cemeteries. This bull was reissued under different titles by subsequent popes fifteen times by the year 1450 CE.[23]

This changed, however, during the Middle Ages when Catholicism aggressively sought to stamp out anything which was deemed to be heresy, including Judaism, Islam, and other groups of Christians whose beliefs didn't conform with those of the Roman church. This transition is evident through the official actions of the popes starting primarily in the 15th century:

Gregory I (the Great), 590–604:	prohibited the mistreatment of Jews
Leo VII, 936–939:	encouraged the archbishop of Mainz to expel Jews, if they refused to be baptized
Alexander II, 1061–1073:	intervened in France and Spain to defend Jews; renewed Gregory I's prohibition against mistreatment of Jews
Innocent III, 1161–1216:	4th Lateran Council in 1215 required Jews and Muslims to wear distinctive dress (Islam also required Christians and Jews to wear distinctive dress).
Clement VI, 1342–1352:	defended the Jews in Avignon against charges that they were responsible for an outbreak of the Black Death
Martin V, 1417–1431:	denounced anti-Jewish preaching and prohibited Jewish children from being required to be baptized
Calistus III, 1455–1458:	banned all social interaction between Jews and Christians
Paul IV, 1555–1559:	restricted Jews in Rome and Papal States to ghettos and required Jews to wear distinctive headwear (upon his death, rioting crowds toppled Paul IV's statue in protest of his policies)
Pius V, 1566–1572:	generally expelled Jews from Papal States
Clement VIII, 1592–1605:	banned all Jewish books (along with other Forbidden Literature)
Leo XII, 1823–1829:	confined Jews to ghettos in Papal States and confiscated their property
Pius XI, 1922–1939:	required a denunciation of Nazism as racist and anti-Christian to be read in the Catholic churches of Germany
Pius XII, 1939–1958:	allowed Jewish refugees sanctuary in Vatican City during World War II, but has been criticized for not being more vocal about the plight of Jews during the War
John XXIII, 1958–1963:	was conciliatory toward Jews[24]

It was in the 15th and 16th centuries that Roman Catholic persecution of Judaism (and all other non-conformists) reached its height.

The Inquisition

The "inquisition" began with seemingly innocent roots. In 1184, Pope Lucius III, instructed all bishops to inquire about the faith of their parishioners. If someone were found to have heretical beliefs they would be excommunicated from the Roman Catholic Church without harm and, if they were to repent, they would be received back. On face value, this seems harmless.

The Inquisition was started to counter heresies within Christianity. Primary among these were the Albigensian movement in France and the Cathari. The Waldensians in France were also targeted, though many contend that they were not heretics at all. As these popular heresies grew (real and perceived), papal methods became more overtly offensive:

- Pope Innocent III allowed for the state to punish heretics and confiscate their property.

- Pope Gregory IX prohibited non-clergymen from possessing the Christian Scriptures and empowered Dominican friars to prosecute suspected heretics in 1229.

- Pope Innocent IV authorized the use of torture to obtain confessions from suspected heretics in 1252.

But, church policy would not allow it to shed blood; so all heretics were turned over to the officials of the state for execution.[25]

It was in this environment that King Ferdinand and Queen Isabella of Spain obtained the authority from the Bishop of Rome (the Pope) to preside over the Spanish Inquisition. They were intent upon purifying Spain of false converts from Judaism (the *conversos*) and from Islam. But their methods were horribly brutal. Their inquisition began in 1478. They expelled all Jews from Spain in 1492. It has been estimated that from 1480 to 1524, 14,344 people were burned alive and 195,937 others were either punished or released as penitents.[26] Most of these were Jews who had converted to Christianity, the *conversos*.

Though they claimed pure religious motives, King Ferdinand and Queen Isabella filled their treasury with the confiscated property of expelled Jews and prosecuted *conversos*.

Refuge In Holland

Fortunately, the Kingdom of Holland was much more gracious. Jewish refugees from Spain *(conversos)* fled to Amsterdam in 1590. Refugees from Germany joined them in 1620. They lived there in peace.

Tolerance In England

In England, religious intolerance toward Jews began primarily in the 12th century. At the time, the entire Jewish population was less than 5,000.[27] Jews were later expelled from the country in 1306. It wasn't until 1656, after the Puritan revolt led by Oliver Cromwell, that the practice of Judaism was allowed again in England.

Eastern Europe

Many of the Jews in Central Europe fled persecution to Eastern Europe during the 13th and14th centuries. But it was during the 15th century that the large migration of Jews to Poland and Lithuania occurred. The management and trading expertise of the Jews were welcomed in these developing nations.

Jews were ultimately granted incredible autonomy in Eastern Europe and formed the Council of the Four Lands, which was essentially a Jewish parliament that governed Jewish affairs. In this favorable environment, the Ashkenazi Jews devoted considerable energy to Talmudic study and established several rabbinic academies. This freedom was interrupted in 1648 when the Ukrainians revolted against the Poles. The Jewish population, who were viewed to be a part of the Polish regime, suffered greatly for almost a decade.[28] Tens of thousands of Jews were killed.

It was likely because of this that Shabbetai Zevi, a false messiah, gained many followers among Eastern European Jews during the 17th century.

From 1880 to 1920, about four million Jews migrated out of Eastern Europe to the west. Almost three million immigrated to the United States. The remainder settled in Jewish communities in Western Europe or migrated further to South America, Canada, South Africa, and Australia. This was the largest population shift in Jewish history.

The Holocaust

The most devastating event in modern Jewish history and certainly one of the most shameful events in human history was the Holocaust. From 1941 to 1945, Adolph Hitler's Third Reich systematically murdered six million Jews, two thirds of the Jews in Europe. One million were killed in mass executions by mobile units (Einsatzgruppen) during the invasion of the Soviet Union in 1941. Most of the remainder were executed in death camps such as the infamous Auschwitz or were worked to death as slave labor.

Country[29]	Jewish population in 1939	Jews killed during Holocaust	% of Jewish Population killed
Austria	185,000	50,000	27%
Belgium	65,700	28,000	43%
Bohemia & Moravia	118,310	78,150	66%
Bulgaria	50,000	-	0%
Denmark	7,800	60	0.8%
Estonia	4,500	1,500	33%
Finland	2,000	7	0.4%
France	350,000	77,320	22%
Germany	566,000	134,500	24%
Greece	77,380	60,000	78%
Hungary	825,000	550,000	67%
Italy	44,500	7,680	17%
Latvia	91,500	70,000	77%
Lithuania	168,000	140,000	83%
Luxembourg	3,500	1,950	56%
Netherlands	140,000	100,000	71%
Norway	1,700	762	45%
Poland	3,300,000	2,900,000	88%
Romania	609,000	271,000	44%
Slovakia	88,950	68,000	76%
Soviet Union	3,020,000	1,000,000	33%
Yugoslavia	78,000	56,200	72%
Total	9,796,840	5,595,129	57%

Had the allies not won the war in Europe, it's certain that European Jewry would have been annihilated.

A JEWISH NATION

After World War II, Israel once again became a nation. By a vote of the United Nations in 1948, Israel was granted a homeland in Palestine. Refugees poured into Israel. In the war that followed with neighboring Arab nations, Israel prevailed and survived.

From 1934 to 1948, about 70,000 Jews had returned to Palestine "illegally." In the year after Israel became a nation, 200,000 Jews from 42 nations immigrated. By 1980 the Jewish population of Israel reached 3 million:[30]

- 800,000 were from Western Europe

- 300,000 were from Eastern European Soviet block nations

- 150,000 were from the Soviet Union

- 600,000 were from Arab nations

- the remainder came from throughout the world

Today, most Jews don't actually live in Israel. Only 36% of the Jews in the world live there. The remainder are still scattered throughout the world, Now, however, it is by choice.

HISTORIC DIVISIONS WITHIN JUDAISM

Prior to the 19th century, the major challenges to the Pharisaic brand of Rabbinic Judaism from within came during the 8th and 18th centuries. Many of these challenges were defeated; others were absorbed.

THE KARAITE CHALLENGE TO THE PHARISEES (8TH CENTURY)

The first significant Jewish splinter group was created by the Karaite challenge to the Oral Law. The Karaites were a Jewish sect in Babylon— possibly the remnant of the Saducees—that essentially revolted against the Talmud. They maintained that only the Scriptures were authoritative.

The leader of the Karaites was Anan ben David, who it seems was passed over to become the Exilarch in Babylon (the spiritual leader of the Jews). Though he was next in line, the rabbinical authorities selected Anan's younger brother. Anan responded by proclaiming himself the counter-Exilarch and the eastern split of Judaism began. It wasn't until the early 10th century, through the efforts of Saadia ben Joseph, the Gaon of the rabbinic academy at Sura, that the rising tide of Karaism was largely stemmed.[31] At that point, there were five large sects of Karaism in existence, possibly comprising 40% of Judaism.[32]

Once again, Rabbinic Judaism as defined by the successors to the Pharisees had prevailed.

KABBALISM (13TH TO 19TH CENTURY)

The *Zohar* (the *Book of Splendor*) was introduced by Moses De Leon during the 13th century in Spain (though he claimed it's teachings originated with Simeon bar Yochai, a sage in the 2nd century). It became the foundation of what is now known as Kabbalistic teaching. After the expulsion of Jews from Spain in the 15th century, the leading Kabbalists settled back in Palestine in Galilee.

Kabbalism is Jewish mysticism. It consists of a broad range of teachings, but generally focuses on seeking to understand God's essence. While 17th century rabbis restricted the study of Kabbalah to "married men over forty who were also scholars of Torah and Talmud," from the 16th through the 19th centuries it was an accepted part of Jewish theology.[33] This is somewhat surprising because Kabbalah espouses ideas such as reincarnation, which is not found in the Hebrew Scriptures.

There have been two significant false Messiahs associated with Kabbalism:

Shabbetai Zevi (17th century)

Shabbetai Zevi was a Kabbalist born in Smyrna (Asia Minor) in the 1626. He led a significant messianic movement, which was taken seriously by the Sephardic and Ashkenazic Jewish communities of Europe and the Ottoman Empire. But he was ultimately excommunicated after "he publicly pronounced the ineffable name of God."[34] When he went to Constantinople to dethrone the sultan, he was arrested and presented with the choice of conversion to Islam or death. He chose conversion. Some of his followers sought to rationalize his conversion and thought him to be the Messiah even after his death.

Jacob Frank (18th century)

The Frankists were a mystical sect in Poland during the mid 18th century. They followed Jacob Frank, a 'pseudo-messiah.' He claimed that he was the incarnation of Shabbetai Zevi. The group was excommunicated by Polish Rabbinic authorities.[35]

HASSIDIM (18TH CENTURY)

Another major internal challenge to Rabbinic Judaism came in the 18th century in Eastern Europe. It was the Hassidic movement. Its founder, Israel ben-Eliezer (the Baal Shem Tov), was an adherent of Kabbalistic teachings.

The Jewish establishment strongly opposed and even banned the Hassidic movement. They took opposition to Hassidic ritual slaughter (sacrifice) and the strong personality cult that surrounded Hassidic leaders. Rabbi Elijah ben-Solomon Zalman (the Vilna Gaon) led the opposition. But unlike, the Karaites, the Hassidic movement ultimately gained acceptance and has since been absorbed into Orthodox Rabbinic Judaism. It has been characterized as the first 'dissident movement' since the destruction of the Temple to be accepted into Rabbinic Judaism.[36]

JEWISH CULTURAL DIVISIONS (13TH TO 19TH CENTURY)

The prolonged geographic dispersion of Jews resulted in cultural divisions within Judaism. The *Sephardi* Jews of Spain and Portugal were educated in both the Talmud and secular matters, cultured, and lived within the Gentile world. They also viewed themselves to be the descendants of the chief families of Judah from the time of the Babylonian captivity. However, the *Ashkenazi* Jews of France, Germany and Eastern Europe were poorer, did not seek to integrate within the Gentile world, wore beards, and limited their academic interests only to study of the Talmud. Consequently, the Sephardi looked upon the Ashkenazi as inferiors. And, the Sephardi looked upon the *Oriental* Jews of the Middle East and North Africa as being even more inferior than the Ashkenazi.

These cultural divisions were evident even after the expulsion of the Sephardi from Spain. Sephardi and Ashkenazi congregations in the same cities were segregated. For example, in 18th century England and Holland the Sephardi prohibited their members from marrying Ashkenazi Jews. The penalty was the loss of synagogue membership and expulsion from the Sephardic community. Ashkenazi Jews who insisted on attending Sephardi synagogues in London and Amsterdam were actually segregated behind wooden barriers. It's reported that Sephardic elitism was still evident in New York City in the early 19th century, almost 450 years after their expulsion from Spain. [37]

REFORM JUDAISM (19TH CENTURY)

The first Reform Synagogue was established in 1818 in Hamburg, Germany. The Synagogue liberalized worship practices by initiating the use of organ music and reciting some prayers in German. Theologically, the Synagogue de-emphasized the desire to return to Palestine (under Ottoman control at the time) and also de-emphasized the focus upon a Jewish Messiah.[38]

During the 1800s a significant number of Ashkenazi Jews immigrated to the United States from Germany. They brought this more liberal perspective of theology and worship practice with them. But it wasn't until 1885 at a conference in Pittsburgh that Reform Judaism was actually formalized.

The "Pittsburgh Platform" of 1885 and subsequent Central Conferences of 1892 and 1895 outlined the basic belief system of Reform Judaism. In summary, Reform Judaism:[39]

- accepted only the moral laws of the Torah and rejected ceremonies which were viewed as inconsistent with modern civilization
- accepted that the soul is immortal but rejected the concept of a physical resurrection of the dead
- rejected the concepts of heaven and hell
- de-emphasized study of the Talmud
- abandoned dietary laws (kosher)
- rejected the desire to return to Palestine and the hope for a Jewish state

- emphasized social justice
- eliminated the requirements of baptism and circumcision for converts
- initiated Synagogue services on Sunday

It has only been recently that Reform Judaism has changed some of these long-held positions. Most notable was the June 2001 vote by of the Central Conference of American Rabbis to recommend conversion guidelines. The recommended guidelines abandoned Reform Judaism's 108-year opposition to conversion rites and suggested that new converts be:

- examined by a *bet din* (a committee of three rabbis or other qualified Jews) to confirm their commitment to Judaism,
- immersed in a ritual bath, and
- circumcised (if the convert is a man).[40]

While Reform rabbis are not required to follow these guidelines, the vote to approve them was nonetheless a major change in the denomination's position.

Some of the other ways that Reform Judaism differs from Orthodox practice include:

- a confirmation ceremony is generally practiced instead of a Bar Mitzvah.
- choirs and organs are used in services.
- members worship with their heads uncovered (no yarmulkas).

Reform Judaism allows for a wide spectrum of beliefs. There are actually no theological criteria for membership in the organization of American Reform rabbis and the Central Conference hasn't gone on record that reform rabbis must even believe in God.[41]

There are now about 2 million members in the 800 Reform synagogues in America.

CONSERVATIVE JUDAISM (20TH CENTURY)

Conservative Judaism had its birth in 1890 with the formation of the Jewish Theological Seminary in New York and was formally organized as the United Synagogue of Conservative Judaism in 1913. It was established as a reaction to Reform Judaism, which had the only rabbinical seminary in the United States at the time.

Conservative Judaism describes itself as being mainline Judaism, in "a sort of twentieth century Pharisee tradition."[42] From the perspective of Conservative Judaism, both Reform and Orthodox branches of Judaism have deviated from traditional Judaism. Conservative Judaism seeks to accept Jewish Law (Halakhah) but seeks to also allow modern application. For example, it's viewed as acceptable to drive on the Sabbath and for women to be rabbis. Orthodox Judaism, however, sees many of these modern applications as being inconsistent with Jewish Law.

Today, there are about 1.3 million members in the roughly 800 Conservative synagogues in America.[43]

RECONSTRUCTIONIST JUDAISM (20TH CENTURY)

Reconstructionist Judaism grew out of the Conservative movement. It has been characterized as the left wing of Conservative Judaism. It's primarily a U.S.-based movement consisting of about 96 congregations with a total of approximately 60,000 members.

Reconstructionism teaches that it is necessary to reinterpret traditional Jewish beliefs and practices. For example, in the 1945 *Sabbath Prayer Book,* "all references to Jews as a chosen people, the concept of revelation of the Torah by God to Moses, the concept of a personal Messiah, restoration of the sacrificial cultus, retribution, and the resurrection of the dead were excised."[44] Reconstructionism is Zionist in that it supports a Jewish homeland for those who wish to live there. It's early social action agenda essentially endorsed socialism by calling for a "cooperative society, elimination of the profit system, and the public ownership of natural resources and basic industries."[45]

ORTHODOX JUDAISM

Orthodox Judaism is not a denomination in the strict sense or even a united movement. It's really a collection of many traditionalist Jewish groups that have more or less collaborated in an effort to counter the Reform and Conservative Jewish movements of the past two centuries. Most of these traditionalist groups have their roots in European

Ashkenazi and Sephardi Judaism and can ultimately trace their origins back to the 1st century Pharisaic sect of Judaism.

While Orthodox Jewish groups do not have a single statement of theology, they do tend to share several common beliefs. They believe in the authority of the written Torah, as found in the Hebrew Scriptures, the oral teachings ("oral Torah") of the Talmud, and the broader set of Jewish Law known as *Halakhah*.[a] They also generally ascribe authority to Rashi's 11th century commentary on the Torah and Moses ben Maimon's 12th century *Thirteen Principles of Faith*.

Maimonides' *Thirteen Principles of Faith*[46]

I believe with perfect faith that:

1. God is the Creator and Ruler of all things. He alone has made, does make, and will make all things.
2. God is One. There is no unity that is in any way like His. He alone is our God—He was, He is, and He will be.
3. God does not have a body. Physical concepts do not apply to Him. There is nothing whatsoever that resembles Him at all.
4. God is first and last.
5. It is only proper to pray to God. One may not pray to anyone or anything else.
6. All the words of the prophets are true.
7. The prophecy of Moses is absolutely true. He was the chief of all prophets, both before and after him.
8. The entire Torah that we now have is that which was given to Moses.
9. This Torah will not be changed, and that there will never be another given by God.
10. God knows all of man's deeds and thoughts. It is thus written (Psalm 33:15), "He has molded every heart together, He understands what each one does."
11. God rewards those who keep His commandments, and punishes those who transgress Him.
12. In the coming of Messiah. How long it takes, I will await His coming every day.
13. The dead will be brought back to life when God wills it to happen.

---

[a] At the core of Jewish Law, *Halakhah*, are the 613 commands (Mitzvahs) that are found in the Torah. Rabbis then added a series of commands (Gereirah) to ensure that the mitzvahs are not broken. Rabbis also added other commands (Tahkanah) that were not originally given in the Torah and elevated some Jewish customs (Minhag) to the status of law.

Sephardic Orthodox Jews traditionally have based their religious practices on the *Shul`han Arukh,* a legal index written by 16th century rabbi, Joseph Karo. Ashkenazi Orthodox Jews have based theirs upon the *Mapah,* which was written by 16th century Rabbi Moshe Isserles' (Rama). In general, both groups' religious practices would include:

- circumcision of males

- observance of dietary laws (Kosher)

- observance of Sabbath (Shabbat)

- use of Hebrew language in services

- emphasis upon Torah and Talmud study

- segregation of men and women in worship services

- observance of the Jewish calendar and religious festivals

There are about 2 million Orthodox Jews in the world today.

MESSIANIC JUDAISM (20TH CENTURY)

An interesting twist in the history of Judaism is the growth, especially during the last several decades, of "Messianic Judaism." Messianic Jews are generally defined as Karaite, Reformed, Orthodox, Conservative, Reconstructionist or previously "non-religious" Jews who have come to believe that Jesus is the promised Messiah of Israel. Many of them participate in the various Christian Denominations. Others have joined together to form new congregations of Messianic Jews.

Their numbers are, in fact, growing fairly rapidly. In the United States there are now about 250 Messianic Jewish congregations spread out over 41 states.[47] In all, there may be as many as 100,000 Messianic Jews in the U.S. There are also congregations in Argentina, Armenia, Australia, Belarus, Belgium, Brazil, Canada, Costa Rica, El Salvador, France, Germany, Guatemala, Holland, Hungary, Israel, Mexico, the Netherlands, New Zealand, Panama, Poland, Puerto Rico, Russia, the Ukraine, the United Kingdom, Venezuela and Zambia.[48]

Messianic Jewish groups are among the most active in the proselytizing of Jews. In the United States, groups such as Jews for Jesus, Chosen People Ministries, and Messianic Vision lead the more visible of these efforts.

RABBINIC JUDAISM TODAY

After all of this, the crushing defeat of Israel by the Romans, the diaspora, subservience to Islamic and Christian kingdoms, failed revolts, peaceful coexistence, persecutions, attempted genocide, and internal division and subdivision, Rabbinic Judaism has survived. *But until the 19th century, it was still Rabbinic Judaism as defined primarily by one sect, the Pharisees.*

In the 1st century, there were about 8 million Jews in the world.[49] By the 11th and 12th centuries, the Roman wars, revolts, persecution, and assimilation had taken their toll. The world's Jewish population had fallen to about 1.5 million. It wasn't until the dawn of the 20th century that the worldwide Jewish population reached 10.5 million.[50] Today there are about 13 to 14 million Jews in the world. Roughly 41% live in the United States (13% in New York City); 36% live in Israel; 9% are in Russia and the nations of the former Soviet Union; 4% are in France; about 3% live in Canada, and 2% live in the United Kingdom. The remainder of the population is spread throughout the world.[51]

The Conservative and Orthodox branches, which more closely resemble 1st through 6th century Pharisaic Judaism than other branches of Judaism, are preferred by about 46% of Jews in America. Reform Jews and Jews with no denominational preference comprise most of the remainder of American Judaism:[52]

Orthodox	6%
Conservative	40%
Reform	39%
No Preference	15%

In Israel, only the Orthodox branch of Judaism is legally recognized. About 15% to 20% of the Jewish population in Israel describe themselves as Orthodox (dati) or Ultra-Orthodox (haderi). Over half of the population classify themselves as secular. The remainder are traditionally observant (masorti) Jews.[53]

14

THE CHRISTIAN BRANCH THRIVED

While the Pharisaic branch of Judaism survived, the now separated Christian branch thrived. From its roots in Palestine, Christianity spread throughout the Roman world in the Middle East, Asia Minor, Europe, and Africa. Christianity's spread was remarkable in that it occurred in spite of opposition from Rabbinic Judaism and severe persecution from the Roman authorities.

THE FIRST THREE HUNDRED YEARS

The first three hundred years of Christianity wasn't confined to the Roman Empire. Christianity also spread into non-Roman Asia, India, and Africa in the 1st century. However, since Christianity started in the Roman-controlled world, that's where we'll start.

JUDEA (PALESTINE)

From its beginnings in the remote Roman province of Judea, Christianity spread across the Roman Empire into Asia Minor, Europe and Africa. Jesus' followers were intent upon spreading the message of the *New Covenant* (the "Gospel") throughout the world. They were further motivated to escape the persecution of the Jewish and Roman authorities in Judea. The reach of Christianity's spread was unintentionally further expanded as Christians sought to escape a series of persecutions under Emperors Nero, Domitian, Marcus Aurelius, Septimus Severus, and Decius.

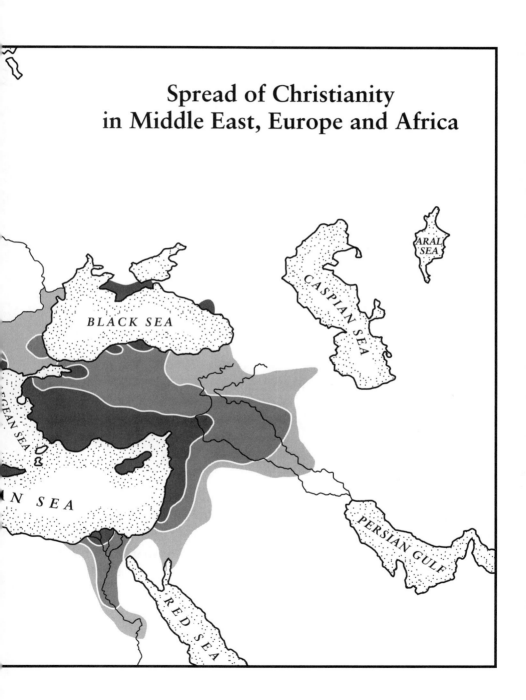

Spread of Christianity
in Middle East, Europe and Africa

How many of Jesus' followers died during these persecutions isn't known. At least two of the persecutions were Empire-wide; the others were regional. But, the death toll must have been high. The persecution by Nero in the 1st century was particularly horrible. The Roman historian Tacitus even considered it excessive. He recorded that a "great number" of Christians were condemned and described the cruelties of Nero:

> Before killing the Christians, Nero used them to amuse the people. Some were dressed in furs, to be killed by dogs. Others were crucified. Still others were set on fire early in the night, so that they might illumine it.[2]

But, rather than stamp out Christianity, the persecutions scattered Christians throughout the Empire.

ASIA MINOR

Through the preaching of Jesus' followers who had fled Jewish persecution in Jerusalem, Christianity took root to the north of Judea in the Roman provinces of Syria, Cilicia, Galatia, Asia, and Lycia by 60 CE. (These provinces are present-day Lebanon, Syria, and Turkey.) They were joined by the apostles Barnabas and Paul (Rabbi Saul) who stayed and taught the new believers. It was actually in Antioch, the Roman capital of Syria, that Jesus' followers were first called "Christians."[3]

CYPRUS

Cyprus was also a Roman province in the 1st century. Again, the apostles Barnabas and Paul were among the first to bring Christianity to the island.[4] They preached there in about 45 CE and won over the Roman proconsul, Sergius Paulus, who became a Christian. Christianity became firmly established and, by the 4th century, Christianity may have been a majority on the Island.[5]

EUROPE

Jesus' disciples Paul, Barnabas, Luke, Mark, and many others evangelized Greece, Crete, and Italy in the 1st century. They were followed in Greece by the apostle Andrew and in Italy by the apostle Peter.

Christianity reached France (Gaul) by the 2nd century. Churches were established there in Vienne and Lyons. Additional missionaries were sent from the church in Rome to France during the 3rd century. It was then that the first church in Paris was founded. The Christian church had also reached Spain and Britain by the 2nd century.[6]

AFRICA

Ethiopia

The first convert to Christianity from Africa in the 1st century was reported to have been the Treasurer of Ethiopia.[7] Unlike the Roman Empire, Christianity in Ethiopia appears to have experienced freedom from its inception. The Church was locally administered and was not subjected to the persecutions that Christians in the Roman Empire endured. In the 4th century, it was actually made the state religion by King Ezana.[8]

Egypt

The apostle Mark is reported to have founded the church in Alexandria, Egypt in the 1st century. Christianity spread throughout the nation within 50 years of his arrival.

The *Coptic Church* in Alexandria held a major position of prominence and leadership within Christianity for several centuries. The Christian Scriptures were translated into Coptic and a school for new converts, the Catechetical School of Alexandria, was founded in the 2nd century. Some of the leading bishops in the world were educated there under the instruction of such noted theologians as Clement and Origen. In addition, the Bishops (Popes) of Alexandria were participants in major church Councils such as the councils at Nicea and Ephesus and led in the development of the Nicene Creed and in the opposition to Gnostic heresies.

Even after the Arab conquest of North Africa in the 7th century and the restrictions upon Christianity that ensued, Egypt remained predominantly Christian until the 11th century.[9]

North Africa

It's clear that the spread of Christianity across the remainder of North Africa was also rapid. By the year 250 CE, there were 130 churches across North Africa, each with their own Bishop. Though their congregations may have been small, their sheer number is indicative of the rapid spread of Christianity on the continent.[10] To the west, Christianity had taken root in Mauritania, Numidia, and Proconsular Africa. In the latter, Carthage (present day Tunis in Tunisia) was a significant center of Christianity. It was here that Tertullian, the 2nd century theologian, lived and where the *Donatist Church* would later form.

ASIA

Edessa and Arbela (Syria and Iraq)

Thaddeus (Addai in Syriac), evidently one of Jesus' disciples who were in the group of seventy referred to in Luke 10:1, evangelized the kingdom of Osrhoene in the 1st century. The kingdom was a buffer state between the Roman and Parthian empires. Its capital city of Edessa (present day Urfa in Turkey) was an important city located at the convergence of two trade routes. The first was the Silk Road, which led to India and China; the other led from Armenia to Egypt. It's reported that its king, Abgar, and the people of the kingdom freely embraced Christianity making it the 1st Christian country.[11]

It appears that two disciples of Addai then took Christianity to the Mesopotamian city of Arbela (Present day Erbil in northern Iraq) in the Persian border kingdom of Adiabene.[12] The churches in Osrhoene and Adiabene were the beginnings of the *Church of the East* (also known as the Nestorian Church). By the 4th century they had established churches and monasteries from Persia to India.

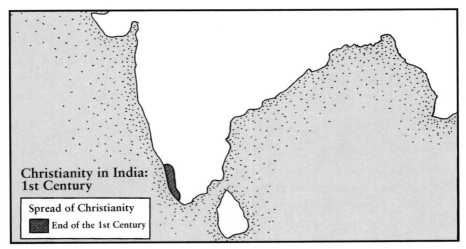

Christianity in India:
1st Century

Spread of Christianity

End of the 1st Century

Source:[14]

The Christian Scriptures were translated from Greek into Syriac, the trading language of the ancient Middle East, in the 2nd century. Syriac became the language of the *Church of the East* in the same way that Latin became the language of the church in much of Western Europe.

India

Jesus' apostle Thomas evangelized southern India and founded seven churches along the Malabar Coast in the 1st century. Pantaenus, a missionary from the church in Alexandria, followed him at the end of the 2nd century. The Church in India is substantially a result of their efforts.[13] Up until the 16th century, Indian Christians were simply known as "Thomas Christians."

The Church in India was locally administered and was independent of the governance of Churches in the West. However, the Indian Church became connected with the Church in Persia through the missionary efforts of the Persian Church and the theological training that was available to Indians at the school in Nisibis (located between Edessa and Arbela in present day Syria).[15]

Armenia

It is believed that Christianity was brought to Armenia in the 1st century by the apostles Thaddeus and Bartholomew. However, it was late in the 3rd century when it became firmly established. It was then that King Tiridates was converted. He made Christianity the state religion in 301 CE.

The *Armenian Church* has been independently administered since its inception, though it accepted the decisions of the major church councils in Nicea (325 CE), Constantinople (381 CE) and Ephesus (431 CE). The Armenian Church also has had its own translation of the Christian Scriptures since the 5th century. Rather than use Greek texts or Syriac translations, they created an alphabet and translated them into the Armenian language.[16]

Elsewhere in Asia

In addition to India, Mesopotamia and Armenia, Jesus' followers could be found scattered in Media, Bactria, Parthia, and Arabia.[17]

THE ROMAN EMPIRE ACCEPTS CHRISTIANITY

It has been estimated that, at the close of the 3rd century, Jesus' followers in the Roman Empire numbered about 10 million people, about a tenth of the population of the Empire.[18] His followers outside of the Empire may have numbered a million as well. This is amazing growth considering the opposition raised by Rabbinic Judaism and the intense persecutions of the Roman Empire.

PERSECUTION BY DIOCLETIAN AND GALERIUS (303 TO 311 CE)

The success of the spread of Christianity was viewed in Rome as a threat. Emperor Diocletion responded in 303 CE with yet another attempt to destroy it. The original aim was to destroy the institution, not the people, but that wasn't the result. Churches were burned, Christian writings were destroyed, observance of religious services was prohibited, and many people were killed. In Egypt, whole villages were massacred. [19] In the Western Empire, the persecution stopped with

Diocletian's resignation in 305 CE, but it continued under Galerius in the Eastern Empire until 311 CE. Unable to stop Christianity, Galerius ultimately gave in and lifted the persecution.[20]

"CHRISTIANITY" BECOMES THE FAVORED RELIGION (312 TO 380 CE)

To make his expansive empire more governable, Diocletian had divided it into two parts, Eastern and Western Roman Empire, each with an Emperor and a Vice-emperor (or caesar). He himself held the title of Emperor in the Western Empire. His western Vice-emperor was Constantius Chlorus. After Diocletian's resignation, Constantius became Western Emperor, but he died a year later in 306 CE. His troops then named his son, Constantine, emperor. After forging an alliance with Licinius in the Eastern Empire, and defeating his principle rival at the Battle of Milvian Bridge, Constantine secured his hold on the Western Empire. He later ousted Licinius to become sole Emperor of the Roman Empire in 324 CE.

It was Constantine who changed the status of Jesus' followers from a persecuted Jewish sect to the favored religion of the Roman Empire. He also took it upon himself to assume a role of protector of the faith. As legend has it, he saw a vision of a cross in the sky while he was praying before the battle of Milvian. In the vision he saw an inscription that said, "conquer by this." He is also said to have seen God's Messiah who told him to make a likeness of the sign of the cross he had seen and to use it as protection.[21] The year after their victory, Constantine and Licinius issued the (so called) *Edict of Milan* that granted religious freedom for *all religions* within the empire.[22]

It was clear, however, that Constantine favored "Christianity." He ordered an officer in North Africa to supply funds to the Bishop of Carthage to pay the expenses of the clergy. When a separatist movement in Africa (the Donatists) challenged Caecilian as Bishop of Carthage, Constantine called a commission of Bishops in Rome to hear the case and ultimately decided the case himself in favor of Caecilian.[23] He gave his Latern palace in Rome to the Bishop of Rome, exempted the clergy from forced labor or military service, and made Sunday a day of rest.[24] He also personally intervened to resolve the Arian heresy controversy.

He did so by calling and presiding over what was essentially the first worldwide council of Bishops to resolve the church governance and doctrinal issues related to the controversy.[25]

At the end of the 4th century, during the reign of Emperor Theodosius, Christianity became the only official religion of the Roman Empire.[26] However, this lofty status came with a high price—the recurring interference of Roman Emperors into the affairs of the church.

PERSIAN PERSECUTION RESULTS

The highest cost of Christianity becoming the state religion in the Roman Empire was borne by Christians in the Persian Empire. For 250 years, Persia had been a safe haven for Christians from Roman persecution. But when Constantine, who was the enemy of Persia, became a Christian this all changed.

Constantine died in 337 CE while preparing to attack Persia. The Persians took advantage of his death and countered with an attack, and the persecution of Christians, who were viewed as allies of Rome, began. Christians were stripped of their rights, double taxes were imposed on them, and many were killed. It's been estimated that during the persecution of 340 to 401 CE, 190,000 Christians were killed.[27]

Like the Jewish and Roman persecutions before it, the Persian persecution had the effect of further scattering Jesus' followers. Some Christians fled Persia to India and Arabia (present-day Saudi Arabia, Yemen, Bahrain, Qatar, United Arab Emirates and Oman).

CHRISTIANITY BECOMES INTERNALLY FRAGMENTED (4TH TO 21ST CENTURY)

Up until the 4th century there was substantial unity within Christianity internationally. While there were Gnostic heresies and the polytheistic heresies espoused by Marcionites to keep out of the church, Christians generally saw themselves as part of a greater brotherhood that transcended race or nationality. This is evident by the writings of the early church fathers and by the international meetings of Bishops that were occurring by the 3rd century in Rome, Carthage and Antioch.[28]

The key subdivisions within Christianity prior to the 4th century were related to:

- The 1st century Jewish followers of Jesus who taught that Gentile followers should be circumcised

- The *Montanist* movement in the 3rd century, which emphasized high standards of moral purity, prophecy, and the early return of the Messiah[29]

- The *Novatian* division, which was initiated by a presbyter (church leader) in Rome during the 3rd century and lasted through the 5th century. Novatian opposed the easy readmission into the church of those who had recanted their faith during the persecution under Emperor Decian.[30]

As Christianity became more geographically dispersed, as Empires rose and fell, and as church governance and theological issues emerged, there came even more subdivisions.

THE DONATISTS (300 TO 400 CE)

One of the primary Christian splinter groups to be formed in the 4th century resulted from the Donatist controversy in North Africa. The controversy that created the split was similar to the one that created the Novatian movement. A formerly "lapsed" leader in the Cathage church had selected Caecilian to be the new bishop. Those who had not recanted their faith during times of Roman Imperial persecution objected and selected Donatus to be the new bishop.

Emperor Constantine himself ultimately intervened with the solution to the controversy by picking Caecilian. So, the losers in the disagreement established the *Donatist Church* in Africa. The split lasted for the rest of the century until Emperor Honorius intervened and dissolved the *Donatist Church* with his *Edict of Unity* in 405 CE.[31]

THE ARIAN HERESY

The Arian Heresy began in Egypt but had a profound impact upon Christianity worldwide. It began with a presbyter named Arius who claimed that "the Word" (Jesus) was not God, but was rather the first of all created beings. He agreed that Jesus existed before his human birth (his incarnation) but contended that Jesus did not exist before the creation of the Universe. Arius thought the belief that Jesus preexisted creation was a denial of monotheism. The Bishop of Alexandria had a major problem with his presbyter's teachings and so did a council of 100 Bishops from the other churches of Egypt and Libya. But, Arius refused to submit to the council and sought to rally support from Antioch.[32]

To settle the controversy, Emperor Constantine called the first major worldwide council of churches. Over 300 bishops from churches in Europe, Asia, and Africa met in Nicea (in Asia Minor) in 325 CE. Bishop Eusebius of Nicomedia (not the historian) presented the Arian case. The Council's conclusion was that Arius' position was heresy in that it denied the deity of Jesus. They developed the *Nicene Creed* to set the record straight.

That would have been the end of the story. But, Emperor Constantine died and his son, the now Emperor Constantinius, was an advocate of the Arian position. He sought to force the Arian position upon the church by banishing Bishops who wouldn't sign a condemnation of the Bishop of Alexandria, who was an ardent proponent of the Nicene Creed. Another church council was even called to reject the outcome of the Nicene Council. But when Constantinius died, Julian the Apostate became Emperor and canceled the orders of banishment. The churches then reconfirmed the Nicene Creed at a Council in Constantinople in 381 CE.[33] The *Church of the East* also adopted the Nicene Creed in 410 CE.[34]

THE NESTORIAN CONTROVERSY

One of the outcomes of the Council in Constantinople was the elevation of the Bishop of Constantinople to a position of supremacy over the churches of Antioch and Alexandria. The churches in Alexandria and Antioch, which had been in existence longer and which had been founded by Jesus' apostles, didn't appreciate being relegated to a subordinate status under Constantinople's authority. To counter the effect of this subordination, they both sought to have their supporters or favorite sons named Bishop of Constantinople. Because Antioch was more successful in doing so, friction developed between the leaders in the two cities. It was in this environment that the Nestorian Controversy erupted.

Nestorius was from the Antiochene School and became Bishop of Constantinople in 428 CE. Members of the church in Constantinople were in disagreement over the use of the term *"Mary Theotokos"* (Mary mother of God). The churches in the West used the phrase widely to emphasize the deity of Jesus. Others, especially those from the Antiochene School, felt that the term "mother of man" should be used to emphasize Jesus' humanity. Nestorius evidently also believed that the phrase detracted from Jesus' humanity. So during a series of Christmas sermons, he proposed a compromise by suggesting the term "mother of Christ." Unfortunately for Nestorius, he had opened a hornet's nest.

Cyril, the Bishop of Alexandria, who was particularly sensitive about any doctrinal error from an Antiochene Bishop of Constantinople, reacted sharply by denouncing Nestorius for denying the deity of Jesus. A church council was called and met in Ephesus in 431 CE. Knowing that Nestorius' defenders from Antioch would be detained for a few weeks, Cyril (who had 50 Bishops in attendance) started the proceedings anyway, over the objections of other Bishops. Though neither Nestorius nor his defenders were in attendance, the Council voted 200 to 0 to excommunicate him. When the 40 Bishops from Antioch arrived, they were incensed and held their own Council to excommunicate Cyril. Ultimately Emperor Theodosius II intervened and arrested both Cyril and Nestorius. He sided with Cyril, who was freed and Nestorius obediently went into exile in Arabia.[35]

It's very likely that both sides in the dispute were actually in substantial agreement. They both believed that Jesus is both fully God and man. The difference was a matter of emphasis and Nestorius' inability to articulate an acceptable theological defense for his position. His explanation that in Jesus there were "two natures and two persons," one human and one divine, was viewed as unacceptable by many. He rationalized that, since God is eternal, only the human part of Jesus was actually born of the

Virgin Mary. But others saw his explanation of splitting the unity of Messiah's deity and humanity into two persons as dangerous.[36]

The Great "Christological" Debates Continued

After the decisions of the Council of Ephesus, the disagreements over how to describe the Jesus' divinity and humanity calmed down, but only briefly. At the risk of over simplifying, the primary conflict was one of theology and supremacy between the Alexanderine and Antiochene schools. The other major players were the Roman church, the church in Constantinople, and the Emperor. All had their views and agendas.

The Robbers Synod

The next council was held at Ephesus in 449 CE and the Bishop of Alexandria, Dioscorus, was appointed by the Emperor to preside. Evidently, Dioscorus railroaded the council to the point that it was called the "robbers synod" by the Bishop of Rome.

The council deposed some of the strongest proponents of the Antiochene view of "Christology." They also agreed that only those who did *not* hold a Nestorian view of the Trinity could be ordained.[37]

The Council of Chalcedon

Within a year, however, the Emperor died. The new Empress, Pulcheria, and her husband called a new council to undo the decisions made in Ephesus. The Council of Chalcedon in 451 CE was the largest ever held. There were 520 bishops and an Imperial delegation of 18 members.

At the conclusion of the Council, Dioscorus was stripped of his position and banished, the bishops who had been deposed by the Council of Ephesus (The Robbers Synod) were restored, and a unifying statement describing the humanity and deity of Jesus was agreed upon. In a way, the Alexandrine and Antiochene views both won and lost. The points that they had all long agreed upon were reiterated: that Jesus is *"truly God and truly man,"* that he was God before the creation, that he was without sin, and that he was born as a man to secure salvation for humanity. But the description said that Jesus was *"...made known in two natures, without confusion, without change, without division, without separation...concurring into one Person*

(prosopon) and one hypostasis—not parted or divided into two persons...".
The *"two natures"* wording was a win for the Antiochenes. The *"not parted or divided into two persons"* was a win for the Alexandrines. It looked
like peace at last.[38]

THE AFRICAN CHURCHES WITHDRAW

Alexandria, however, did not accept the Byzantine bishop who was
sent to replace the banished Dioscorus. The result was that the African
churches of Egypt and Ethiopia rejected the decisions of Chalcedon and
withdrew from the other churches. They came to be known as *monophysite* (one nature) Christians.

However, the Coptic Church today is adamant that it has never
believed in *monophysitism* as it was described by the Council of
Chalcedon in the 5th century.[39]

THE ROMAN AND BYZANTINE CHURCHES EXPERIENCE A RIFT

After the Western Roman Empire fell to the barbarians in 476 CE,
Zeno, the Emperor in the Eastern Roman Empire (Byzantium) feared
the same result. Because he needed the political support of Africa to
keep his throne, he sided with *monophysitism*. This caused the Roman
Bishop, Felix III, to excommunicate both him and the Patriarch (Bishop)
of Constantinople. In like manner, the Patriarch of Constantinople
excommunicated Felix III. The split lasted for 36 years.[40]

CHURCHES OUTSIDE THE ROMAN EMPIRE GO INDEPENDENT (400 TO 500 C.E.)

The Church of the East

During period from 420 to 457 CE came another wave of Zoroastrian
persecution of Christians in Persia. Because of the severe persecution
under the Persians, the *Church of the East* was primarily focused upon
survival rather than the Nestorian and Monophysite controversies. It was
during this time (424 CE) that the *Church of the East* declared itself to be
independent and that its patriarchs were equal in jurisdiction to those of
the west. Distancing itself from the Byzantine world, which was the

enemy of Persia, was likely essential to self-preservation.

The primary link between the western church and the *Church of the East* that remained was through their theological school in Byzantine-controlled Edessa. The *School of the Persians* was the most prominent of the three schools in Edessa and, unlike the *Armenian* and *Syrian* schools, it was decidedly Nestorian in theology. But, its Nestorian views led to its demise. In 489 CE, the monophysite-leaning Byzantine Emperor Zeno ordered the *School of the Persians* closed. He did so to placate the monophysite Bishop of Edessa. The result was that the last real bridge between the churches of the west and the east was collapsed.[41]

The Armenian Church

The Armenians were at war with the Persians during the Council of Chalcedon so they didn't attend. After Chalcedon, they reaffirmed their support of the Councils of Nicea, Constantinople, and Ephesus, but rejected the decisions of Chalcedon. The Council was viewed as a "Nestorianizing Assembly."[42] This was a significant schism within Christianity because even by the 4th century, the size of the *Armenian Church* was estimated to be several million people.[43]

The division was perpetuated by the Muslim conquest of Armenia in the 7th century and the later emergence of the Ottoman Turks. The Armenian Christians effectively became cut-off from European and African Christianity.

The Church In India

The *"Thomas Christians"* in India had long been isolated from western Christianity. Their primary bridge to the rest of Christianity was through the *Church of the East* in Persia. With the closure of the *School of the Persians* and the isolation of the *Church of the East,* India was even more isolated.

In addition, because India was supplied with theological training from the Nestorian *School of the Persians,* the *Church in India* was labeled as "non-Chalcedonian" by the west.

NEW INDEPENDENT CHURCHES ARE BORN

While the churches of the Roman and Byzantine world were debating theology, new churches were being planted in Britain and Africa.

The Celtic Churches

An independent *Celtic Church* was firmly established in Britain before the 4th century. It then spread to Ireland and Scotland during the 4th and 5th centuries through the missionary efforts of Patrick and Columba. These churches, however, didn't recognize the authority of the *Roman Church* and subsequently became rivals of Rome in Britain.[44]

The Celtic Churches also evangelized parts of Germany and France.

The Nubian Church

The three states that made up Nubia in Eastern Africa were converted to Christianity through the missionary efforts of both *Monophysite* and *Chalcedonian* missionaries. This occurred from 543 CE through 580 CE.

After Egypt fell to the Arabs in 641 CE, Christianity in Nubia developed in relative isolation. The Nubians had repelled the Arab invaders, but were now cutoff from Christianity in neighboring nations.[45]

THE ROMAN AND EASTERN ORTHODOX CHURCHES SPLIT (400 TO 1200 CE)

The political division of the Roman Empire into two parts during the 4th century set the stage for the split between the church in Rome and the churches in the Eastern half of the Empire. The language barrier that existed by the 7th century also created a huge cultural gulf as few Europeans could read Greek and few Byzantines could speak Latin. But there were probably five incidents which, more than any other, caused the split.

The Filioque: The Constantinople and Nicene gatherings of Bishops resulted in the Nicene Creed, a simple unified pronouncement of what Christianity is. The church in Rome, however, added a phrase to the creed in reference to the Holy Spirit without consulting of the other churches. This was considered to be an affront by these churches.

The Crowning of Charlemagne: Pope Stephen (754 CE) saw the "barbarian" advance prevailing against the vestiges of the Western Empire and aligned himself with the Franks. Pope Leo crowned the King of the Franks, Charles the Great (Charlemagne), as the Emperor of the "Holy Roman Empire" in 800 CE. But, the Byzantines viewed Charlemagne as a foreign intruder and the coronation by Leo to be an act of schism within the Empire.[46]

Claims of Papal Authority: The Byzantine Bishops had seen the Bishop of Rome (the Pope) to be a Bishop among equals. They had even granted Rome a place of first among equals. But when Pope Nicolas sought to exert authority over the entire earth in 865 CE., they essentially said, "no way." By 1009 CE. the Roman church and the Byzantine churches were no longer communicating.

Mutual Excommunications: Pope Leo IX sent three representatives to meet with Michael Cerularius, the patriarch of Constantinople, who was critical of the Roman church's use of unleavened bread in the observance of the Lord's Supper. The meeting succeeded only in widening their disagreement. The Roman church's response was to excommunicate the patriarch in 1054 CE. He responded, in turn, by excommunicating the Bishop of Rome.[47]

The Crusades: The Crusades intensified the division between the Byzantine Orthodox Churches and the Church of Rome. After the first Crusade, the prevailing crusaders established competing churches under Roman governance in Byzantine cities. This created incredible division at a local level. But the ultimate affront to the Byzantines came in 1204 CE, during the fourth crusade, when the European crusaders sacked and pillaged Constantinople, the Byzantine capital.[48]

THE CATALYST FOR DISSENT IN THE ROMAN CHURCH: 300 YEARS OF POOR LEADERSHIP (1300 TO 1600 CE)

From the late 13th century into the 16th century, the Roman church was plagued by poor leadership, compromised doctrine, corruption and immorality.

Popes expanded claims of the monarchical authority of the papacy.

They authorized the use of torture and capital punishment against Christian and non-Christian dissenters. They sold "forgiveness" and church offices as a means of raising funds. They practiced nepotism. Some were sexually immoral. This was not a good time for Roman Catholicism. Many liken this period to the kingdom of Judah before its fall to the Babylonians—the sin of its leaders had led to Judah's downfall.[49]

Some of the Popes during this era were probably genuinely seeking to protect Roman Catholic orthodoxy. But, the methods that they used were clearly inconsistent with teachings of the Messiah that they claimed to follow.[50]

Bishop of Rome (Pope)	Tenure	Leadership Deficiency[51]
Boniface VIII	1295–1303	Declared that every creature is subject to the Pope
Clement V	1305–1314	Asserted papal authority; used up the papal treasury
John XXII	1316–1334	Accused of heresy; Inquisition killed Albigenses and Waldensians
Benedict	1335–1342	Inquisitor; ordered heretics burned at the stake
Clement VI	1342–1352	Corrupt; sold indulgences (forgiveness)
Innocent VI	1352–1362	Persecuted other Christians
Gregory XI	1371–1378	Repressed Christian "heretics" (such as John Wycliffe)
Urban VI	1378–1389	Unstable; caused the great schism (2 competing Popes)
Boniface IX	1389–1404	Committed Nepotism and sold church offices
Paul II	1464–1471	Has been characterized as a playboy
Sixtus IV	1471–1481	Spanish Inquisition: persecuted Christians and Jews
Innocent VIII	1484–1492	Was corrupt
Alexander VI	1492–1503	Given to unbridled sensuality
Julius II	1503–1513	Was a military Pope
Leo X	1513–1521	Sold indulgences (forgiveness)
Paul III	1534–1549	Had four illegitimate children
Julius III	1550–1555	Was given to sensual pleasures
Paul IV	1555–1559	Reactivated the Inquisition

ROMAN CATHOLIC DISSENT AND SEPARATION (1100 TO 1600 CE)

Given the leadership problems that were experienced by the *Roman Catholic Church*, it isn't surprising to see a direct parallel in dissent. There were many who sought change. Some of the more notable reformers included:

1100 to 1200 C.E.

Peter Waldo (c. 1150–1218) and the *Waldensians* independently translated the Bible from Latin into French and traveled in twos throughout the French countryside teaching the common people from the Christian Scriptures. They were excommunicated by the archbishop of Lyons and later by Pope Lucius III in 1184. Those who didn't conform and submit to Roman Catholic authority by 1214 were declared to be heretics by Pope Innocent III. The Inquisition under Pope John XXII ordered many of them killed.[52]

Francis of Assisi was an Italian reformer of sorts who stayed within the structure of the Roman Church during the early 1200s. He renounced wealth and established a new order within Catholicism. Catholicism now regards him as a "saint".

1300 to 1400 C.E.

John Wycliffe (c. 1329–1384), an Oxford theologian in England, was another independent Bible translator. He and his colleagues translated the entire Bible from Latin into English. In addition, he questioned the pope's authority, challenged the sale of indulgences (forgiveness), rejected the doctrine of transubstantiation, and spoke against the hierarchies in the Roman Catholic Church. He then organized a group of parishioners (the *Lollards*) who went throughout England reading the Bible in English. He was protected from papal reprisals by Oxford University and sympathetic government officials.[53]

Jan Huss (1373–1415), a Roman Catholic priest and dean of philosophy at the University of Prague, was influenced by the teachings of John Wycliffe. Huss criticized the papacy, demanded church reforms, and opposed the selling of indulgences. He was condemned by the Roman church for heresy and burned at the stake.[54] His legacy was the *Moravian Church* in Bohemia, Moravia, and Poland.

Girolamo Savonarola (1452–1498) was a Roman Catholic priest in Florence, Italy. He spoke out against the worldliness and corruption in the Catholic Church and openly condemned Pope Alexander VI's character and leadership. He was arrested, tortured, hanged and burned.[55]

1500 to 1600 C.E.

Martin Luther (1483–1546), a German Roman Catholic priest denounced the sale of indulgences, claimed that the Scriptures had supreme authority above church authority, challenged teachings on the celibacy of priests, and translated the Bible into German. He also taught that righteousness is imparted by God through faith. Prince Frederick the Wise of Saxony protected him from papal reprisals.[56]

In support of the papacy, the Emperor of the Holy Roman Empire moved his army against the protestant German princes. But the resulting Peace of Augsburg in 1555 left the *Lutheran Church* on a legal parity with Catholicism. By this time, Lutheranism had also spread outside of Germany and had become the state religion of several nations:[57]

- Sweden in 1527
- Finland in 1530
- Denmark & Norway in 1539
- Iceland in 1554

Henry VIII (1491–1547), King of England, rejected the authority of the Roman Catholic Church and in 1534 had parliament declare him to be the head of the *Church of England*.

Ulrich Zwingli (1484–1531), a Swiss Roman Catholic priest, was a leader in the Swiss reformation. Led by Zwingli the church in Zurich translated the Bible, ended priestly celibacy and the Lenten fast, removed images from churches, and replaced the Latin Mass with a plain Communion.[58]

John Calvin (1509–1564) broke from Catholicism and left his home in France to settle in Switzerland. It was there that he published his *Institutes of the Christian Religion*. His impact upon the reformation movement may have been second only to Martin Luther.

John Knox (1514–1572), a Scottish Roman Catholic priest, was a leader of the Calvinist Reformation in Scotland. This laid the groundwork for the *Presbyterian Church*, which became the state church of Scotland in 1592.

THE COUNTER REFORMATION

The Roman Catholic Church responded to the reformers with internal reform of its own. The Council of Trent (1545–1563) resulted in a crack down on immorality in the church and abolished the sale of indulgences (forgiveness). But, for most Protestants, the reforms didn't go far enough. The mass was still to be conducted only in Latin, the Scriptures were still not to be translated into the languages of the people, the doctrine of transubstantiation was upheld, and seven sacraments were reconfirmed. The reforms were viewed as too little and too late.

More significant change didn't come until 500 years later via Vatican II in 1962. It was then that:

- the observance of the mass in the local languages of the people was approved

- the Scriptures could be translated into local languages (versus Latin)

- other non-Roman Catholic followers of Jesus were regarded as Christians

- doctrines on Mary were clarified and Mary veneration was toned down

- it was emphasized that the Bible, not tradition, was the primary source of divine truth.

REFORM IN THE CHURCH OF ENGLAND

Henry VIII split from the Roman Catholic Church primarily so that he could divorce his spouse. But the *Church of England* was still basically Roman Catholic in doctrine. Then after Henry died, Thomas Cranmer, the archbishop of Canterbury, set about instituting the following reforms:

- images were removed from churches

- confessions to priests ceased

- Calvinist scholars were welcomed at Oxford and Cambridge Universities

- *The Book of Common Prayer* replaced the Roman Catholic liturgical worship service[59]

When Mary, Queen of Scots, became queen, she had Cranmer burned at the stake and sought to turn England back to Roman Catholicism. But the Anglican Reformation, which Cranmer encouraged, had too much momentum. The early reformers were followed by Baptists, Puritans, Quakers and others. Many of them, like persecuted Jews, found refuge in Holland. About 20,000 fled to America during the Great Migration in the 1630s and 1640s. But ultimately, reformers were tolerated and the Church of England became substantially *"protestantized."*

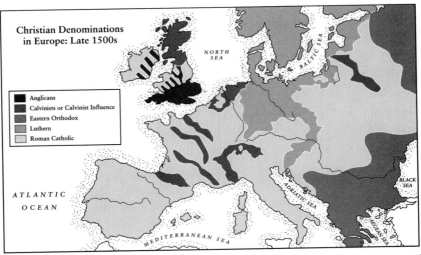

Source:[60]

FURTHER MISSIONARY MOVEMENTS

Though various Emperors and Kings through history did seek to force their subjects to convert to Christianity, the primary spread of Christianity was through evangelism (proselytizing).

China   Missionaries from the *Church of the East* reached China in the 7th century.

Russia   *Eastern Orthodox Christianity* was accepted by the Czar and became the state religion of Russia in the 11th century.

South America   European military conquest brought *Roman Catholicism* to South America in the 15th and 16th centuries.

North America   European colonization during the 17th and 18th centuries brought many Christians seeking opportunity and religious freedom to the continent. The *Great Awakening* of the 18th century resulted in an even broader acceptance of Christianity in North America.

Africa   European colonization and the significant missionary efforts of the 18th and 19th centuries further expanded Christianity into central and southern Africa.

CHRISTIANITY TODAY

About 33% of people worldwide are now generally classified as Christians, making it the world's largest religious faith. But perhaps a more significant way to measure the acceptance Christianity has received is to look at the number of the world's people groups that have accepted Jesus as Messiah and the wide geographic distribution of these groups.

PEOPLE GROUPS THAT FOLLOW JESUS

The term *people group* represents an ethnic or linguistic group within a country. Based upon this definition, there are about 11,874 people groups in the world. Of these, about 67% have a measurable population of Christians. In about 46%, Christianity is the primary faith of the group (comprising over 60% of their population). This reflects a significant level of acceptance by a broad base of peoples throughout the world.

WORLD REGIONS THAT FOLLOW JESUS

Estimates by Christian sources also show a wide geographic distribution of Christians throughout all regions of the world. The only regions where Christianity is not broadly accepted are the Islamic world of the Middle East and North Africa, and Southern and Eastern Asia.

World Region and % of population that is Christian[62]	
Central and Southern Africa	48%
Southern and Eastern Asia	7%
Eurasia	46%
Caribbean	70%
Europe	77%
Latin America and South America	91%
Middle East and North Africa	4%
North America	71%
Australia and Pacific Islands	67%

It's interesting to note that the center of Christianity is no longer in the Middle East or Europe. The faith has so spread that 20% of all Christians now live in Africa. There are 393 million African Christians.[63]

THOUSANDS OF DENOMINATIONS AND GROUPS

There are now thousands of Christian denominations and independent churches in the world. In 1992, there were over 130 Christian denominations with over 1,000 members in the United States alone.[64] In addition to the official denominations, there are thousands of unaffiliated churches and missions.

WITH SO MANY DENOMINATIONS, WHAT DO THEY AGREE ON?

Today there are about 1.9 billion followers of Jesus. The many Christian denominations include *Coptic, Malankara Orthodox, Ethiopian Orthodox, Church of the East, Eastern Orthodox, Roman Catholic, Armenian, Maronite, Syrian Church of Antioch, Church of England (Anglican), Lutheran, Presbyterian, Moravian, Methodist, Baptist, Congregationalist, Quaker, Pentecostal,* and many more. Although they disagree on many points of theology and practice, but considering their numbers, what they do agree upon is remarkable.

Almost without exception, the many denominations of Christians agree on at least one of the two core statements of faith that had emerged by the 4th century. One of these is the Nicene Creed. It was developed by bishops at meetings in Nicea and Constantinople in 375 and 381 CE. It still remains almost universally accepted by Jesus' followers:

> We believe in ONE GOD THE FATHER Almighty, Maker of heaven and earth, And of all things visible and invisible, And in one Lord JESUS CHRIST, the only-begotten of the Father before all worlds; Light of Light, Very God of very God, Begotten, not made, Being of one substance with the Father; By whom all things were made; Who for us men, and for our salvation, came down from heaven, And was incarnate by the Holy Ghost of the Virgin Mary, And was made man; He was crucified for us under Pontius Pilate; And suffered and was buried; And the third day he rose again, according to the Scriptures; And ascended into heaven, And sitteth on the right hand of the Father; And he shall come again with glory, to judge the quick and the dead; Whose kingdom shall have no end. And in the HOLY GHOST, the Lord and Giver of life; Who proceedeth from the Father; Who with the Father and the Son together is worshiped

and glorified; And who spake by the Prophets. And in one holy catholic and apostolic Church; We acknowledge one baptism for the remission of sins; And we look for the resurrection of the dead; And the life of the world to come.[65]

—The Nicean Constantinople Creed of 381 CE

Another interesting point of substantial agreement is how Jesus' followers view themselves. Though they are now predominately made up of Gentiles, the majority of Christian denominations still view themselves to be a branch of the tree of Judaism through their *New Covenant*. They don't claim to be Jewish in the ethnic sense, but they point to Rabbi Saul's characterization of the Gentiles being like a wild olive branch that has been grafted into the tree of Israel.[66] They believe that God's promise to Abraham is being fulfilled: *"all the families of the earth shall bless themselves by you."*[67]

15

So, How Could This Be Judaism?

Jesus' followers acknowledge that by late in the 2nd century, most of the converts to their "branch of Judaism" were coming from the Gentiles.[1] By the time of Constantine, in the 4th century this was especially true. So, how can a branch of Judaism, which by the 4th century is primarily made up of Gentile converts and the uncircumcised descendants of original Hebrew followers, be considered Jewish?

How Could This Be Judaism?

Jesus' followers respond to this question with several points:

Judaism is not just a Race, It is a Covenant

While the promise of the Abrahamic covenant was to Abraham and his descendants (through his son Isaac), and the *Mt. Sinai Covenant* was between God and the soon to be Nation of Israel, both covenants were open to others. Abraham's servants who were circumcised participated in the blessings of the covenant[2] and any foreigners who accepted the conditions of the *Mt. Sinai Covenant* were also explicitly included in the covenant.[3]

There are many examples of this throughout the Scriptures. For example, neither of Moses' wives appear to have been descendants of Jacob. His first wife was from Midian and his second wife was from

Cush (Ethiopia).[4] Similarly, King David's great great grandmother was Rahab who had been a harlot in Jericho before she accepted the covenant. Likewise, King David's great grandmother was Ruth who was from Moab (a nation hostile to Israel) before she accepted the covenant.[5] Yet, they were all included in the covenant.

Even today it is widely acknowledged that Rabbinic Judaism is not a race. Anyone can convert to Judaism.[6] Jesus' followers hold to the same position. They merely maintain that the *New Covenant,* which Jesus taught, is the new covenant of *Judaism.*

> *The Rabbinic Jewish population in the world was small,*
> *so of course more converts would be coming from the Gentiles.*

Rabbinic Judaism had been highly effective in winning converts from the Gentiles up to the 1st century.[7] These converts were circumcised and baptized, offered a sacrifice and accepted the Torah. Then they were considered to be Jews, regardless of their ethnic backgrounds.

Jesus' followers took a similar view, with the following exceptions:

- Circumcision was not the sign of the *New Covenant.*

- Jesus was their atoning sacrifice for sin; not an animal.

- The Torah was seen as the definition of righteous living but not as the means of being accounted righteous by God.

But, just like Rabbinic Judaism, converts were accepted from every nation and ethnic background.

They reason that since there were more Gentiles in the world than Rabbinic Jews, it's reasonable to expect that more converts would come from the Gentiles.

If Jesus Really Is Messiah, Then The New Covenant Really Is Jewish

This argument at first sounds like circular reasoning. But, Jesus' followers do have a point: If Jesus really did fulfill all of the Scriptural prophecies about Messiah, especially rising from the dead, then he really is the Messiah. And, if he really is the Messiah, then the *New Covenant,* which he taught, really is the fulfillment of Jeremiah's and the other prophets' teachings about a new covenant to come. The bottom line would be that the *New Covenant* really is Judaism and anyone who accepts the *New Covenant* really is Jewish.

It was Pharisaic Judaism which defined Jesus' followers
as being non-Jewish

It was the Sanhedrin who rejected Jesus and it was the Pharisees who wrote him out of Rabbinic Judaism. What if they were wrong? What if they missed the real Messiah? After all, the Pharisees regarded the Saducees (the former priests) as heretics, waged theological war on the Karaites, and for generations rejected the Hassidic movement. They controlled the Rabbinic academies, the offices of Patriach in Palestine and Exilarch in Babylon, and the codification of the Mishnah and the Talmuds. What if, in their attempts to preserve the Judaism of the *Mt. Sinai Covenant,* they really did miss the Messiah and the *New Covenant?*

Jesus' followers point to modern-day Israel as a parallel. In 1997, the Agudath Ha-Rabonim (Ultra-Orthodox rabbis) made a pronounce-ment that the Reform and Conservative movements of Judaism are "outside of Torah and outside of Judaism."[8] Through this statement, they essentially took it upon themselves to declare that the beliefs of 79% of American Jews are non-Jewish. Jesus' followers state that this is essentially what happened during the 1st and 2nd centuries. They con-tend that the same desire to control the definition of orthodoxy in Judaism is at work, but what if they're wrong?

WOULDN'T GOD LET HIS PEOPLE IN ON WHO MESSIAH IS?

If Jesus really is Messiah, how could so many Rabbinic Jews not have understood it? Wouldn't everyone have known? Surely God wouldn't send Messiah without declaring it to all of Israel.

Jesus and his 1st century followers believed that God, in fact, did *not* let all of Israel understand who Messiah is. They claimed that Israel had become spiritually calloused and that God intentionally didn't let most Jews see and understand that Jesus is Messiah.

BLINDNESS ON THE PART OF RABBINIC JUDAISM

Jesus is recorded as saying that the people of Israel could not hear his message because of the callousness of their hearts. He contended that this was in fulfillment of Isaiah's prophecy in Isaiah 6:9-12:

> *The disciples came to him and asked, "Why do you speak to the people in parables?" He replied, "The knowledge of the secrets of the kingdom of heaven has been given to you, but not to them. Whoever has will be given more, and he will have an abundance. Whoever does not have, even what he has will be taken from him. This is why I speak to them in parables:*
> > *Though seeing, they do not see; though hearing, they do not hear or understand.*
>
> *In them is fulfilled the prophecy of Isaiah:*
> > *You will be ever hearing but never understanding; you will be ever seeing but never perceiving. For this people's heart has become calloused; they hardly hear with their ears, and they have closed their eyes. Otherwise they might see with their eyes, hear with their ears, understand with their hearts and turn, and I would heal them.*
> > > —Matthew 13:10-15 (NIV®)

Jesus' disciple John is recorded as further contending that it was God who allowed this spiritual blindness to occur:

> *Even after Jesus had done all these miraculous signs in their presence, they still would not believe in him. This was to fulfill the word of Isaiah the prophet:*
> > *"Lord, who has believed our message and to whom has the arm of the Lord been revealed?"*

*For this reason they could not believe, because, as Isaiah
says elsewhere:*

> *"He has blinded their eyes and deadened their
> hearts, so they can neither see with their eyes, nor
> understand with their hearts, nor turn— and I
> would heal them."*

*Isaiah said this because he saw Jesus' glory and spoke
about him. Yet at the same time many even among the
leaders believed in him.*

—John 12:37-43 (NIV®)

If this were really the case, does it mean that God rejected the Jews
and violated his own covenants and promises to Abraham and
Abraham's descendants? Rabbi Saul passionately claimed, in the quota-
tion that follows, that no, God did not reject Israel:

> *I ask then: Did God reject his people? By no means! I am
> an Israelite myself, a descendant of Abraham, from the
> tribe of Benjamin. God did not reject his people, whom
> he foreknew. Don't you know what the Scripture says in
> the passage about Elijah— how he appealed to God
> against Israel:*
>
>> *"Lord, they have killed your prophets and torn
>> down your altars; I am the only one left, and they
>> are trying to kill me"?*
>
> *And what was God's answer to him?*
>
>> *"I have reserved for myself seven thousand who
>> have not bowed the knee to Baal."*
>
> *So too, at the present time there is a remnant chosen by
> grace. And if by grace, then it is no longer by works; if it
> were, grace would no longer be grace. What then? What
> Israel sought so earnestly it did not obtain, but the elect
> did. The others were hardened, as it is written:*
>
>> *"God gave them a spirit of stupor, eyes so that*

they could not see and ears so that they could not hear, to this very day."

And David says:

"May their table become a snare and a trap, a stumbling block and a retribution for them. May their eyes be darkened so they cannot see, and their backs be bent forever."

Again I ask: Did they stumble so as to fall beyond recovery? Not at all! Rather, because of their transgression, salvation has come to the Gentiles to make Israel envious. But if their transgression means riches for the world, and their loss means riches for the Gentiles, how much greater riches will their fullness bring! I am talking to you Gentiles. Inasmuch as I am the apostle to the Gentiles, I make much of my ministry in the hope that I may somehow arouse my own people to envy and save some of them. For if their rejection is the reconciliation of the world, what will their acceptance be but life from the dead? If the part of the dough offered as firstfruits is holy, then the whole batch is holy; if the root is holy, so are the branches. If some of the branches have been broken off, and you, though a wild olive shoot, have been grafted in among the others and now share in the nourishing sap from the olive root, do not boast over those branches. If you do, consider this: You do not support the root, but the root supports you. You will say then, "Branches were broken off so that I could be grafted in." Granted. But they were broken off because of unbelief, and you stand by faith. Do not be arrogant, but be afraid. For if God did not spare the natural branches, he will not spare you either. Consider therefore the kindness and sternness of God: sternness to those who fell, but kindness to you, provided that you continue in his kind-

ness. Otherwise, you also will be cut off. And if they do not persist in unbelief, they will be grafted in, for God is able to graft them in again. After all, if you were cut out of an olive tree that is wild by nature, and contrary to nature were grafted into a cultivated olive tree, how much more readily will these, the natural branches, be grafted into their own olive tree! I do not want you to be ignorant of this mystery, brothers, so that you may not be conceited: Israel has experienced a hardening in part until the full number of the Gentiles has come in. And so all Israel will be saved, as it is written:

> *"The deliverer will come from Zion; he will turn godlessness away from Jacob. And this is my covenant with them when I take away their sins."*

—Romans 11:1-27 (NIV®)

Jesus' 1st century followers contended that this blindness was to be temporary. Many of his present-day followers agree and assert that the blindness is now being taken away. They point to the rising numbers of Messianic Jews as evidence of their contention.

MESSIANIC JUDAISM, ARE EYES OPENING?

As previously mentioned, there are about 250 Messianic Jewish congregations with possibly 100,000 members in the United States. This is about 1.6% of the U.S. Jewish population. There are also Messianic Congregations in about 20 other countries. Although this doesn't sound like many, it is. There are now more Messianic Jews than Reconstructionist Jews.

Some Christians believe that the growing number of Jews who are becoming followers of Jesus may be the beginning of broad acceptance by Jews of Jesus as the Jewish Messiah. They believe that God is taking away the "blindness" so that Jews can accept Jesus as Messiah. Their hope is for a reunification of the branches of Christianity and Judaism (Messianic-style) to refocus the followers of Jesus on the *New Covenant* that Jesus taught and its historic roots in the covenants that God made with Abraham, Isaac, Jacob and the nation of Israel.

BUT CHRISTIANS PERSECUTED JEWS!

The first response that many Jews have to the contention that Jesus' followers (Christians) are a branch of Judaism is, "but Christians persecuted Jews!" And, they're right. Christians did persecute Jew, and Jews also persecuted Christians. Clearly, neither group is without fault. From the 1st century on they have been theological opponents and each has behaved inappropriately toward the other.

But, the real question is, what is true? Christians concede that at many points in history their Christian predecessors failed. They acknowledge that many who claimed to be Christians persecuted Jews and, at times, even persecuted each other. But, they contend that this doesn't mean that Jesus is not who he claimed to be. They offer the following points to consider:

Those who persecuted Jews were not obeying Jesus

Jesus' 1st century disciples recorded that he taught them to love their enemies and to do good to those who meant them harm. He warned them that they would be persecuted and taught them to "turn the other cheek." He even set the example by not resisting his accusers and by not retaliating against those who sought to kill him.[9]

This was also the mindset of Jesus' early disciples. Historians confirm that when persecuted by the Jews, the Romans, and the Persians, the vast majority didn't retaliate. Nor did they persecute those who didn't agree with them.

Later generations of those calling themselves Christians who persecuted Jews (or anyone else) weren't following Jesus' teachings or the example set by his early followers.

Even the leaders of ancient Israel failed morally

Christians point to the many kings of Israel who failed and ask if their failures mean that God is not God and that His covenant with Israel is not true? They contend that the failures of the kings and people of ancient Israel doesn't mean that their covenant with God wasn't real. It just means that they failed. Some examples of their failure include:

Eli's sons—were corrupt priests[10]

King Solomon—in spite of his wisdom, disobeyed God by building places of worship for his many wives' false gods[11]

King Jeroboam—introduced false worship in the northern kingdom of Israel[12]

King Ahab—allowed and funded the worship of the false god, Baal[13]

King Ahaz—sacrificed his son to false gods[14]

King Manasseh—built altars to false gods in the Temple in Jerusalem, sacrificed his son to false gods, and killed the innocent[15]

The people of Israel—because of the sins of the people of the northern kingdom of Israel, God allowed them to be defeated by the Assyrians and taken away into captivity[16]

The people of Judah—God allowed the southern kingdom of Judah to be defeated because of their sins and taken away into captivity by the Babylonians [17]

Christians confess that many of their predecessors also failed.

The Politics of Kings and Empires

Christians also contend that much of the persecution directed at Jews was the result of the politics of kings and rivalries between empires. In many cases the same persecution was directed at both Christians and Jews. For example:

The Inquisition

The early targets of the Inquisition were the *Albigenses* and *Waldensians* in France in the 12th and 13th centuries. The *Albigenses* were a heretical semi-Christian sect and the *Waldensians* were Christians who were the forerunners of the *Protestants*. The *Roman Catholic Church* persecuted them both and had many burned at the stake.[18]

Similarly, the Inquisition in Spain during the 15th century was not primarily directed at Jews. It was directed at Jewish and Muslim *converts* to Christianity (*the conversos*). Jews who had not converted were not subjected to the Inquisition, they were expelled.

Expulsions

Probably no other people group on earth has been expelled from so many countries as the Jews. Jews were useful to kings because of their proven skills in trade, finance, medicine and administration. They frequently served as doctors and courtesans to kings. Yet, they were often viewed with distrust and were resented by the rest of the population. Jews had rejected the Christian Messiah, they assisted the Persians and the Moors in their conquests of Christian kingdoms, they extracted high interest rates, they were often wealthy, they served as tax collectors, and they generally remained separated from the rest of society.[19] In this generally anti-Semitic environment, a change in leadership could result in their ouster from a kingdom, and it often did.

It was common in medieval Europe for Kings to expel any person or group from their kingdom that didn't meet their approval. Monarchs were supreme. For the most part, there were no civil rights. And, Jews weren't alone in being the victims of expulsions:

- Count Leopold Von Firmian of Salzburg, Austria, who was both a Count and a Catholic Archbishop, expelled 22,000 *Lutherans* in 1731. This was after 30,000 *Lutherans* had already fled in 1723.

- King Louis XIV made *Protestant Christianity* illegal in France in 1685. This forced them to leave the country in droves.[20]

State Ordered Violence

It was also common for Kings to use force to rid their realms of unwanted subjects or ideologies. Again, both Jews and Christians were victims:

- Queen Catherine de Medici of France ordered the deaths of Huguenot (*Calvinist Christian*) leaders in Paris in 1572. By the time the violence ended, 30,000 to 100,000 Huguenots were dead.[21]

- In the Netherlands, the Spanish Duke of Alva killed thousands of dissident *Calvinist* Christians in 1567.[22] Some estimate that between 50,000 to 100,000 Christians died.

The Crusades

The 1st Crusade to liberate the Holy Land from Islam was initiated in 1095 by Pope Urban II at the request of the Byzantine Emperor. The military advance of the Islamic Ottoman Turks was dangerously close to Constantinople and Emperor Alexis needed western help in pushing them back. There were several crusades to free the Holy Land. It was during the first that mob violence erupted against the Jews in the Rhineland; the subsequent crusades were also accompanied by violence against Jews.[23]

But these weren't the only crusades. There were crusades against the pagans threatening the Baltic churches of Prussia, Estonia, Livonia and Finland starting in 1199; against Markward of Anweiler in 1199; against the Moors in Spain in 1212, and against the invading Mongols in 1241.[24] And there were others.

But of all the medieval crusades, none actually targeted the Jews. Much of the persecution that Jews fell victim to was from anti-Semitic mob violence and armies run amok. This may seem of little consolation, but it is significant because there was little hesitation to initiate theological crusades against those perceived to be heretics and separatists Christians:

- Pope Innocent III ordered a crusade against the *Albigenses* in France in 1209 after the papal legate sent to them was murdered.[25] In the four years that followed, about 200,000 *Albigenses* were killed.[26]

- A crusade against peasant 'heretics' in Germany was fought in 1234.

- Popes Honorius III and Gregory IX authorized crusades against 'heretics' in Bosnia in 1227 and 1234. [27]

- In 1420, Pope Martin ordered a crusade against the *Hussites,* who were Christian dissenters, in Bohemia.[28]

Again, no similar crusades were called against Jews.

The Holocaust

Well before the infamous Crystal Night in November 1938, when the Nazis burned 177 Jewish synagogues, a large percentage of the German population and the Christian Church had already been silenced. Freedom of speech was rescinded in 1933. In the same year, an effective police state was imposed and the concentration camp at Dachau was opened to house political dissenters. Journalists were among the first arrested.[29]

Hitler detested Christianity but sought to manipulate both *Protestants* and *Roman Catholics* to achieve his objective of a Third Empire. He nationalized the *German Evangelical Church* (the federation of *Lutheran, Reformed,* and *United territorial* churches) in 1933, forming the *Reich Church,* and took control of its leadership. Dissenting pastors responded by forming an emergency league and sending a letter of protest signed by 6,000 clergy to Hitler. They were countered by a muzzling order from the *Reich Bishop* and a scathing meeting with Hitler after which a dissident leader's residence was bombed. In the midst of this intimidation, about 2,000 pastors resigned from the league, but many of the others formed the *Confessing Church* in 1934. They actively protested what they viewed as the pagan theology of the *Reich Church* and Nazi encroachments into the church. Hitler had little patience for them. A memo of protest to him in 1936 resulted in the arrest and imprisonment of 800 clergy of the *Confessing Church.* Then, in early 1938, the Nazi government required that all pastors sign a personal oath of allegiance to Hitler. The few pastors who did not comply joined those already in concentration camps.[30]

After initially trying to deal with him, the *Catholic Church* also resisted Hitler. From 1933 to 1936, Pope Pius XI objected to the government of Germany thirty-four times for restrictions on religious liberties.[31] He also had a denunciation of Nazi neo-paganism smuggled into Germany and read in the *Catholic Churches* in 1937.[32] When Italy issued anti-Semitic laws in 1938, he spoke out repeatedly, saying:

"It [anti-Semitism] is a deplorable movement, a movement in which we, as Christians, must have no part."[33]

Albert Einstein actually wrote that the Christian Church in Germany was the one institution that raised the greatest resistance to Hitler:

> Being a lover of freedom, when the [Nazi] revolution came I looked to the universities to defend it, knowing that they had always boasted of their devotion to the cause of truth; but no, the universities were immediately silenced. Then I looked to the great editors of the newspapers, whose flaming editorials in days gone by had proclaimed their love of freedom; but they, like the universities were silenced in a few short weeks...Only the Church stood squarely across the path of Hitler's campaign for suppressing the truth. I never had any special interest in the Church before, but now I feel a great affection and admiration for it because the Church alone has had the courage and persistence to stand for intellectual and moral freedom. I am forced to confess that what I once despised I now praise unreservedly.[34]

There were anti-Semites among the Protestant and Catholic clergy in Germany. That is clear. But it is also clear that the Christian Church was the one institution that continued to resist Hitler long after others had been silenced.

Christians Also Protected Jews

Finally, Christians point out that many of Jesus' followers have come to the aid of Jewish people through the centuries. For example:

- Constantine granted Jews a place as the only recognized religion other than Christianity in the Roman Empire.

- Charlemagne granted considerable religious freedom and protection to Jews.

- Pope Gregory the Great (590–604) prohibited the mistreatment of Jews.[35] His prohibition was reissued in various forms by fifteen subsequent popes.

- During the first crusade, the Bishop of Spier hanged the ringleaders behind violence against Jews. The Archbishop of Cologne also stopped the rioters.

- In 1063, Pope Alexander II defended the Jews of southern France and Spain who had suffered during the crusade against the Moors in Sicily and Spain. He prohibited the mistreatment of Jews.[36]

- Pope Clement VI defended the Jews in 1348–49 by issuing a bull stating that the devil was responsible for the Black Death plague, not the Jews. King Peter of Aragon, Emperor Charles IV and other leaders issued similar pronouncements.[37]

- Pope Martin V (1413–1431) opposed anti-Semitic preaching and prohibited forced baptism of Jewish children[38]

- The Netherlands gave both Christian *Pilgrims* and Jews sanctuary in the 1600s.

- Many Christians protected Jews during the Holocaust: priests in the *Bulgarian Orthodox Church* performed mass 'conversions' to hide Jews,[39] *Lutheran* Denmark ferried 7,000 Jews to safety in Sweden; Christians in the Netherlands hid Jews in their homes, and Swedish diplomat Raoul Wallenberg, a Protestant Christian, saved 100,000 Jews in Hungary.

Christians don't raise these points to excuse the sins of the past. They admit that people who professed to be Christians did persecute Jews. They fostered anti-Semitism; restricted religious liberties; attempted forced baptisms and conversions; required Jews to wear distinctive dress; taxed them unfairly; expelled Jews from their nations; relegated Jews to ghettos, and even killed them. People who called themselves Christians did repeatedly persecute the Jews. But, Christians contend, that is not what Jesus taught and it is not what his noblest followers did. Those who persecuted Jews were wrong.

CONCLUSIONS

Jesus' followers contend that Christianity is the *New Covenant* of Judaism. They say that God kept many in the nation of Israel from seeing it and ushered in a new era of grace toward the Gentiles. But, they say that the blindness of Israel was to be temporary and contend that the Messianic Jewish movement is evidence that it may be ending. They say that the Hebrew Scriptures will be fulfilled, and that all of Israel will be saved.

Jesus ' followers also readily confess that many of their predecessors unjustly persecuted the Jewish people. But, they contend that this is not what Jesus taught or what his early disciples practiced. They confess that those who persecuted Jews were wrong. They also point to the failures of ancient Israel in following God and say that, like them, the failures of their predecessors do not invalidate the truth that Jesus is Messiah.

16

Is There Proof?

If Jesus really is the Messiah and his *New Covenant* really is true, then we should expect that there would be evidence to support it. Surely something so significant would have a factual basis to support the legitimacy of its claim.

As you might expect, Jesus' followers contend that there is a solid base of evidence to conclude that he is the Messiah. But, other groups make similar claims. Menachem Mendel Schneersen's followers claim that they have evidence to support that he's the Messiah. Both groups can't be correct. It's obvious that their evidence should be tested. So, how do we do it?

A good way to test the evidence presented in support of Christianity or any other "religious group" is to apply the same tests that support the validity of 1st century Judaism.

What Is the Evidence for Judaism?

The evidence to support the legitimacy of 1st century Judaism is compelling. Archaeologists, historians, theologians, and scientists have spent centuries evaluating the claims of Judaism. They have assessed the Hebrew Scriptures' history, theology, prophecy, science, and textual reliability. In every category, Judaism has borne up well under evaluation.

To demonstrate this, an overview of a few categories of these assessments include the following:

HISTORICAL ACCURACY

The Hebrew Scriptures are remarkable in that they not only describe theology; they are also the story of God's relationship with the world, with his nation of priests (Israel), with other nations, and with individual men, women, and children. And, the theology is so interwoven with the story of these relationships, that the truth of the Scriptures cannot be separated from the truth of the people and events described. To put it another way: if the people and events described in the Scriptures are not true, then the theology isn't true either.

Archaeology and third-party historians, however, have provided a wealth of evidence to support the accuracy of the stories of the Scriptures. There really was a King David.[1] Ruins of cities that fit the description of the account of Sodom and Gomorrah really have been found.[2] Jabin, the king of Hazor, and Japhia, the king of Gezer, really lived in the 14th century BCE.[3] There really was a 9th century BCE king of Israel named Jehu the son of Omri.[4] Assyrian King Sennacherib really did besiege Jerusalem.[5] King Cyrus of Persia really did issue a decree allowing Jews to rebuild the Temple in Jerusalem.[6] There really were other nations of people called Hitties, Moabites, and Canaanites.[7] There really were cities named Ur, Jericho, Ashkelon, Hazor, Shechem, and Dan.[8] The volume of evidence is immense. And, while the historical accuracy of the Hebrew Scriptures of itself doesn't conclusively prove their theological accuracy, it is evidence, without which, the theological claims of the Scriptures would have little credibility.

FULFILLED PROPHECIES

According to the Hebrew Scriptures, the mark of a true prophet of God is whether or not what they claim will happen does happen. Applying this same measure, a mark of true Scripture from God would also be whether or not the prophecy it contains actually happens.

The Hebrew Scriptures excel so incredibly using this measure that most debate now centers on the date of authorship rather than the accuracy of its prophecy. This is because the prophecy it contains is so accurate, when compared to actual historical events, that some scholars find it easier to believe that it was written after the events actually happened.

A good example of this is the prophet Daniel, a contemporary of the prophet Ezekiel during the reign of King Nebuchadnezzar of Babylon. Daniel prophesied in the 6th century BCE that the Babylonian Empire would be conquered by the Medo-Persian Empire and that it would in turn, be overtaken by the Greeks. He further said that the Greek Empire would split into four parts and he provided details on the conflicts that would ensue between two of the factions. All of these things actually happened, as prophesied. The Persians did defeat the Babylonians in 539 BCE. Alexander the Great then defeated the Persians in 331 BCE. After his death, Alexander's kingdom was split among four of his generals: Ptolemy, Seleucas, Lysimachus, and Cassander. And, as prophesied, Ptolemy (Egypt) and Seleucas (Syria) became adversaries.

The prophecies of Daniel are so accurate that Porphyry, a 3rd century atheist, theorized that the book of Daniel was a 2nd century fake. It's legitimacy, however, was confirmed when a copy of Daniel was found among the 1st and 2nd century BCE Dead Sea Scrolls written about four hundred years before it was supposedly faked.[9]

TEXTUAL RELIABILITY

What is meant by 'reliability' is the certainty that the copies are an accurate reflection of the original writings.

There are at least two general tests that can be applied. The first is based on the number of manuscript copies that still exist from close to the date of the original writing. Using this criteria, if many copies of a manuscript still exist from close to the date of the original and the copies match each other, it is more likely that the copies were accurately transcribed from the original. A second test is to look at the methods employed in making copies. If a controlled process of copying manuscripts was used, one tends to have greater confidence in the text's authenticity than if no controls existed at all.

The Hebrew Scriptures do especially well when applying the second test. The methods and controls applied by the scribes and later by the Massoretes were exacting. Sir Frederic G. Kenyon, the former director of the British Museum attested to their methods of transmitting the Scriptures:

> Besides recording varieties of reading, tradition, or con-
> jecture, the Massoretes undertook a number of calcula-
> tions which do not enter into the ordinary sphere of tex-
> tual criticism. They numbered the verses, words, and let-
> ters of every book. They calculated the middle word and
> middle letter of each. They enumerated verses which
> contained all the letters of the alphabet, or a certain
> number of them; and so on. These trivialities, as we may
> rightly consider them, had the effect of securing minute
> attention to the precise transmission of the text; and they
> are but an excessive manifestation of a respect for the
> sacred Scriptures which in itself deserves nothing but
> praise. The Massoretes were indeed anxious that not one
> jot nor tittle—not one smallest letter or one tiny part of
> a letter—of the Law should pass away or be lost.[10]

The accuracy of transmission is borne out by the 202 biblical manuscripts that were found among the Dead Sea Scrolls.[11] Before this archaeological discovery, the oldest copy of Isaiah was from the 10th century. One copy of Isaiah found among the Dead Sea Scrolls, however, was dated from the 2nd century BCE. After comparing the two, using one chapter as an example, it was found that after over 1,000 years there was essentially only one word different (three letters) in the chapter between the two manuscripts.[12]

Robert Dick Wilson, a theologian from Westminster Seminary in Philadelphia, attested to the accuracy of transmission of the Hebrew Scriptures:

> In 144 cases of transliteration from Egyptian, Assyrian,
> Babylonian and Moabite into Hebrew and in 40 cases of

the opposite, or 184 in all, the evidence shows that for 2300 to 3900 years the text of the proper names in the Hebrew Bible has been transmitted with the most minute accuracy. That the original scribes should have written them with such close conformity to correct philological principles is a wonderful proof of their thorough care and scholarship; further, that the Hebrew text should have been transmitted by copyists through so many centuries is a phenomenon unequaled in the history of literature.[12]

EVIDENCE TO SUPPORT MIRACULOUS EVENTS

In addition to the historical and archeological evidence, which confirms the historical accuracy of the Hebrew Scriptures, there is also a significant amount of evidence to support the miraculous events recorded in the Scriptures. For example, evidence suggests that there really was a cataclysmic flood.[14] The walls of Jericho really did fall outward.[15] Cities matching the descriptions of Sodom and Gomorrah really did exist and really were destroyed by fire and buried in ash.[16] Sennacherib really did besiege Jerusalem during the reign of King Hezekiah and then unexpectedly broke off his campaign, like the Scriptures say, and returned home.[17]

Again, this evidence may not conclusively prove that the miracles recorded in the Scriptures really occurred. However, the evidence is extremely consistent with these and the many other miracles described.

CONSISTENCY OF THE AUTHORS' HISTORY AND THEOLOGY

There are many books of the Hebrew Scriptures (the *Tanakh*) which were written by contemporaries or which describe the same historical events. For example, Ezekiel and Daniel were both prophets that were taken captive and exiled in Babylon during Nebuchadnezzar's reign, and both 1st and 2nd Kings and 1st and 2nd Chronicles describe the same historical events. By comparing the consistency of the statements made by these authors, conclusions can be reached about the reliability of their theology. The assumption being, that if the history contained in the books of the Hebrew Scriptures is contradictory, their theology is likely not reliable either.

In actuality the theology and history of the Hebrew Scriptures are remarkably consistent. The themes of God's righteousness and forgiveness; sacrificial atonement; God in relationship (covenant) with man; blessing from obedience to God and disaster from disobedience; redemption; Messiah; the triumph of good over evil; heaven, and the resurrection of man after death are consistent throughout the Scriptures. This is especially remarkable since the 39 books of the Hebrew Scriptures were written by people from all walks of life over a span of about 1,000 years. Even detailed prophecies are theologically consistent. For example, the prophecies about Messiah which were written by Malachi, Ezekiel, Daniel, Isaiah, Jeremiah and Zechariah—over a span of 3 centuries—all fit within a consistent theology.

The Lives Of The Authors

An additional test for the truthfulness of any historical document is the credibility of its author as judged by the life they lived.

It's obviously difficult to obtain evidence about the lives of the authors of the Hebrew Scriptures thousands of years after their deaths. This is especially true for those who were neither kings nor people of prominence. But, there is internal evidence in the Scriptures themselves. For example, several authors attest to the righteous lives and prophet credentials of other authors:

- Ezekiel described his contemporary Daniel as being a righteous man.[18]

- Daniel and the author of 2 Chronicles considered Jeremiah to be a prophet.[19]

- The authors of 2 Chronicles and 2 Kings considered Isaiah to be a prophet.[20]

- Ezra considered Haggai to be a prophet.[21]

Perhaps even more telling, however, is their forthrightness in describing their own failings and imperfections as they sought to follow

God. In addition to their great successes, they had some great failures: Moses killed an Egyptian, Elijah ran from evil Queen Jezebel, King David committed adultery, and Gideon was afraid to tear down his father's altar to the pagan god Baal.[22] This apparent honesty makes texts like the Hebrew Scriptures, which convey the good and bad, strengths and weaknesses, of the authors and others appear to be more plausible that those which do not.

The Hebrew Scriptures convey the history of God's interactions with people who (though imperfectly) learned to walk with God.

SCIENTIFIC STATEMENTS

While there will likely be debate about the origins of the universe for years to come, the core scientific statements within the Hebrew Scriptures appear to have a solid scientific basis. They record that:

- God created the universe out of nothing. Whether this is called the "big bang" or not, it is consistent with the view that everything (matter and energy) did have a beginning.

- Life didn't just happen, it was designed. This is consistent with the Law of Biogenesis.

- All people on earth had common ancestry. Genetic studies suggest that this is true.[23]

- There was a monumental flood, which has been established.

- The sphere of the earth doesn't sit on anything, and it doesn't.[24]

The Scriptural theme of creation is obviously worthy of an extended discussion and there are many noteworthy books on this topic.[25] However, suffice it to say, there is voluminous evidence to support a God-directed creation view.

SUMMARY

On balance, there is a significant body of evidence to support the validity of the Hebrew Scriptures. So much so, that is seems logical to conclude that the theology they describe is also true. But how do the Christian Scriptures stand up under these same tests of evidence?

WHAT IS THE EVIDENCE FOR CHRISTIANITY?

When the question is asked, "What evidence is there to support the validity of Christianity," there are really many questions being asked. The primary questions are whether there is evidence to support that:

- Jesus is the Messiah

- Jesus is God in the flesh

- Jesus really did die as a sacrifice for the sins of mankind

- Jesus did rise from the dead, appeared to his followers, and ascended into heaven

- the *New Covenant* is really true

Using the same tests that have been historically used to assess the validity of Judaism as recorded in the Hebrew Scriptures, let's see how Christianity as recorded in the Christian Scriptures compares.

HISTORICAL ACCURACY

Jesus' followers point out that, like the Hebrew Scriptures, the *New Testament* provides an incredible volume of details. These details include: historical events within the Roman Empire, Judea, and Galilee; the names of political leaders, religious leaders, and average people; the names, locations, and physical proximity of cities and towns; social customs; and religious observances. Both books convey theology *and* history. In fact, they provide so much detail that they invite evaluation of their historical accuracy—both of the direct events and the historical context described.

The *New Testament* has been critically evaluated for centuries and has also borne up well through the process. For example, one of the world's greatest archeologists, Sir William Ramsay, after many years of evaluation, concluded that the historical details recorded by Luke were unsurpassed in trustworthiness:

> Luke is a historian of the first rank; not merely are his statements of fact trustworthy...this author should be

placed along with the greatest of historians. [26]

This statement about Luke is especially significant in that he wrote both the *Gospel of Luke* and the *Acts of the Apostles*. He and Rabbi Saul (Paul) actually both wrote more words of text in the *New Testament* than any of its other authors.

While the accuracy of the history recorded in the *New Testament* doesn't prove that Jesus is the Messiah, his followers claim that it attests to the reliability of the people (like Luke) who claimed that he is—it is evidence.

TEXTUAL RELIABILITY

Using this test, the *New Testament* actually surpasses all other ancient manuscripts. By having more copies available which were made closer to the reported date of authorship and bearing greater consistency than any other text, it is the most reliable of all ancient manuscripts.

According to Bruce Metzger, chairman of the Revised Standard Version Bible Committee, there are 5,664 ancient Greek manuscript copies of the *New Testament* today. The oldest fragment, five verses of the *Gospel of John,* was found in Egypt and has been dated at 100 to 150 CE. In addition to these texts, there are over 8,000 Latin manuscripts and collectively about 8,000 ancient Ethiopian, Slavic and Armenian manuscript copies. By comparison, the ancient document with the second greatest number of copies in existence is Homer's Iliad with about 650 Greek manuscript copies in existence and the oldest fragment of it in existence is dated roughly 1,000 years after Homer wrote it.[27]

Even without the manuscript copies, it's possible to reconstruct almost the entire *New Testament* from the quotations imbedded in the writings of the early church fathers. These were the 2nd and 3rd century leaders of the earliest Christian churches.[28]

Sir Frederic G. Kenyon, is quoted as saying:

> The interval then between the dates of original composition and the extant evidence becomes so small as to be in fact negligible, and the last foundation for any doubt that the Scriptures have come down to us substantially as

they were written has now been removed. Both the
authenticity and the general integrity of the books of the
New Testament may be regarded as finally established.[29]

Scholars do point out that there are many minor variants between
the thousands of ancient manuscripts. However, where there have been
differences between ancient manuscripts, such as in word order—which
the ancient Greek language allows—there have been no Christian doctrines compromised.[30] In 95% of the cases, the meaning of the passage
hasn't changed.[31]

Again, this doesn't prove that Jesus is the Messiah, but his followers
say that it does mean that what his 1st century followers wrote about
him hasn't been changed. They say that it is evidence that the original
eyewitness accounts of Jesus' life have not been altered.

EVIDENCE TO SUPPORT MIRACULOUS EVENTS

JESUS' MIRACLES

As mentioned previously, a primary reason why Jesus' disciples
believed that Jesus is the Messiah is the miracles they claimed to have
witnessed. They even cited the names of people they claimed were
healed and raised from the dead by Jesus. But, while it's difficult two
thousand years later to corroborate their written accounts, the fact
that they did actually name people and their city of residence is
viewed as evidence in its own right. Jesus' present-day followers contend that, if the New Testament writers were lying, they would have
been easily exposed by being so specific. The locals would have
known that it was fiction.

Jesus' followers also point to Flavius Josephus and to the Talmud as
evidence to support that something miraculous was happening.
Josephus, writing in the 1st century, said that Jesus was a "doer of wonderful works."[32] In contrast, the 5th century Babylonian Talmud called
Jesus a sorcerer,[33] evidently attributing the reported miracles to tricks or
magic. Both references, however, are evidence that something unusual
was happening.

One of the more interesting documents in support of Jesus' miracles, however, is a letter reportedly written by Agbarus, the prince of Edessa, in the 1st century. It was found in the public records of the city of Edessa and translated by Eusebius, the 3rd and 4th century historian in his book, *Ecclesiastical History*. The letter was a couriered message from Agbarus to Jesus:

> Agbarus, prince of Edessa, sends greeting to Jesus the excellent Savior, who has appeared in the borders of Jerusalem. I have heard the reports respecting thee and thy cures, as performed by thee without medicines and without the use of herbs. For as it is said, thou causest the blind to see again, the lame to walk, and thou cleansest the lepers, and thou castest out impure spirits and demons, and thou healest those that are tormented by long disease, and thou raisest the dead. And hearing all these things of thee, I concluded in my mind one of two things: either that thou art God, and having descended from heaven, doest these things, or else doing them, thou art the son of God. Therefore, now I have written and besought thee to visit me, and to heal the disease with which I am afflicted. I have, also, heard that the Jews murmur against thee, and are plotting to injure thee; I have, however, a very small but noble state, which is sufficient for us both.[34]

This letter is significant in that Jesus' fame as a healer had reached beyond the Euphrates to Edessa. It is also significant because Eusebius reported that the same archives record that a follower of Jesus named Thaddeus did go to Agbarus after Jesus' death and healed Agbarus of his illness.

MIRACULOUS EVENTS IN NATURE

Events that occur in nature are often easier to corroborate, since they're often observed by a large number of people. Frequently, more than one person has recorded the same event.

In the case of Jesus, his followers point to third-party sources to confirm the reported miracles in nature that occurred during his crucifixion. There are 1st and 3rd century sources that support the claims that a solar eclipse[35] and an earthquake[36] occurred while Jesus was being crucified. Of course, it could have been coincidence that both events occurred during the same time frame as Jesus' execution and that they weren't a confirmation of his deity. But, Jesus followers contend that this was not the case.

CONSISTENCY OF THE AUTHORS' HISTORY AND THEOLOGY

Like the Hebrew Scriptures, Jesus' followers' theology, as recorded in the *New Testament,* is remarkably consistent. Assuming that Rabbi Saul (Paul) wrote the *letter to the Hebrews,* there were eight authors of the twenty-seven 'books' of the *New Testament.* These authors included three of Jesus' earliest disciples (Matthew, Peter, and John), two 'second wave' followers (Luke and Mark), a former enemy (Rabbi Saul), and two of Jesus' 'half-brothers' (James and Jude).

Saul (Paul) was a highly educated rabbi and a Roman citizen. Peter and John were uneducated Galilean fishermen. Matthew was a tax collector. Luke was a Greek medical doctor and accompanied Paul on several missionary journeys. Mark (John Mark), who was evidently from Jerusalem, was a relative of the apostle Barnabas and was close to Peter. Jude and James were from Galilee and, like their father, were probably carpenters. But, in spite of their differences in education, profession, social position, and nationality, the events and theology that they recorded are, in fact, remarkably consistent.

History

The events recorded by the authors of the *New Testament* are actually very consistent. By just comparing three 'books' or letters of the *New Testament,* this point must be conceded to Jesus' followers. F.F. Bruce, professor of biblical criticism and exegesis at the University of Manchester, provides attestation to this fact:

> It requires no very detailed study to discover that these three have a considerable amount of material in common.

> We find, for example, that the substance of 606 out of 661
> verses of Mark appears in Matthew, and that some 350 of
> Mark's verses reappear with little material change in Luke.
> Or, to put it another way, out of the 1,068 verses of
> Matthew, about 500 contain material also found in Mark;
> of the 1,149 verses of Luke, about 350 are paralleled in
> Mark. Altogether, there are only 31 verses in Mark which
> have no parallel either in Matthew or Luke.[37]

The authors of the *New Testament* each recorded events that were viewed to be significant. They didn't all uniformly include every event. But when they did describe the same events, they were consistent.

Theology

The theology recorded by the authors of the *New Testament* also seems to be internally consistent. For example:

- Matthew, Mark, Luke, John and Saul all called Jesus the son of David.[38]

- Seven of the eight authors called Jesus the Messiah (Christ means Messiah).[39]

- All eight authors called Jesus Lord.[40]

- Six authors called Jesus the *"Son of God"*.[41] The other two described him as *"glorious Lord"* and *"Sovereign."*[42]

- Saul and John explicitly said, multiple times, that Jesus is God.[43]

- Seven authors said that Jesus died on the cross as a sacrifice to enable mankind to have forgiveness for sin and spiritual salvation.[44]

- All eight authors spoke of the Holy Spirit being at work in the lives of Jesus' followers.[45]

- Three authors, Matthew, Mark, and Saul, spoke of a *New Covenant* with God through Jesus.[46]

- Six authors stated that Jesus had fulfilled the prophecies of the Scriptures and/or the requirements of the Law.[47]

- All of the authors said that Jesus will return from heaven.[48]

- Four authors, Peter, Luke, John and Saul, said that Jesus will reign as king of kings forever.[49]

In addition to noting the points where these authors made theological statements that were in agreement, it is also worth noting that they did not make any theological statements that contradicted one another. For example, while only five authors explicitly said that Jesus is the descendant of King David, the other three didn't say that he wasn't. They didn't say anything at all on the topic.

The two *New Testament* authors who are most frequently cited for an apparent inconsistency in theology are Saul and James. Saul said that we are only saved from judgment by God's unmerited favor (God's grace) through putting our *"faith"* in Messiah Jesus. He further said that this 'salvation' is not based upon our *"works."*[50] James, however, contended that, *"faith by itself, if it is not accompanied by actions is dead."*[51] Consequently, many have concluded that this indicates a theological inconsistency. But, it seems evident from Luke's account of the first church council in Jerusalem that James was in agreement with Saul.[52] James appears to have been emphasizing that if people have faith it should be *evidenced* by their actions. If not, they don't really believe what they claim. It doesn't appear that he believed that people could achieve 'salvation' based upon their own efforts or good deeds.

In addition to being internally consistent, Jesus' followers contend that the theology recorded in the *New Testament* is also consistent with the Hebrew Scriptures (the *Tanakh*). They quoted frequently from the three sections of the Scriptures: the Law, the Prophets and the Writings. They also contended that Jesus had fulfilled the prophecies about Messiah in the Scriptures. But they would also likely acknowledge that they were carrying a 'new' message (or gospel) which included several elements that were rooted in the Hebrew Scriptures.

What was "new" about their message?

The 'new' element of Jesus' teaching and his followers' message essentially was that:

- The Messiah is here, now.
- The *New Covenant* is here, now.
- The Law is still valid, but:
  —While obeying the Law is an act of *faith* in God, merely obeying the Law doesn't give you a relationship with God and secure your forgiveness, your *faith* in God does.
  —Circumcision is not the sign of the *New Covenant,* Jesus' blood shed on the cross is.
  —The requirements in the Law of a sacrifice for sin were *fulfilled* by Jesus. He came into the world to die as the Passover sacrifice. But, the gift of his sacrifice must be *accepted* to have any effect.
- The promise of the Holy Spirit, as part of the *New Covenant,* is here now.

Probably the most dramatic element of this theology to 1st century Judaism was its claim that the Messiah and the *New Covenant* were here now! And, this Messiah wasn't primarily here as a conquering king, he was here as a sacrificial savior to pay the price for mankind's sin. And, not only that, they said that this Messiah is God!

All of the writers of the *New Testament* were consistent in this basic message. And, while their consistency doesn't prove that their theology or message is true, a lack of consistency would definitely discredit their message.

THIRD-PARTY CONFIRMATION OF JESUS' TEACHINGS

It is possible that the writers of the New Testament all got together and fabricated the entire story. Jesus' initial apostles (Matthew, John and Peter), the second wave of his followers (Mark and Luke), his family (James and Jude), and his enemy, Saul, could have all gotten together to create the story of the events of Jesus' life, his teachings, his crucifixion, and his resurrection from the dead. It's possible. Jesus' followers contend, however, that it isn't likely.

Among the evidence that they point to is a third-party confirmation of Jesus' teachings that was recorded while Jesus was still alive. In the same archives that recorded the Prince of Edessa's letter to Jesus, requesting that he come to heal the prince, was Jesus' reply. The courier recorded Jesus' answer as follows:

> Blessed art thou, O Agbarus, who, without seeing, hast believed in me. For it is written concerning me, that they who have seen me will not believe, that they who have not seen may believe and live. But in regard to what thou hast written, that I should come to thee, it is necessary that I should fulfill all things here, for which I have been sent. And after this fulfillment, thus to be received again by Him that sent me. And after I have been received up, I will send to thee a certain one of my disciples, that he may heal thy affliction, and give life to thee and to those who are with thee.[53]

In the response are many of the same theological points that the New Testament quotes Jesus as having said. For example:

Response to Agbarus	New Testament
Blessed art thou, O Agbarus, who, without seeing, hast believed in me.	*Then Jesus told him, "Because you have seen me, you have believed; blessed are those who have not seen and yet have believed."* —John 20:29
...it is written concerning me, that they who have seen me will not believe, that they who have not seen may believe and live.	*This is why I speak to them in parables: "Though seeing, they do not see; though hearing, they do not hear or understand. In them is fulfilled the prophecy of Isaiah: "'You will be ever hearing but never understanding; you will be ever seeing but never perceiving.*

Response to Agbarus	*New Testament*
	For this people's heart has become calloused; they hardly hear with their ears, and they have closed their eyes. Otherwise they might see with their eyes, hear with their ears, understand with their hearts and turn, and I would heal them." —Matthew 13:13-15
...it is necessary that I should fulfill all things here, for which I have been sent.	"My food," said Jesus, "is to do the will of him who sent me and to finish his work. —John 4:34
...after this fulfillment, thus to be received again by Him that sent me.	Jesus said, "I am with you for only a short time, and then I go to the one who sent me. —John 7:33
	I came from the Father and entered the world; now I am leaving the world and going back to the Father." —John 16:28
...after I have been received up, I will send to thee a certain one of my disciples, that he may heal thy affliction	When Jesus had called the Twelve together, he gave them power and authority to drive out all demons and to cure diseases, and he sent them out to preach the kingdom of God and to heal the sick. —Luke 9:1-2
...and give life to thee and to those who are with thee.	For I have come down from heaven not to do my will but to do the will of him who sent me. And this is the will of him who sent me, that I shall lose none of all that he has given me, but raise them up at the last day. For my Father's will is that everyone who looks to the Son and believes in him shall have eternal life, and I will raise him up at the last day." —John 6:38-40

We do know that Edessa really was the capital of the small kingdom of Osrhoene, a buffer state between the Roman Empire and Persia. We also know that Abgar the Black (Agbarus) was its king at the time of Jesus, and that a Thaddeus (Addai in Syriac), a follower of Jesus, brought Christianity to the kingdom.[54] Given the accuracy of these details, it's possible that Eusebius' record of the Edessa archives is accurate. If it is correct, it is confirmation that Jesus' theology was not fabricated by his disciples after his death.

THE LIVES OF THE AUTHORS

A significant point made by Jesus' present-day followers is that his 1st century followers lived like they believed that Jesus was God, that he had risen from the dead, and that his *New Covenant* was true. This may seem like a trivial point at first. There have been many false Messiahs who convinced many people to follow them. Simon Bar–Kokbha evidently had Rabbi Akiva, the 2nd century Torah scholar, convinced that he was the Messiah. The difference is that after Simon Bar–Kokhba was killed by the Romans, he had no more followers.

The same is true of Theudas in the 1st century and David Reubeni in the 16th century. After they were killed, they had no more followers. But, after Jesus was executed by the Romans, his followers claimed that he rose from the dead and that they and hundreds of other people saw him over a forty-day period of time. They say that he taught them, telling them that he would return at the end of the age, and then ascended up into heaven. This, of course, could have all been a lie. But, Jesus' followers point out, that *it would have been such a monumental lie that most of his followers would have known it*. Yet, they didn't live like it was a lie:

- They quit their professions to travel throughout the world proclaiming that Jesus is Messiah.
- They suffered extreme persecution at the hands of the Jewish Sanhedrin, the Romans, and even the Greeks.
- They didn't personally gain wealth, prestige, or power from their efforts.
- They didn't seek to use religion for political purposes to overthrow either the Romans or the Sanhedrin; they didn't even participate in

the Jewish revolts against Rome
- They spent the rest of their lives insisting that Jesus rose from the dead.
- Many of them were killed because of their beliefs (James, Stephen, Saul, Peter, Mark, James the brother of Jesus, Thomas, etc.).
- They lived selfless lives preaching that man can be reconciled to God through Jesus (God in the flesh) and that we should live lives of forgiveness and love for one another.
- None of them recanted their faith in Jesus.

Jesus' present-day followers contend that, if Jesus' resurrection were a fraud, that Jesus' followers would have known it and they wouldn't have lived lives like this. They say that this is evidence for the truth of Jesus' resurrection.

FULFILLED PROPHECIES

Jesus' followers claim that his life fulfilled the prophecies about Messiah that were recorded in the Hebrew Scriptures. In addition to this, they also point out that Jesus himself prophesied many things. They cite these prophecies as evidence that he passed the test of a prophet. Jesus is recorded as having prophesied about:

- his betrayal[55]
- the manner of his crucifixion and death[56]
- Peter denying that he knew Jesus[57]
- his resurrection from the dead after three days[58]
- the out pouring of the Holy Spirit[59]
- the persecution of Jesus' disciples[60]
- the destruction of Jerusalem and the Temple[61]

Jesus' 1st century followers contended that all of these things happened just as Jesus said they would.

It is possible that Jesus' followers colluded after his death and contrived these stories to make it appear that Jesus had accurately predicted the events of his death and even the destruction of the Temple. However, it appears that at least the *Gospel of Mark* was written before the destruction of the

Temple (in about 64 or 65 CE) and some scholars believe that the *Gospel of Luke* may have been too.[62] If they're correct, then Jesus did prophesy the destruction of the Temple about thirty-eight years before it happened.[63]

Other prophecies

Jesus also prophesied about things that were to happen after the destruction of the Temple:

- False Messiahs and prophets will appear.
- There will be signs in the heavens.
- The "Son of Man will come in the clouds with great power and glory".[64]

He essentially said that he is the "Son of Man" prophesied by the Prophet Daniel and that he is coming back to reign.[65] Obviously, if he does this, there's no question, he is the Messiah.

THEY DIDN'T FIND THE BODY

Perhaps the strongest evidence that Jesus' followers present to support Jesus' resurrection from the dead is that neither the Romans nor the Sanhedrin found the body. When the would-be-messiah Theudas was defeated, the Roman army literally brought back his head. When John the Baptist was executed by Herod, he presented his wife with John's head on a platter. It seems that neither the Roman army nor the local government were reluctant about graphic displays to keep the populace in line. So why didn't they merely exhume Jesus' body and drag it through the streets? This would have killed the upstart sect of Judaism on the spot. The answer seems obvious—they didn't find the body.

So, what happened to it?

- *Did they forget where it was?*   That's not likely.
- *Did Jesus' followers overpower the Roman guards who were recorded to have been guarding Jesus' tomb?*   If they had, it would have been tough to convince everyone that a dead body was a living resurrected Messiah.

- *Did they payoff the guards for the body?*   Not likely, for the same reasons.
- *Was Jesus not really dead?*   The Talmud, Josephus, and Jesus' followers all say that he was dead.
- *Did they actually find the body and drag it through the streets and Jesus' followers just omitted that part?*   Neither the Talmud, Josephus, nor any 1st or 2nd century sources record that a body was ever found.

None of these scenarios seem plausible. Jesus' followers agree and point to the empty tomb as additional evidence that Jesus is who he claimed to be.

BUT, WHAT IS THE PROOF?

Jesus' followers point out that all of the evidence to support the validity of the claims that he made about himself is precisely that, evidence. They believe that the body of evidence is overwhelming in its support of Jesus' resurrection and that the logical conclusion to be reached is that Jesus is, in fact, the Messiah. But, while they say that this should be enough to reach this conclusion, they contend that there is even more convincing proof.

The proof that Jesus' followers point to is the Holy Spirit of God. They point out that the prophet Joel said that the Holy Spirit of God would be given not only to the nation of Israel, but to all people.[66]

Jesus' followers contend that this is exactly what happened. They say that the Holy Spirit was given to Jesus' followers at the Feast of Pentecost (*a feast of harvest*) after Jesus ascended up into heaven. They also contend that now all of his followers 'receive' the Holy Spirit at the moment they place their faith in Jesus as Messiah. They also contend that the Holy Spirit is at work in the lives of 'believers' to help them to follow God.

So, if Jesus is the Messiah and if he did usher in God's *New Covenant,* then shouldn't it be evidenced by the Holy Spirit as his followers claim?

ASSESSING THE "PROOF"

How do you assess whether claims like this are true? If you can't actually see God's Holy Spirit, how could you assess if His spirit is at work in someone's life? There are three ways to do this:

Versus Scripture

The first way to assess this claim is to evaluate it against the Hebrew Scriptures, by looking at the prophecies about the Holy Spirit and how the Holy Spirit worked in other people's lives.

What does the Scripture say that the Holy Spirit will do? Based upon the prophecies of Joel, Ezekiel, and Jeremiah the Holy Spirit of God will:

- give life[67]
- cause people to prophesy, dream dreams, and see visions[68]
- put God's law in people's minds and write it on their hearts[69]
- move people to follow God's decrees and keep His laws[70]

In addition, it's obvious from the Scriptures that the Holy Spirit of God empowers people to do God's will. In one instance it was to build a temple to worship God. In others it was to liberate the nation of Israel from its enemies. In yet others, it was to proclaim the word of God.

This is essentially what the *New Testament* teaches as well.[71]

Personal Experience

The second way to assess this claim is based upon your own personal experience. The challenge with this 'proof', however, is that it's an experiential proof. In other words, you are supposed to receive the Holy Spirit (the proof) *when* you accept Jesus as your Messiah, *not before*. So you can't personally test the 'proof' ahead of time.

Many of those who profess to be Christians claim to have had this experience. Some call it being "born again."[72] It's difficult to debate what someone claims to be his or her personal experience. However, if a person contends that they've received the Holy Spirit of God, their life should be part of the evidence.

Observing Others

If Jesus' followers, or anyone else for that matter, claim to have received the Holy Spirit of God, there should be evidence of it in their lives. You should be able to observe a difference in them. But, in what way? According to the Scriptures what would we see?

- *Would people with the Holy Spirit of God in their lives be perfect?*

  Likely not—they would still be human. Even King David, who was a prophet of God and a man with whom the Holy Spirit dwelt, wasn't perfect. He committed adultery. But, David was a man who had a heart to seek after God. He wasn't perfect, but he wanted to know, obey, and worship God. He was not a man who merely obeyed God out of a sense of duty or guilt. He *loved* God.

  Likewise, people with the Holy Spirit of God in their lives would love God and would want to follow Him.

- *Would people with the Holy Spirit of God in their lives be able to do miraculous things?*

  Maybe, if God wanted them to. God used Moses, Elijah, Elisha, and others to do miraculous things. He showed his power though their obedience. But, others like Gideon, Othniel, King Saul and King David, who were also directed by God's Holy Spirit, didn't raise the dead or part the waters.[73] They were used and directed in different ways by the same Holy Spirit of God.

- *Would people with the Holy Spirit of God love sin?*

  No, sin is contrary to the nature of God. They might sin, but it would make them miserable. Again, King David is a good example of this. Though he was a man through whom the Holy Spirit of God spoke, he was not a puppet; he was still capable of sinning. But, when he did sin, he was miserable.[74]

- *Isn't the Holy Spirit the same as a conscience?*

  No. Everyone, in every culture, seems to have a conscience—a consciousness of the difference between right and wrong. But, according to Scriptures, that's not the Holy Spirit. The Holy Spirit is the presence of God interacting with people.

The Holy Spirit doesn't just make us conscious of our sin, though He does. God's Holy Spirit teaches us His Law, guides us in life decisions, empowers and strengthens us, and allows us to experience God's presence on earth.

- *Would the Holy Spirit come and go from people's lives?*

  The Scriptures record that the Holy Spirit of God filled, came upon, or rested upon many people to accomplish specific objectives: Bezalel, Moses, the elders of Israel, Othniel, Gideon, Jephthah, Samson, Azariah, Jahaziel, Zechariah, Balaam, King David, King Saul, and many others.[75] The Scriptures also record that the Holy Spirit departed from King Saul after he presumptuously disobeyed God.[76] However, the new covenant that God promises doesn't appear to be one where His Holy Spirit comes and goes. It appears to be a part of an ongoing covenant that never ends.[77]

- *How would you tell if the Holy Spirit were in someone's life?*

  Since the Holy Spirit will place God's law in the hearts of mankind and move people to follow Him, the lives of people with the Holy Spirit would be identifiable by a loving and obedient attitude toward God[78] and an attitude of kindness and love toward other people.[79]

The likely evidence of the Holy Spirit of God being at work in a person's live would be a changed life. A person wouldn't necessarily be perfect, but they would love God and want to follow and obey Him. They would also want to treat others in a way that's consistent with the Scriptures.

Again, this is basically what Jesus' 1st century followers taught and what his present day followers also believe. But, if what they say is true, their lives should be part of the evidence.

Don't Other Faiths Also Pass These Tests?

Some people might contend that all religious faiths fair equally well against these tests. In fact, they don't. A quick example of this (without intending offense toward adherents of this faith) is the Church of Jesus Christ of Latter Day Saints (the Mormons). Critics of Mormonism point out that, even without exploring the many theological differences between Mormonism and 1st century Judaism, Mormonism doesn't rate well against these tests. Their points of criticism include:

History: No archaeological evidence has been found in South America to support the *Book of Mormon's* claims of Hebrew people settling there in the 6th century BCE.[80]

Science: Animals that are reported in the *Book of Mormon* to have lived in South America at the time of Nephi's reported arrival (cows, horses, and oxen)[81] weren't indigenous to the continent.[82]

Lives of the Authors: The *Book of Mormon* includes an attestation by eleven witnesses who claimed to see the golden tablets that Joseph Smith, Jr. is said to have found in upstate New York and translated as the *Book of Mormon*. Critics report that all three of the original witnesses left the Mormon Church; they were all denounced by the church and at least two were excommunicated.[83] By 1838, of the other eight witnesses, only three remained in the Church (two had died). The three remaining were Joseph Smith's father and two brothers.[84]

Theological Consistency: Unlike Judaism, Mormonism teaches that there are many gods. It also teaches that people can become gods.[85]

Method of Transmission: Joseph Smith, Jr. is said to have translated the golden tablets by deciphering their 'Egyptian hieroglyphics.' This translation is reported to have occurred in the 1820s. However, entire chapters of the *Book of Mormon* are essentially identical to the translation of the Bible commissioned by King James of England in 1611.[86]

It isn't easy for a religious faith to pass these tests. Consequently, it's notable that both the Judaism of the *Hebrew Scriptures* and the Christianity of the *New Testament* do.

CONCLUSIONS

Jesus' followers contend that Christianity is the promised *New Covenant* of the Hebrew Scriptures. To support their claim, they point to the tests that validate the truth of Judaism and cite evidence to suggest that Christianity passes the same tests. In fact, they do present a strong case, which seems to be at least as compelling as the case for the Judaism of the Scriptures. This is significant because the case in support of the Judaism of the Scriptures is overwhelming.

WHAT DID YOU EXPECT?

When you started reading this book, what did you expect about God and Messiah? Did you even have any expectations? And, if you did, what were they based upon? If you're like many people, your expectations were loosely based upon some combination of personal experience, what you were taught, what you could comprehend, popular thought, or merely what you *wanted* to be true. But the problem is that all of these approaches are limited, and some are inherently flawed.

THE BASIS FOR EXPECTATIONS?

PERSONAL EXPERIENCE

Personal experience is important and we should definitely use it as a basis for our beliefs, but it shouldn't be the sole basis for beliefs. After all, our own experiences are limited. We weren't with Moses in the wilderness when he encountered God or on Mt. Sinai when the nation of Israel received the Law from God. But that doesn't mean that these events didn't happen. On the contrary, the mere existence of the nation of Israel and a group of people called the Jews is evidence to suggest that they did. If we limit our expectations totally based upon our own experiences we can miss the truth—simply because we weren't there.

WHAT WE WERE TAUGHT

We also base our expectations of God upon what we've been taught by others. A person who was raised in a polytheistic culture likely believes in many gods and a person who was raised in a monotheistic culture likely believes in one. But, by definition, both people cannot be right. At least one of them was taught something that wasn't true.

Whether we learned it as a child, as an adolescent, or as an adult, most of us don't really test what we've been taught for ourselves. When the subject is God, most of us throw up our hands because we don't really know how to test what we've been taught. The result tends to be a convictionless belief system. We believe it, but we don't *really* believe it.

WHAT WE CAN COMPREHEND

We often limit our expectations based upon what we can intellectually grasp or explain. But, by definition, as mortal physical beings, we can only comprehend an eternal spiritual God at a very finite level. In fact, we can't even fully understand or explain what's in our own physical world. But, that doesn't mean that those things don't exist. They do. So, why do some assume, merely because they don't understand, God, that He doesn't exist? If we could understand everything about God, He would be an incredibly small God.

POPULAR CULTURE

Whether we like it or not, our expectations about God are continually influenced by popular culture. The entertainment industry pumps out thousands of movies, talk shows, songs and commercial messages that shape our perspectives. But, unfortunately, entertainment is intended to be entertainment, not truth.

MAKING OUR OWN "GOD"

Probably worst of all, we frequently "make our own god" by basing what we believe about God on what we *want* to be true, not what is true.

When we take bits and pieces of what we have been taught, add what we have experienced, then mix in some drama, and disregard the things we don't like, we are effectively making our own "god." The obvious problem is that, if there really is a God (and the evidence suggests that there is), He is likely not amused. It makes you wonder if God looks at us and says, "You worship something you call god, but that's not Me!"

Almost no one would really do this by intent. But, when we fail to search out the truth or at least look for evidence upon which to base our beliefs, we at minimum have a view of God that is based on ignorance. Yet, if God is real and Messiah is really coming, then honestly seeking to understand more about Him is likely the most important mission of our lives!

A SOLID BASIS FOR EXPECTATIONS

The most solid basis for any expectation is always truth. We should base our expectations upon what we know to be true or have reasonable evidence to believe is true. But finding truth usually requires two things: effort and an open mind. You generally won't find truth if you just sit there with your eyes shut. You should look for truth.

You might ask, "How do you find the truth?" The response is, you know how—you assess truth every day. You do it in a number of ways. For example, the following simple statement can be assessed in at least fourteen different ways:

> "I saw Tom and Mary yesterday at the N train station in Brooklyn Heights. They were soaking wet."

The truth of this statement can be assessed based upon personal experience, physical confirmation of facts, third-party historical confirmation, eyewitness reliability, and other eyewitness accounts:

PERSONAL EXPERIENCE:

- Did I see Tom and Mary yesterday soaking wet, in Brooklyn Heights, or at the N train station?
- Do I know anything else about Tom and Mary that would be inconsistent with this statement?

PHYSICAL CONFIRMATION:

- Is there really a place called Brooklyn Heights?
- Is there really an N train station there?
- Are there really people named Tom and Mary?
- Is there any evidence of water or something that would have made them wet in Brooklyn Heights yesterday?
- Is there any evidence of water or something that would have made them wet anywhere along the N train line yesterday?

THIRD-PARTY HISTORICAL CONFIRMATION:

- Was rain reported in Brooklyn Heights on the evening news or in the newspaper?
- Was rain reported elsewhere along the N train line yesterday?

EYEWITNESS RELIABILITY:

- Is the person reporting the event reliable?

OTHER EYEWITNESS CONFIRMATION:

- Did anyone else see Tom and Mary in Brooklyn Heights or soaking wet yesterday?
- Did Tom confirm that he was soaking wet at the Brooklyn Heights N train station yesterday?
- Did Mary confirm that she was soaking wet at the Brooklyn Heights N train station yesterday?
- Did anyone else see something that could have made Tom and Mary wet yesterday?

Other statements can be assessed through even more tests: the sciences, archaeology, history, logic and other means. Generally, the more information available, the easier it is to assess truth; the greater the evidence to support a statement, the greater the likelihood that it is true. Truth is not inconsistent with itself; truth is true at all levels.

THE CASE FOR JESUS

This book has essentially been an investigation into the case for Jesus. It presents the results of many of his followers' search for truth. These results are a part of the fact base upon which they have based their beliefs.

Jesus' followers present a case that God is so intimately involved in the lives of people and His creation, that He entered His creation as the human Messiah (Jesus) so that we could know Him and understand His plan of forgiveness, reconciliation, and salvation. They say that His many appearances and interactions with ancient Israel, His nation of priests, foreshadowed His appearance as Messiah. They point to the sacrificial system required by the Torah, and contend that Jesus entered the world to fulfill it, to be the sacrifice that makes us righteous in God's eyes. They also point to the covenants, which God made with His creation, and the promised new covenant to come and say that Jesus is their fulfillment. Then they point to the many prophecies of the Hebrew Scriptures and claim that Jesus is their embodiment.

They base their case upon the history, theology, and prophecy of the Hebrew Scriptures, which they believe to have been proven true by a large body of evidence. They also base their case upon eyewitness testimony and third party testimony in the form of histories written by credible sources of the 1st century era, which corroborate the eyewitness accounts. They point to archeological validation of data recorded in the eyewitness testimonies. They point to the lives and teachings of Jesus and his followers. They cite the fulfillment of prophecies made by Jesus. They even cite their own personal experiences. They also point to the absence of negative evidence as evidence—Jesus' body was not found and his disciples did not recant, even at the cost of their lives. They make their case based upon evidence.

WHAT IS YOUR CASE?

But, back to the original question, *"What did you expect?"* You had expectations of your own when you started reading this book. You had a set of beliefs about God and about the Messiah. What were they based upon? Did you have a case for what you believed?

The objective of this book has been to take you on a mental journey. The first several chapters were intended to provide a frame of reference for the trip from the Hebrew Scriptures. The remaining chapters then provide the case made by Jesus' followers. The intent has been that you would be prompted to reflect upon *your* expectations, specifically about God and Messiah, and to assess them. Assess them in light of what the Hebrew Scriptures say. Assess them versus the case that Jesus' followers make. And, assess them for truth.

Now that you have made the journey and reflected upon your original expectations, what have you concluded? Was the case for your expectations as compelling as you thought, or has it proven to be weak? How has it borne up under scrutiny? Most importantly, was your case based upon truth?

It is my hope that this book prompts you to search for truth. It is my prayer that you find it.

NOTES

CHAPTER 1: WHY DID GOD CALL ABRAM?

1. Eli Barnavi, *A Historical Atlas Of The Jewish People*, © 1992 by Hachette Litterature, published in the U.S. by Schocken Books, New York, page 2.
2. Genesis 18:19 (JPS)
3. Isaiah 42:5-12, Psalms 67:2-8, and Psalms 100
4. Joshua 24:2
5. Genesis 11:26-32
6. Genesis 14:17-20
7. Genesis 9:24-27
8. Genesis 12:10-20 and Genesis 20:1-18
9. Genesis 16:1-6
10. Isaiah 41:8
11. Jonah 3:1-10
12. Daniel 4:31-34
13. Ezra 1:2-4

CHAPTER 2: WHO WAS THAT MAN?

1. Exodus 22:21-26 (in some translations: Exodus 22:21-27)
2. Genesis 2:15-17, 3:8-19, 6:13-14, 26:2-5 and Exodus 3:1-6
3. Genesis 18:22 (JPS)
4. Genesis 18:33-19:1
5. Genesis 12:1-4
6. Genesis 12:7
7. Genesis 13:14-18
8. Genesis 15:1-20
9. Genesis 17:1-22
10. Deuteronomy 10:14-15
11. Isaiah 41:8
12. Exodus 33:20
13. Genesis 18:22-33
14. Exodus 3:1-6
15. Exodus 24:17
16. Deuteronomy 4:9-14
17. Exodus 33:7-11
18. Isaiah 6:1-8, Ezekiel 1:25-28, Daniel 7:11-28
19. Deuteronomy 10:12-15

CHAPTER 3: WHATEVER HAPPENED TO THE SACRIFICE?

1. Joseph Telushkin, *Jewish Literacy*, © 1991 by Rabbi Joseph Telushkin, William

Morrow and Company, Inc., New York, page 61
2. Flavius Josephus, *The Wars of the Jews*, (6.9.3)
3. Paul Johnson, *A History of the Jews*, © 1987 by Paul Johnson, Harper & Row, New York, NY, page 171.
4. Moses Maimonides, *The Guide for the Perplexed*, 1956 (1904 translation by M. Friedlander), Dover Publications, Inc, New York, page 323
5. Genesis 3:21
6. Genesis 4:3-5 (JPS)
7. Genesis 8:20-21 (JPS)
8. Genesis 15:7-21 (JPS)
9. Genesis 22:1-14
10. Exodus 12:1-29
11. Exodus 25:8-28:43
12. Exodus 29:1-46
13. Exodus 30:22-30
14. Numbers 28:1-15
15. Leviticus 3:1-4 and 7:15-33
16. Exodus 35:22-24, Leviticus 7:29-32 and Leviticus 23:20
17. Leviticus 4:1-5:13
18. Leviticus 5:5-13
19. Leviticus 5:14-26
20. Leviticus 1:2-13 (JPS)
21. Leviticus 23:4-8, Leviticus 23:9-14, Leviticus 23:15-21, Leviticus, 23:23-25, Leviticus 23:33-36
22. Leviticus 16:1-34
23. Leviticus 16:21 (JPS)
24. Numbers 18:25-31
25. Jeremiah 33:17-18
26. Isaiah 1:1-20
27. Joseph Telushkin, *Jewish Literacy*, © 1991 by Rabbi Joseph Telushkin, William Morrow and Company, Inc., New York, page 61
28. *Babylonian Talmud*, (Megillah 3b)
29. Micah 1:15 and 3:12

CHAPTER 4: A NEW DEAL WITH GOD?

1. Genesis 1:26, 2:15-20
2. Genesis 3:16-24
3. Genesis 6:1-22 and 7:1-5
4. Genesis 9:1-17

5. Exodus 12:1-7
6. Genesis 15:1-20
7. Genesis 17:9-14
8. Exodus 19:8 (JPS)
9. Deuteronomy 26:16-19 and 28:1-69
10. 1 Samuel 8:7-22
11. 2 Samuel 7:16 (JPS)
12. Malachi 2:4-9
13. Moshe Miller trans. *The Chofetz Chaim on Awaiting Mashiach,* ©1993 by Moshe Miller, Targum Press, Southfield, MI, page 13.

CHAPTER 5: A MESSIAH FOR ISRAEL?

1. Maimonides, *Mishneh Torah, Hilchot Melachim U'Milchamoteihem,* Rabbi Eliyahu Touger, trans. © 1987 by Moznaim Publishing Corporation, New York, NY, page 232.
2. Micah 4:1-5
3. Genesis 35:19-21
4. 2 Samuel 7:16
5. Isaiah 9:1-4
6. Jeremiah 23:5-6
7. Malachi 3:1
8. Moses ben Maimon, *Yad haHazaqa (Mishne Torah), Shoftim, Hilkhot Melachim* 11-12
9. Isaiah 11:11-12
10. Daniel 7:1-28 (JPS)
11. Leviticus 6:20, 2 Kings 9:33, Isaiah 63:3
12. Zechariah 13:7
13. *Babylonian Talmud* (Sukkah 52a and 52b)
14. Daniel Chapter 12
15. Sa'adiah ben Joseph, *Book of Doctrines and Beliefs*
16. Jeremiah 23:5-6, Isaiah 11:1, and Zechariah 10:4
17. Isaiah Chapter 53
18. Daniel 9
19. Daniel 7:1-28
20. *The Bible Almanac,* © 1980 by Thomas Nelson Publishers, Nashville, TN page 152, (Ezra 1:2-3 and 2 Chronicles 36:22-23)
21. John F. Walvoord, *Daniel, The Key To Prophetic Revelation,* © 1971 by the Moody Bible Institute, Moody Press, Chicago, IL , pages 226-227. (Nehemiah 2:1)
22. Rabbi Hersh Goldwurm, *Daniel,* © 1988 by Mesorah Publications, Ltd., Brooklyn, NY, pages 259-262. And TANAKH. A *New Translation of THE HOLY SCRIP-*

TURES According to the Traditional Hebrew Text, © 1985 by The Jewish Publication Society, Philadelphia, New York, and Jerusalem., p.1487

Also referenced in support of footnotes:

e, g: *The Chofetz Chaim on Awaiting Messiah,* Moshe Miller, trans. © by Moshe Miller, Targum Press, Southfield, MI, pages 13 and 40.

f: *Three Jewish Philosophers,* Harper & Row Publishers, 1965, New York, NY, page 179.

g,h,i: Raphael Patai, *The Messiah Texts, Jewish Legends of Three Thousand Years,* © by Raphael Patai, Wayne State University Press, Detroit, MI, pages 21, 83, and 113.

CHAPTER 6: IS MESSIAH THE SON OF GOD?

1. Psalms 89:27
2. 2 Samuel 7:14 and Deuteronomy 14:1
3. James C. VanderKam, *The Dead Sea Scrolls Today,* © 1994, William B. Eerdmans Publishing Company, Grand Rapids, Michigan, page 178.
4. Genesis Chapter 18
5. Daniel 7:27
6. *Babylonian Talmud,* Sanhedrin 98A
7. Daniel 7:17
8. 2 Samuel 7:16
9. Isaiah Chapter 53, Zechariah 13:7-8, and Daniel 9:20-27
10. Leviticus 4:1 through 5:13
11. Ecclesiastes 7:20, Psalms 14:1-3, and Psalms 53:1-5
12. Psalm 49:7-9 and 49:15
13. Isaiah 53:10-12
14. 1 Kings 17: 17-24
15. 2 Kings 4:18-37
16. Isaiah 45:18, 45:21-22, and 46:9
17. Jacob Neusner, *Dictionary of Judaism In The Biblical Period,* © 1996 by Macmillan Library Reference USA, Hendrickson Publishers, Peabody, MA, page 259.
18. C.D. Yonge, trans. *The Works of Philo, Complete and Unabridged, (On the Creation)* © 1993 by Hendrickson Publishers, Peabody, MA, page11
19. Genesis 1:27,Nehemiah 9:6, Job 9:8, Isaiah 44:24

20. Deuteronomy 6:4 and Isaiah 43:10-11

CHAPTER 7: IS JESUS THE MESSIAH?

1. *The World Almanac and Book of Facts 2002,* © 2002 by World Almanac Education Group, Inc., New York, NY, page 684
2. Flavius Josephus, *Antiquities of the Jews* 15.3.3, 15.7.4-8, and 16.11.6
3. Flavius Josephus, *Antiquities of the Jews* 18.3.3
4. Flavius Josephus, *Antiquities of the Jews* 20.5.1
5. Hershel Shanks, ed., *Christianity and Rabbinic Judaism,* (Louis Feldman, Chapter 1), © 1992, Biblical Archaeology Society, Washington, DC, page 16
6. Rabbi Joseph Telushkin, *Jewish Literacy,* © 1991, William Morrow and Co., Inc., New York, pages 143-146
7. Isaiah 9:55
8. Luke 1:1-16 and Matthew 3:23-38
9. *Babylonian Talmud,* Tractate Sanhedrin (43a), © 1987 by Soncino Press, London
10. Micah 4:6-8 and Micah 5:1
11. Luke 2:1-7
12. Flavius Josephus, *The Antiquities of the Jews* (18:1.1-3)
13. Flavius Josephus, *The Wars of the Jews* (7.8.1)
14. Josh McDowell and Bill Wilson, *He Walked Among Us, Evidence for the Historical Jesus,* Here's Life Publishers, San Bernadino, CA, © 1988, page 203
15. Merrill F. Unger, *Ungers Bible Dictionary,* © 1980, Moody Press, Chicago. page 233
16. Josh McDowell and Bill Wilson, *He Walked Among Us, Evidence for the Historical Jesus,* Here's Life Publishers, San Bernadino, CA, © 1988, page 201
17. Leviticus 25:8-34
18. Flavius Josephus, *The Antiquities of the Jews,* 18.1.1 (1-8)
19. Luke 3:23
20. Luke 3:1-2
21. Malachi 3:23
22. Luke 1:5
23. Luke 1:36
24. Luke 1:80 and Matthew 3:1-6
25. William Whiston, trans. *The Works of Josephus, Complete and Unabridged,* The Antiquities of The Jews, (18.5.2) © 1987 by Hendrickson Publishers, Inc., Peabody, MA
26. John 1:21
27. Matthew 11:11-14 and Luke 7:27
28. John 1:15-34
29. John 3:22-30
30. John 1:34
31. John 1:29 and 1:36
32. Zechariah 9:9-10
33. Matthew 21:1-11
34. Zechariah 9:9-10 (JPS)
35. Malachi 3:1
36. John 7:14 and 18:19-20
37. Isaiah 52:10-15 and Chapter 53
38. Luke 23:1-25
39. John 19:14-18
40. *Babylonian Talmud,* Sanhedrin 43a
41. William Whiston, *The Works of Josephus, Complete and Unabridged,* © 1987, Hendrickson Publishers, Peabody, MA., page 480.
42. Pines, Shlomo, *An Arabic Version of the Testimonium Flavium and its Implications,* Jerusalem, Jerusalem Academic Press, 1971, pages 9-10.
43. 1 Corinthians 15:3-8, Acts 1:2-3
44. *Babylonian Talmud,* (Nazir 32b and Yoma 54a), 1938, Soncino Press, London
45. Zechanah 13:7 (JPS)
46. Flavius Josephus, *Wars of the Jews,* 5.13.7
47. Hershel Shanks, ed., *Christianity and Rabbinic Judaism,* (Lee I. A Levine, Chapter 4), © 1992, Biblical Archaeology Society, Washington, DC, page 16
48. Isaiah Chapter 11
49. Isaiah 53:8-12
50. Daniel 7:13-14 (JPS)
51. Isaiah 9:5-6
52. Jeremiah 23:5-6
53. 1 Corinthians 5:7, Hebrews 9:11-28
54. Romans 5:6-21
55. Isaiah 11:1-10 and Daniel 7:13-14
56. Isaiah 53:7-12, Daniel 9:26, and Zechariah 12:10 and 13:7
57. *Three Jewish Philosophers,* 1965, Harper & Row Publishers, New York (Saadya Gaon, *Book of Doctrines and Beliefs*).

CHAPTER 8: WHY WAS JESUS KILLED?

1. Flavius Josephus, *Antiquities Of The Jews,* (18.3.3)

2. *Babylonian Talmud,* Tractate Sanhedrin (43a), © 1987 by Soncino Press, London
3. Luke 4:14-19
4. Luke 4:20-29 (NIV®)
5. John 4:25-26 and Matthew 16:13-17
6. Luke 9:20-21 and Matthew 16:20
7. Matthew 26:26-32, Matthew 16:21, Mark 8: 31-32, Mark 10:32-34 and John 12:31-36
8. 1 John 2:1-2, 1 John 4:10, and Hebrews 9:1-28
9. Isaiah Chapter 53
10. Luke 9:22
11. Luke 5:17-25
12. Psalms 89:27 and 2 Samuel 7:14
13. Deuteronomy 14:1 and Jeremiah 31:17
14. Exodus 3:14
15. 1 John 5:20
16. John 19:7 (NIV®)
17. 1 Peter 1:18-20 and Ephesians 1:4-8

CHAPTER 9: WHY DID THEY BELIEVE JESUS?

1. Matthew 10:1-42
2. John 1:44
3. Matthew 4:18 and Luke 5:10
4. John 1:26-42
5. Mark 3:17
6. Mark 1:20, John 18:15
7. Mark 2:14
8. John 1:44
9. Merrill F. Unger, *Unger's Bible Dictionary,* © 1980, Moody Press, Chicago, page 126
10. John 21:2 and John 1:45
11. Merrill F. Unger, *Unger's Bible Dictionary,* © 1980, Moody Press, Chicago, page 1086
12. Rabbi Joseph Telushkin, *Jewish Literacy,* © by Rabbi Joseph Telushkin, William Morrow and Company, New York, pages 133-135.
13. Merrill F. Unger, *Unger's Bible Dictionary,* © 1980, Moody Press, Chicago, page 615
14. John 12:4-6
15. Matthew 27:3-10
16. Acts 2:7
17. *Nelson's Illustrated Bible Dictionary,* © 1986, Thomas Nelson Publishers
18. *Christianity and Rabbinic Judaism,* (Chapter 1 by Louis Feldman), ©1992, Biblical Archaeology Society, Washington, D.C., page 5
19. Matthew 3:16-17, Mark 1:9-11, and Luke 3:21-22
20. Matthew 17:5, Mark 9:5-9, Luke 9:33-36, 2 Peter 1:16-18
21. John 12:26-33
22. John 2:1-11
23. John 11:1-44
24. Luke 8:40-56, Matthew 9:18-25
25. Luke 7:11-17
26. Matthew 14:13-21 and John 6:1-14
27. Matthew 15:32-38
28. Matthew 15:29-31, John 5:1-8, Matthew 20:29-34, Mark 10:46-52, Mark 1:29-31, Mark 6:54-56, Luke 17:11-19, Luke 5:17-26 John 18:10-11
29. John 6:16-21, Matthew 14:22-32, and Mark 6:45-51
30. Luke 8:22-25
31. Matthew 8:28-34
32. *Babylonian Talmud,* (Sanhedrin 43A)
33. Flavius Josephus, *Antiquities of the Jews* 18.3.3
34. Matthew 27:45 and 27:51-53
35. The Ages Digital Library Collections, *The Ante-Nicene Fathers, Volume 6,* (Edited by A. Roberts and J. Donaldson), © 1997 by Ages Software, Albany, OR, pages 261-262.
36. Shlomo Pines, *An Arabic Version of the Testimonium Flavium and its Implications,* ©1971 by The Israel Academy of Sciences and Humanities, Jerusalem Academic Press, Jerusalem, pages 6-8.
37. John 20:1-18, Matthew 28:1-10 and Mark 16:9
38. Luke 24:33-34
39. Luke 24: 13-32
40. Luke 24:33-49 and John 20:19-25
41. John 20:26-29
42. I Corinthians 15:7 and *The New Bible Commentary: Revised,* © 1970 Inter-Varsity Press, London, page 1071.
43. Matthew 28:16-20
44. John 21:1-23
45. I Corinthians 15:6
46. Acts 1:3
47. Luke 24:49-51 and Acts 1: 3-12
48. Matthew 13:34-36, Mark 1:22
49. Matthew 23:13-36
50. John 12:32-33, Mark 10:32-39, and John 2:18-22)
51. 1 Peter 1:3-21
52. Luke 10:1-17
53. Joel 2:28-32 and Acts 1-36
54. 2 Peter 1:16-21

55. Romans 1:17, 2:6, 2:24, 3:4, 3:10-12,
3:13, 3:14, 3:15-17, 3:18, 4:7, 4;17, 4:18,
7:7, 8:36, 9:7, 9:9, 9:12, 9:13, 9:15, 9:17,
9:25-26, 9:27-28, 9:29, 9:33, 10:5, 10:6,-
7, 10:8, 10:11, 10:13, 10:15, 10:16,
10:18, 10:19, 10:20, 10:21, 11:3-4, 11:8,
11:9-10, 11:26-27, 11:34, 11:35, 12:19,
12:20, 13:9, 14:11, 15:9, 15:10, 15:11,
15:12, 15:21
56. Philippians 2:5-11
57. Acts 24:27, 2 Corinthians 11:23-25, Acts
16:19-24, Acts 24:27, Acts 21:31-34 and
Romans 16:7
58. Philip Schaff, *History of the Christian
Church,* Volume 1, 1996, Hendrickson
Publishers, Peabody , MA pages 329-330
(originally Published by Charles Scribner's
Sons in 1858).
59. Acts 22:27-29
60. John 7:5
61. Jude 1:1-4 and James 1:1
62. Acts 21:18
63. Galatians 1:19
64. Flavius Josephus, *Antiquities of The Jews,*
20.9.1
65. Eusebius, *Ecclesiastical History,* (2.23.1-
25), trans. C.F. Cruise, © 1998 by
Hendrickson Publishers, Inc. Peabody,
MA, page 59.
66. Acts 12:1-3 and *Nelson's Illustrated Bible
Dictionary,* © 1986, Thomas Nelson
Publishers
67. Acts 4:1-3
68. Acts 5:41
69. Revelation 1:9
70. Acts 12:1-4
71. Philip Schaff, *History of the Christian
Church,* Volume 1, 1996, Hendrickson
Publishers, Peabody , MA page 251 (originally Published by Charles Scribner's Sons
in 1858).
72. Aziz S. Atiya, *History of Eastern
Christianity,* © 1967 by Aziz S. Atiya,
University of Notre Dame Press, Notre
Dame, IN, Page 27.
73. Samuel Hugh Moffett, *A History of
Christianity in Asia,* Volume 1, © 1998 by
Samuel Hugh Moffett, Orbis Books,
Maryknoll, NY, page 34.
74. Philip Schaff, *History of the Christian
Church,* Volume 1, 1996, Hendrickson
Publishers, Peabody , MA (originally
Published by Charles Scribner's Sons in

1858). pages 381-382
75. Acts 2:44-46, Acts 4:32-37
76. 1 Corinthians 3:3-23
77. Matthew 5:44-48 and 1 Peter 2:13-20
78. Matthew 27:62-66

CHAPTER 10: DID JESUS REJECT JUDAISM?

1. Lawrence H. Schiffman, *Who Was A Jew?
Rabbinic and Halakhic Perspectives on the
Jewish Christian Schism,* © 1985
Lawrence H. Schiffman, KTAV Publishing
House, Inc., page 51
2. Flavius Josephus, *The Antiquities of the
Jews,* (18.1.2-6)
3. Flavius Josephus, *The Antiquities of the
Jews,* (18.1.3)
4. *Nelson's Illustrated Bible Dictionary,* ©
1986, Thomas Nelson Publishers
5. *Ibid.*
6. Flavius Josephus, *The Antiquities of the
Jews,* (18.1.4)
7. Flavius Josephus, *The Wars of the Jews,*
2.8.14
8. C.D. Yonge, trans., *The Works of Philo,*
Hypothetica: Apology for the Jews, 11.1-
11.18 and Every Good Man Is Free, 75-
89, © 1993 by Hendrickson Publishers,
Inc. and Flavius Josephus, *The Wars of
the Jews,* (2.8.2-13)
9. *Nelson's Illustrated Bible Dictionary,* ©
1986, Thomas Nelson Publishers
10. Flavius Josephus, *The Antiquities of the
Jews,* (18.1.5)
11. Flavius Josephus, *The Antiquities of the
Jews,* (18.1.6) and *The Wars of the Jews,*
(8.1)
12. Deuteronomy 6:5 (JPS)
13. Matthew 15:21-28
14. Luke 16:17
15. Matthew 23:1-39 and Luke 11:37-54
16. Matthew 22:29-32
17. John 7:19a (NIV®)
18. John 10:22-23, John 7:1-10, John 2:23,
and Mark 14:12
19. Leviticus Chapters 11 through 14
20. Matthew 8:1-4
21. Matthew 12:9-14
22. Luke 13:10-17
23. John 5:1-16
24. John 9:1-16
25. Matthew 12:1-8

26. Leviticus Chapter 18 and Leviticus 20:10-21
27. Deuteronomy 24:5 and 25:5-10 and Genesis 28:1
28. Deuteronomy 22:13-19 and 24:1-4
29. Luke 24: 13-27
30. John 12:31-36 and 14:28-29
31. John 3:26-36
32. Isaiah Chapter 53
33. Jeremiah 23:1-8, 31:31-40, 33:14-22 and Malachi 3:1-5
34. Joel 2:28-32, John 14:16-17, John 14:25-26, John 16:7-15 and Acts 1:4-8
35. John 16:5-15

CHAPTER 11: DID JESUS FOLLOWERS REJECT JUDAISM?

1. Acts 15:1 (NIV®)
2. Acts 15:5 (NIV®)
3. Acts 15: 19-21(NIV®)
4. Max I. Dimont, *Jews, God and History,* © 1962 by Max I. Dimont, Signet, New York, NY, page 142.
5. Acts 24:14 (NIV®)
6. 1 Timothy 1:8 and 1 Corinthians 14:33-34
7. 1 Corinthians 9:19-21
8. Romans 3:20
9. Romans 4:3 (NIV®)
10. Galatians 3:6-29
11. Romans 9:30-33
12. Galatians 2:15-21
13. Galatians 3:24
14. Romans 10:4
15. Galatians 3:25
16. Colossians 2:13-17 and Ephesians 2:6-16
17. Acts 20:16
18. Hebrews 9:1-28 and 10:1-22
19. Genesis 17:1-14
20. Exodus 12:43-49 and Leviticus 12:3
21. Leviticus 23:3
22. Exodus 20:8-11, Exodus 35:2-3 and Exodus 16:23
23. John 20:1-20
24. 1 Corinthians 16:1-4
25. Thomas Bokenkotter, *A Concise History of the Catholic Church,* © 1990 by Thomas Bokenkotter, Doubleday, New York, page 39.
26. Exodus 12:1-51
27. Mark 14:12-29 and Luke 22:1-30
28. 1 Corinthians 11:20-34
29. Exodus 23:14-19, Deuteronomy 16:9-19, and Leviticus 23:9-21
30. Acts 2:1-24
31. *Nelson's Illustrated Bible Dictionary,* © 1986 by Thomas Nelson Publishers
32. Esther 9:1-32
33. Deuteronomy 16:13-17 and Leviticus 23:34-44
34. Deuteronomy 31:9-13
35. John 7:1-14
36. Leviticus 23:23-25 (JPS)
37. F.F. Bruce, *Israel & the Nations, The History of Israel from the Exodus to the Fall of the Second Temple,* © 1997 The Estate of F.F. Bruce and D.F. Payne, Intervarsity Press, Downers Grove, IL, pgs. 144-150.
38. Jeremiah 41:1-5
39. Barry W. Holtz, ed., *Back To The Sources, Reading The Classic Jewish Texts,* © 1984 by Barry W. Holtz, Touchstone Books, New York, (Chapter 2 by Robert Goldenberg), pages 129-135
40. Rabbi Joseph Telushkin, *Jewish Literacy,* © 1991 by Rabbi Joseph Telushkin, William Morrow and Company, Inc., New York, pages 166-168.
41. Patrick Johnstone, *Operation World The Day-by-Day Guide To Praying For the World,* ©1993 by Patrick Johnstone, Zondervan Publishing, Grand Rapids, MI, pages 23-24, and Infoplease.com 7/4/2000, © 2000 by the Family Education Network (citing The 1999 Encyclopedia Britannica Book of the Year, © 1999 by Encyclopedia Britannica, Inc.)
42. *The World Almanac and Book of Facts 2002,* © 2002 by World Almanac Education Group, Inc., New York, NY, pages 684 and 867.
43. A. Kenneth Curtis, J. Stephen Lang, and Randy Petersen, *The 100 Most Important Events In Christian History,* © 1991 by Christian History Institute, Fleming H. Revell, Grand Rapids, MI, page 46.
44. Rabbi Joseph Telushkin, *Jewish Literacy,* © 1991 by Rabbi Joseph Telushkin, William Morrow and Company, Inc., New York, pages 477-478.
45. Merrill F. Unger, *Unger's Bible Dictionary,* © 1980 The Moody Bible Institute of Chicago, Moody Press, Chicago, pages 70-71.
46. *Wycliffe Dictionary of Theology,* © 1960 by Baker Books, 1999 edition by

Hendrickson Publishers, Peabody, MA, page 54.

47. Daniel B. Clendenin, *Eastern Orthodox Theology, A Contemporary Reader,* © 1995 by Daniel B. Clendenin, (Chapter 5 by John Meyendorff), Baker Books, Grand Rapids Michigan, page 82.

48. Thomas Bokenkotter, *A Concise History of the Catholic Church,* © 1990 by Thomas Bokenkotter, Doubleday, New York, pages 41-42.

49. Peter L'Huillier, *The Church of the Ancient Councils,* © 1996 by St. Vladimir's Seminary Press, Crestwood, NY, pages 17-142.

50 Philip Schaff, *History of the Christian Church,* Volume 3, (original printing in 1867), 1996 Hendrickson Publishers, Peabody, MA, pages 414-423.

51. Matthew 13:53-58, John 2:11-12 and 7:1-5, and Mark 3:31-35

52. *Wycliffe Dictionary of Theology,* © 1960 by Baker Book House, Grand Rapids, MI, page 344.

53. Wolfganag Beinert and Francis Schussler Fiorenza, *Handbook of Catholic Theology,* © 1995 by The Crossroad Publishing Company, New York, NY, pg 644

54. Bill Huebsch with Paul Thurmes, *Vatican II in Plain English/The Constitutions,* © by Bill Huebsch, Thomas More Publishing, Allen Texas, pages 61-68

55. Daniel B. Clendenin, *Eastern Orthodox Theology, A Contemporary Reader,* © 1995 by Daniel B. Clendenin, (Chapter 4 by Sergius Bulgakov), Baker Books, Grand Rapids Michigan, pages 66-67.

56. Matthew 1:23

57. Daniel B. Clendenin, *Eastern Orthodox Theology, A Contemporary Reader,* © 1995 by Daniel B. Clendenin, *(Chapter 4 by Sergius Bulgakov),* Baker Books, Grand Rapids Michigan, pages 68-75.

58. Genesis 16:7-13, 22:11-18, 31:11-13, Exodus 3:2-4:31, Numbers 22:18-35, Judges 2:1-5, and 13:2-23

59. Daniel 8:16-27 and 9:21-27

60. Revelation 19:10 and 22:8-9

61. Deuteronomy 26:13-14, 18:10-12, 14:1

62. 1 Samuel 28:6-20

63. 1 Corinthians 11:23-26

64. Merrill F. Unger, *Unger's Bible Dictionary,* © 1980 The Moody Bible Institute of Chicago, Moody Press, Chicago, page 1119.

65. Genesis 1:26-27 and 3:22

66. Isaiah 44:6 and 44:24 and Isaiah 45:12 and 45:18

67. Ezekiel Chapter 1

68. Daniel 7:9-12

69 Exodus 24:9-11

70. Exodus 33:18-23

71. 1 Kings 8:27 and 2 Chronicles 6:18

72. Isaiah 44:6-28 and 2 Chronicles 7:13-16

73. *Babylonianm Talmud,* Sanhedrin 98A

74. Isaac Leeser, *The Twenty-Four Books of the Holy Scriptures,* 1856, Tribner & Co., London, page 859.

75. Josh McDowell and Don Stewart, *Handbook of Today's Religions,* © 1983 by Campus Crusade for Christ, Inc., Thomas Nelson Publishers, Nashville, TN, page 27.

CHAPTER 12: HOW DID THE BRANCH BECOME SEPARATED FROM THE TREE?

1. John 9:18-23

2. Acts 4:1-22, Acts 5:17-42

3. Acts 6:8-8:3, Acts 9:1-2

4. Acts 12:1-4

5. Flavius Josephus, *The Antiquities of the Jews,* (20.9.1) and *Eusebius' Ecclesiastical History,* C.F. Cruise, trans. © 1988 by Hendrickson Publishers, Peabody, MA, (2.23.1-19) pages 59-61 and J.D. Douglas, *Who's Who in Christian History,* © 1992 by Tyndale House Publishers, Inc., Wheaton, IL, page 352.

6. *Eusebius' Ecclesiastical History,* C.F. Cruise, trans., © 1988 by Hendrickson Publishers, Peabody, MA, (2.6.1-8, 3.19.1, 3.32.1-7, 3.33.1-3) pages 42-43, 84, and 97-99

7. *Nelson's Illustrated Bible Dictionary,* © 1986 by Thomas Nelson Publishers

8. A. Kenneth Curtis, J. Stephen Lang & Randy Petersen, *The 100 Most Important Events In Christian History,* © 1991 by Christian History Institute, Fleming H. Revell, Grand Rapids, MI, page 14.

9. F.F. Bruce, *Israel & the Nations,* © 1997 by the Estate of F.F. Bruce and D.F. Payne, Intervarsity Press, Downs Grove, IL, pages 220-222.

10. *Ibid.,* pages 220-223.

11. Titus 3:1 and 1 Peter 2:13

12. *Eusebius' Ecclesiastical History,* C.F. Cruise, trans., © 1988 by Hendrickson Publishers, Peabody, MA, (3.5.3) page 70.
13. Flavius Josephus, *The Wars of the Jews,* (6.9.3)
14. Flavius Josephus, *The Wars of the Jews,* (6.6.1)
15. Hershel Shanks, ed., *Christianity and Rabbinic Judaism, (Chapter Four by Lee I. A. Levine),* © 1992 by the Biblical Archeology Society, Washington, DC, pages 133-136.
16. Michael L. Rodkinson, *The History of the Talmud,* © 1916 by the New Talmud Publishing Society, Boston, Volume 1, page 8.
17. Lawrence H. Schiffman, *Who was a Jew? Rabbinic and Halakhic Perspectives on the Jewish Christian Schism,* © 1985 by Lawrence H. Schiffman, KTAV Publishing House, Inc., Hoboken, NJ, page 55
18. *Ibid.,* pages 53-61
19. *Ibid.,* page 51
20. Colossians 1:21-23 and 2:8-17
21. Hershel Shanks, ed., *Christianity and Rabbinic Judaism, (Chapter Four by Lee I. A. Levine),* © 1992 by the Biblical Archeology Society, Washington, DC, page 146.
22. *Ibid.,* pages 144-146.
23. David S. Ariel, *What Do Jews Believe?* © 1995 by David S. Ariel, Schocken Books, New York, page 238-239.
24. Rabbi Joseph Telushkin, *Jewish Literacy,* © 1991 by Joseph Telushkin William Morrow and Company, Inc., New York, page 146.
25. George Foot Moore, *Judaism,* Volume 1, © 1927 by the President and Fellows of Harvard College, Hendrickson Publishers, Peabody, MA, page 93.
26. Hershel Shanks, ed., *Christianity and Rabbinic Judaism, (Chapter Four by Lee I. A. Levine),* © 1992 by the Biblical Archeology Society, Washington, DC, pages 147-148.
27. Michael L. Rodkinson, *The History of the Talmud,* © 1916 by the New Talmud Publishing Society, Boston, Volume 1, page 14 of Introduction.
28. *Ibid.,* page 12.
29. Joan Comay, *The Diaspora Story,* © 1980 by Joan Comay and Beth Hatefutsoth, The Nahum Goldmann Museum of the Jewish Diaspora, Random House, New York, page 120.
30. Louis Finkelstein, *The Jews: Their History,* © 1970 by Louis Finkelstein, Schocken Books, NY, pages 183-185.
31. Michael L. Rodkinson, *The History of the Talmud,* © 1916 by the New Talmud Publishing Society, Boston, Volume 1, pages 2-4.

CHAPTER 13: RABBINIC JUDAISM SURVIVED

1. Eli Barnavi, *A Historical Atlas of the Jewish People,* © 1992 by Hachette Litterature, Schocken Books, Inc., New York, page 55 and *The Baker Atlas of Christian History,* © 1997 Angus Hudson Ltd / Tim Dowley & Peter Wyatt trading as Three's Company, Baker Books, Grand rapids, MI, page 66.
2. Joan Comay, *The Diaspora Story,* © 1980 by Joan Comay and Beth Hatefutsoth, The Nahum Goldmann Museum of the Jewish Diaspora, Random House, New York, pages 124-125.
3. Louis Finkelstein, *The Jews: Their History,* © 1970 by Louis Finkelstein, Schocken Books, NY, page 226.
4. Raymond P. Scheindlin, *A Short History of the Jewish People,* © 1998 by Raymond P. Scheindlin, MacMillian, New York, page 66.
5. Joan Comay, *The Diaspora Story,* © 1980 by Joan Comay and Beth Hatefutsoth, The Nahum Goldmann Museum of the Jewish Diaspora, Random House, New York, pages 124-125.
6. Raymond P. Scheindlin, *A Short History of the Jewish People,* © 1998 by Raymond P. Scheindlin, MacMillian, New York, pages 67-69.
7. Joan Comay, *The Diaspora Story,* © 1980 by Joan Comay and Beth Hatefutsoth - The Nahum Goldmann Museum of the Jewish Diaspora, Random House, New York, page 128.
8. Elizabeth Isichei, *A History of Christianity in Africa,* © 1995 by Elizabeth Isichei, William Eerdmans Publishing, Grand Rapids, MI, page 17.
9. Joan Comay, *The Diaspora Story,* © 1980 by Joan Comay and Beth Hatefutsoth, The Nahum Goldmann Museum of the

Jewish Diaspora, Random House, New York, page 120.

10. *The Baker Atlas of Christian History,* © 1997 Angus Hudson Ltd / Tim Dowley & Peter Wyatt trading as Three's Company, Baker Books, Grand rapids, MI, pages 86-89.

11. Raymond P. Scheindlin, *A Short History of the Jewish People,* © 1998 by Raymond P. Scheindlin, MacMillian, New York, pages 73-75.

12. Paul Johnson, *A History of the Jews,* © 1987 by Paul Johnson, Harper & Row, New York, NY, page 177.

13. *Ibid.,* page 178.

14. www.Britannica.com, © 1997 Encyclopedia Britannica, Inc.

15. Raymond P. Scheindlin, *A Short History of the Jewish People,* © 1998 by Raymond P. Scheindlin, MacMillian, New York, pages 125-134.

16. Kevin Alan Brook, *The Jews of Khazaria,* © 1999 by Kevin Alan Brook, Jason Aronson Inc, Northvale, NJ, pages 133-143.

17. Max I. Dimont, *The Jews In America, The Roots, History and Destiny of American Jews,* © 1978 by Max Dimont, Touchstone Books, New York, Pages 22-23.

18. Frederick M. Schweitzer, *A History of the Jews Since the First Century A.D.,* © 1971 by the Anti-Defamation League of B'nai B'rith, The MacMillan Company, New York, pages 80-85.

19. Paul Johnson, *A History of the Jews,* © 1987 by Paul Johnson, Harper & Row, New York, NY, page 207-208.

20. Armenians In The Holy Land, website: www.holyland.org/deeproot.html, December 12, 2001

21. Max I. Dimont, *The Jews In America, The Roots, History and Destiny of American Jews,* © 1978 by Max Dimont, Touchstone Books, New York, Pages 24-26.

22. Louis Finkelstein, *The Jews: Their History,* © 1970 by Louis Finkelstein, Schocken Books, NY, pages 226.

23. Frederick M. Schweitzer, *A History of the Jews Since the First Century A.D.,* © 1971 by the Anti-Defamation League of B'nai B'rith, The MacMillan Company, New York, page 77.

24. Richard P. McBrien, *Lives of the Popes,* © 1997 by Richard P. McBrien, Harper Collins, New York, NY, pages 155, 180,

183, 211, 241, 255, 261, 286, 290, 297, 334, 362, 364, 374.

25. A. Kenneth Curtis, J. Stephen Lang & Randy Petersen, *The 100 Most Important Events In Christian History,* © 1991 by Christian History Institute, Fleming H. Revell, Grand Rapids, MI, pages 91 and 92.

26. Philip Schaff, *History of the Christian Church,* Volume 6, (originally published in 1910), Hendrickson Publishers, Peabody MA, page 553.

27. Paul Johnson, *A History of the Jews,* © 1987 by Paul Johnson, Harper & Row, New York, NY, page 208.

28. Raymond P. Scheindlin, *A Short History of the Jewish People,* © 1998 by Raymond P. Scheindlin, MacMillian, New York, pages 151-153.

29. *America and the Holocaust,* PBS Online (www.pbs.org/wgbh/holocaust/maps.htm), (source of data: Encyclopedia of the Holocaust; editor in chief, Israel Gutman) October 25, 2000

30. Joan Comay, *The Diaspora Story,* © 1980 by Joan Comay and Beth Hatefutsoth, The Nahum Goldmann Museum of the Jewish Diaspora, Random House, New York, page 273.

31. Louis Finkelstein, *The Jews, Their History,* © 1970 by Louis Finkelstein, Schocken Books, NY, pages 199-209.

32. www.jewfaq.org/movement.htm, © 1999 by Tracey R. Rich, October 16, 2000.

33. Joseph Telushkin, *Jewish Literacy,* © 1991 by Joseph Telushkin, William Morrow and Co., Inc., New York, pages 200-203.

34. Raymond P. Scheindlin, *A Short History of the Jewish People,* © 1998 by Raymond P. Scheindlin, MacMillian, New York, page 133.

35. Joan Comay, *The Diaspora Story,* © 1980 by Joan Comay and Beth Hatefutsoth, The Nahum Goldmann Museum of the Jewish Diaspora, Random House, New York, page 73.

36. *Ibid.,* pages 74-77.

37. Raphael Patai, *The Tents of Jacob: The Diaspora - Yesterday and Today,* © 1971 by Raphael Patai, Prentice Hall, Inc., Englewood Cliffs, NJ, pages 279-285.

38. Bernard Lazerwitz, J. Alan Winter, Arnold Dashefsky, and Ephraim Tabory, *Jewish Choices: American Jewish*

Denominationalism, © 1998 by State University of New York, State University of New York Press, Albany, NY, page 16.

39. Jacob Neusner, ed., *Understanding American Judaism,* © 1975 by Jacob Neusner, KTAV Publishing House, Inc., New York, pages 6-29.

40. New Jersey Star-Ledger, June 28, 2001, page 18.

41. Jacob Neusner (editor), *Understanding American Judaism,* © 1975 by Jacob Neusner, KTAV Publishing House, Inc., New York, page 54.

42. *Ibid.*, page 249.

43. www.jewfaq.org/movement.htm, © 1999 by Tracey R. Rich, October 16, 2000.

44. Jacob Neusner, ed., *Understanding American Judaism,* © 1975 by Jacob Neusner, KTAV Publishing House, Inc., New York, page 227.

45. *Ibid.*, page 226.

46. OU.ORG, (www.ou.org/torah/rambam.html), © 2002 by the Union of Orthodox Jewish Congregations of America

47. *The Messianic Times,* Volume 10, Number 2, Messianic Times, Inc., Niagara Falls, NY pages 29-31.

48. Internet sites: Messianic Jewish Association of America (www.mjaa.org), Chosen People Ministries (www.chosen-people.com) and International Federation of Messianic Jews (www.ifmj.org), Messianic.com (www.messianic.com), the International Alliance of Messianic Congregations and Synagogues *(http://iamcs.mjaa.org/)*, and *The Messianic Times,* Volume 10, Number 2, Messianic Times, Inc., Niagara Falls, NY pages 29-31.

49. Paul Johnson, *A History of the Jews,* © 1987 by Paul Johnson, Harper & Row, New York, NY, page 171.

50. Raphael Patai, *The Tents of Jacob: The Diaspora - Yesterday and Today,* © 1971 by Raphael Patai, Prentice Hall, Inc., Englewood Cliffs, NJ, pages 76-79.

51. *The Jewish Population of the World,* AICE, The Jewish Student Online Research Center (JSOURCE), Sept. 14,2000, www.us-israel.org/jsource/judaism/jew-pop.html, © 2000 by The American-Israel Cooperative Enterprise

52. Bernard Lazerwitz, J. Alan Winter, Arnold Dashefsky, and Ephraim Tabory, *Jewish Choices: American Jewish Denominationalism,* © 1998 by State University of New York, State University of New York Press, Albany, NY, page 40.

53. www.jewfaq.org/movement.htm, © 1999 by Tracey R. Rich, October 16, 2000.

CHAPTER 14: THE CHRISTIAN BRANCH THRIVED

1. J.B. Lightfoot, J. R. Harmer, ed. and revised by Michael W. Holmes. *The Apostolic Fathers.* 2nd edition. Baker Books. 1989 and Tim Dowley, *Introduction To The History Of Christianity,* © 1990 by Lion Publishing, Fortress Press, Minneapolis, MN, pages 64-65.

2. Justo L. Gonzalez, *The Story of Christianity,* © 1984 by Justo L. Gonzalez, Prince Press, Peabody, MA, page 35.

3. Acts 8:1-5 and 11:19-26

4. Acts 13:4-12

5. Britannica.com, November 1, 2000, © 1999-2000 Britannica.com, Inc.

6. Philip Schaff, *History of the Christian Church,* Volume 2, Hendrickson Publishers, Peabody MA, pages 29-30.

7. Acts 8:34-40

8. The Ethiopian Orthodox Tewahedo Church, (www.students.uiuc.edu~moges/orth.html), August 9, 2000

9. Encyclopedia Coptica, www.coptic.net, © 1992-2000 Copt-Net

10. Adrian Hastings, *A World History of Christianity,* © 1999 by Adrian Hastings and the contributors, William B. Eerdmans Publishing Company, Grand Rapids, MI, pages 25-26.

11. Samuel Hugh Moffett, *A History of Christianity in Asia, Volume I: Beginnings to 1500,* © 1998 by Samuel Hugh Moffett, Orbis Books, Maryknoll, NY, pages 46-57.

12. *Ibid.*, pages 70-71.

13. *Ibid.*, pages 25-39.

14. *Ibid.*, page 34.

15. Dr. Paulos Mar Gregorios, *The Malankara (Indian) Orthodox Church, A Historical Perspective,* www.members.aol.com/manj/odox1.htm, August 9, 2000

16. *The Armenian Church in Cilicia: Centuries*

of Tradition, © 1997 by The Armenian Prelacy, www.armprelacy.org/his02.htm, March 6, 2000

17. Philip Schaff, *History of the Christian Church,* Volume 2, Hendrickson Publishers, Peabody MA, page 23.

18. *Ibid.,* page 22.

19. Adrian Hastings, *A World History of Christianity,* © 1999 by Adrian Hastings and the contributors, William B. Eerdmans Publishing Company, Grand Rapids, MI, pages 34-35.

20. A. Kenneth Curtis, J. Stephen Lang and Randy Petersen, *The 100 Most Important Events In Christian History,* © 1991 by Christian History Institute, Fleming H. Revell, Grand Rapids, MI, page 33.

21. Mark A. Noll, *Turning Points,* © 1997 by Mark Noll, Baker Books, Grand Rapids, MI, page 50.

22. A. Kenneth Curtis, J. Stephen Lang and Randy Petersen, *The 100 Most Important Events In Christian History,* © 1991 by Christian History Institute, Fleming H. Revell, Grand Rapids, MI, page 33.

23. J.D. Douglas, *Who's Who in Christian History,* © 1992 by Tyndale House Publishers, Inc., Wheaton, IL, page 172.

24. Thomas Bokenkotter, *A Concise History of the Catholic Church,* © 1990 by Thomas Bokenkotter, Doubleday, New York, NY, page 39.

25. Timothy Ware, *The Orthodox Church,* © 1997 by Timothy Ware, Penguin Books, NY, pages 19-23.

26. Mark A. Noll, *Turning Points,* © 1997 by Mark Noll, Baker Books, Grand Rapids, MI, page 50.

27. Samuel Hugh Moffett, *A History of Christianity in Asia, Volume I: Beginnings to 1500,* © 1998 by Samuel Hugh Moffett, Orbis Books, Maryknoll, NY, pages 137-145.

28. Adrian Hastings, *A World History of Christianity,* © 1999 by Adrian Hastings and the contributors, William B. Eerdmans Publishing Company, Grand Rapids, MI, page 33.

29. Kenneth Scott Latourette, *A History of Christianity,* Volume 1, © 1975 by HarperSanFrancisco, Prince Press Edition, Peabody, MA, pages 128-129.

30. *Ibid.,* pages 138-139.

31. Thomas Bokenkotter, *A Concise History of the Catholic Church,* © 1990 by Thomas Bokenkotter, Doubleday, New York, NY, page 73.

32. Peter L'Huillier, *The Church of the Ancient Councils,* © 1996 by St. Vladimir's Seminary Press, Crestwood, NY, pages 17-18.

33. Justo L. Gonzalez, *The Story of Christianity,* © 1984 by Justo L. Gonzalez, Prince Press, Peabody, MA, pages 158-179.

34. Samuel Hugh Moffett, *A History of Christianity in Asia, Volume I: Beginnings to 1500,* © 1998 by Samuel Hugh Moffett, Orbis Books, Maryknoll, NY, page 70.

35. *Ibid.,* pages 169-175.

36. Justo L. Gonzalez, *The Story of Christianity,* © 1984 by Justo L. Gonzalez, Prince Press, Peabody, MA, pages 250-254.

37. Justo L. Gonzalez, *A History of Christian Thought, Volume 1: From the Beginnings to the Council of Chalcedon,* © 1987 by Abingdom Press, Nashville, TN pages 368-376.

38. *Ibid.,* pages 376-380.

39. *Encyclopedia Coptica,* © 1992-2000 Copt-Net, (www.Coptic.net) page 3, August 8, 2000

40. Samuel Hugh Moffett, *A History of Christianity in Asia, Volume I: Beginnings to 1500,* © 1998 by Samuel Hugh Moffett, Orbis Books, Maryknoll, NY, pages 192-193.

41. *Ibid.,* pages 186–204.

42. *The Armenian Church in Cilicia: Centuries of Tradition,* The Armenian Church in Cilicia, (www.armprelacy.org/his02.htm), © 1997 by the Armenian Prelacy, September 8, 2000.

43. Earle E. Cairns, *Christianity Through The Centuries,* 3rd Edition, © 1996 by Earle E. Cairns, Zondervan Publishing House, Grand Rapids, MI, page 121.

44. *Ibid.,* pages 123-124.

45. Elizabeth Isichei, *A History of Christianity in Africa,* © 1995 by Elizabeth Isichei, William B. Eerdmans Publishing Company, Grand Rapids, MI, pages 30-31.

46. Timothy Ware, *The Orthodox Church,* © 1997 by Timothy Ware, Penguin Books, NY, page 45.

47. Earle E. Cairns, *Christianity Through The Centuries*, 3rd Edition, © 1996 by Earle E. Cairns, Zondervan Publishing House, Grand Rapids, MI, page 198.

48. Timothy Ware, *The Orthodox Church*, © 1997 by Timothy Ware, Penguin Books, NY, pages 59-60.

49. 2 Kings 21:1-26

50. Luke 6:27-36

51. Richard P. McBrien, *Lives of the Popes*, © 1997 by Richard P. McBrien, Harper Collins, New York, NY.

52. A. Kenneth Curtis, J. Stephen Lang and Randy Petersen, *The 100 Most Important Events In Christian History*, © 1991 by Christian History Institute, Fleming H. Revell, Grand Rapids, MI, pages 77-78.

53. J.D. Douglas, *Who's Who in Christian History*, © 1992 by Tyndale House Publishers, Inc., Wheaton, IL, page 735.

54. *Ibid.*, pages 334-335.

55. *Ibid.*, pages 607-608.

56. *Ibid.*, pages 433-437.

57. Earle E. Cairns, *Christianity Through The Centuries*, 3rd Edition, © 1996 by Earle E. Cairns, Zondervan Publishing House, Grand Rapids, MI, pages 289-291.

58. *Ibid.*, pages 745-747.

59. A. Kenneth Curtis, J. Stephen Lang and Randy Petersen, *The 100 Most Important Events In Christian History*, © 1991 by Christian History Institute, Fleming H. Revell, Grand Rapids, MI, pages 108-109.

60. *Modern History Sourcebook*, www.fordham.edu/halsall/mod/map16rel.gif, September 29, 2000 and *The Baker Atlas Of Christian History*, © 1997 by Angus Hudson Ltd / Tim Dowley & Peter Wyatt trading as Three's Company, Baker Books, Grand Rapids, MI, pages 116-117.

61. Patrick Johnstone, *Operation World*, © 1993 by Patrick Johnstone, Zondervan Publishing, Grand Rapids, MI, page 21.

62. *Ibid.*, page 21.

63. Elizabeth Isichei, *A History of Christianity in Africa*, © 1995 by Elizabeth Isichei, William B. Eerdmans Publishing Company, Grand Rapids, MI, page 1.

64. *The World Almanac and Book of Facts 1992*, © 1991 by Pharos Books, New York, NY, pages 724-725.

65. Philip Schaff, *The Creeds of Christendom*, reprinted 1998 by Baker Books, Grand Rapids, MI, pages 27-29.

66. Romans 11:1-36

67. Genesis 12:3 (JPS)

CHAPTER 15: SO, HOW COULD THIS BE JUDAISM?

1. Adrian Hastings, *A World History of Christianity*, © 1999 by Adrian Hastings and the contributors, William B. Eerdmans Publishing Company, Grand Rapids, MI, page 28.

2. Genesis 17:9-14

3. Exodus 12:48-50

4. Exodus 2:16-21 and Numbers 12:1

5. Joshua 2:1, Ruth 1:4-5 and Matthew 1:2-6

6. Raphael Patai, *The Tents of Jacob, The Diaspora—Yesterday and Today*, © 1971 by Raphael Patai, Prentice Hall, Englewood Cliffs, NJ, pages 73-74.

7. Hershel Shanks, ed., *Christianity and Rabbinic Judaism*, © 1992 by the Biblical Archaeology Society, Washington, DC, pages 5-7.

8. *Who is a Jew?* (www.jewfaq.org/whois-jew.htm), © 1995-1999 by Tracey R Rich, pages 3-4.

9. Matthew 5:38-48, John 16:2-4, John 18:1-40 and 19:1-11

10. 1 Samuel 2:12-17

11. 1 Kings 11:1-8

12. 1 Kings 12:25-33 and 13:33-34

13. 1 Kings 18:17-19

14. 2 Kings 16:1-4

15. 2 Kings 21:1-17

16. 2 Kings 18:11-12

17. Jeremiah 29:1-23

18. A. Kenneth Curtis, J. Stephen Lang and Randy Petersen, *The 100 Most Important Events In Christian History*, © 1991 by Christian History Institute, Fleming H. Revell, Grand Rapids, MI, page 78.

19. Philip Schaff, *History of the Christian Church*, Volume 5, 1996 Hendrickson Publishers, Peabody, MA, pages 442-444.

20. Justo L. Gonzalez, *The Story of Christianity*, © 1984 by Justo L. Gonzalez, Prince Press, Peabody, MA, page 145.

21. A. Kenneth Curtis, J. Stephen Lang and Randy Petersen, *The 100 Most Important Events In Christian History*, © 1991 by Christian History Institute, Fleming H. Revell, Grand Rapids, MI, pages 111-112.

22. *Britannica.com*,
(http://www.britannica.com/seo/c/council-of-troubles/), © 1999-2000 Britannica.com Inc.

23. Louis Finkelstein, *The Jews, Their History*, © 1970 by Louis Finkelstein, Schocken Books, New York, NY, pages 233-234.

24. Jonathan Riley-Smith, *The Crusades, A Short History*, © 1987 by Jonathan Riley-Smith, Yale University Press, New Haven, CT, pages 130-139 and 161-166.

25. Thomas Bokenkotter, *A Concise History of the Catholic Church*, © 1990 by Thomas Bokenkotter, Doubleday, New York, NY, page 118.

26. R.C. Wetzel, *A Chronology of Biblical Christianity*, The Ages Digital Library, Version 1.0, © 1997 by Ages Software, Albany, OR, page 131.

27. Jonathan Riley-Smith, *The Crusades, A Short History*, © 1987 by Jonathan Riley-Smith, Yale University Press, New Haven, CT, pages 166-167.

28. *Ibid.*, pages 233-234.

29. *Concentration Camp Dachau 1933-1945*, © 1978 by Comite International de Dachau, Munich, Germany, pages 37-45.

30. Erwin W. Lutzer, *Hitler's Cross*, © 1995 by Erwin W. Lutzer, Moody Press, Chicago, pages 111-149.

31. Richard McBrien, *Lives of the Popes*, © 1997 by Richard McBrien, Harper Collins, New York, NY, page 362.

32. Georges Passelecq and Bernard Suchecky, *The Hidden Encyclical of Pius XI*, © 1997 by Harcourt Brace & Company, New York, NY, pages 101-110.

33. *Ibid.*, page 138

34. Arthur C. Cochrane, *The Church's Confession Under Hitler*, © 1976 by Pickwick Press, Pittsburgh, PA, (Reprinted from the 1962 Westminster Press edition), page 40.

35. Richard McBrien, *Lives of the Popes*, © 1997 by Richard McBrien, Harper Collins, New York, NY, page 180.

36. *Ibid.*, page 180.

37. Paul Johnson, *A History of the Jews*, © 1987 by Paul Johnson, Harper & Row, New York, NY, page 216.

38. Richard McBrien, *Lives of the Popes*, © 1997 by Richard McBrien, Harper Collins, New York, NY, page 255.

39. Nechama Tec, *When Light Pieced The Darkness, Christian Rescue Of Jews In Nazi-Occupied Poland*, © 1986 by Oxford University Press, New York, page 10.

CHAPTER 16: IS THERE PROOF?

1. Alfred J. Hoerth, *Archaeology & the Old Testament*, © 1998 by Alfred J. Hoerth, Baker Books, Grand Rapids, MI, page 326.

2. Randall Price, *The Stones Cry Out*, © 1977 by World of the Bible Ministries, Inc., Harvest House Publishers, Eugene, OR, pages 114-123.

3. Frederic G. Kenyon, *Our Bible and the Ancient Manuscripts Being a History of the Text and its Translations*, © 1998 by Lazarus Ministry Press, (originally published by Eyre and Spottiswoode, London, 1895), page 17.

4. Randall Price, *The Stones Cry Out*, © 1977 by World of the Bible Ministries, Inc., Harvest House Publishers, Eugene, OR, pages 77-78.

5. *Ibid.*, page 67.

6. *Ibid.*, page 67.

7. *Ibid.*, pages 66-69.

8. Alfred J. Hoerth, *Archaeology & the Old Testament*, © 1998 by Alfred J. Hoerth, Baker Books, Grand Rapids, MI, pages 72, 82, 91, and 106.

9. John F. Walvoord, *Major Bible Prophecies*, © 1991 by John F. Walvoord, Zondervan Publishing House, Grand Rapids, MI, pages 149-153.

10. Frederic G. Kenyon, *Our Bible and the Ancient Manuscripts Being a History of the Text and its Translations*, © 1998 by Lazarus Ministry Press, (originally published by Eyre and Spottiswoode, London, 1895), page 33.

11. James C. Vanderkam, *The Dead Sea Scrolls Today*, © 1994 by Wm. B. Eerdmans Publishing Co., Grand Rapids, MI, pages 30-31.

12. Norman Geisler and William E. Nix, *A General Introduction to the Bible*, 1968, Moody Press, Chicago, page 263 as quoted in: Josh McDowell, *Evidence That Demands A Verdict*, Volume 1, © 1979 by Campus Crusade for Christ, Here's Life Publishers, San Bernadino, page 58.

13. Robert Dick Wilson, *A Scientific*

Investigation of the Old Testament, Moody Press, Chicago, IL, 1959 as quoted in: Josh McDowell, *Evidence That Demands A Verdict*, Volume 1, © 1979 by Campus Crusade for Christ, Here's Life Publishers, San Bernadino, page 55.

14. William Ryan and Walter Pitman, *Noah's Flood*, © 1998 by Walter C. Pitman III and William B. F. Ryan, Simon & Schuster, New York, NY

15. Alfred J. Hoerth, *Archaeology & the Old Testament*, © 1998 by Alfred J. Hoerth, Baker Books, Grand Rapids, MI, page 210.

16. Randall Price, *The Stones Cry Out*, © 1977 by World of the Bible Ministries, Inc., Harvest House Publishers, Eugene, OR, pages 114-123.

17. Alfred J. Hoerth, *Archaeology & the Old Testament*, © 1998 by Alfred J. Hoerth, Baker Books, Grand Rapids, MI, page 351.

18. Ezekiel 14:13-14

19. Daniel 9:1-2 and 2 Chronicles 36:12

20. 2 Kings 20:1-21 and 2 Chronicles 32:1-33

21. Ezra 5:1

22. Exodus 2:11-15, 1 Kings 19:1-4, 2 Samuel 11:1-5, and Judges 6:25-27

23. Asian DNA Enters Human Origins Fray, *Science News*, October 3, 1996 and *The New York Times*, November 23, 1995 (A 1:1) and May 26, 1995 (A 16:1)

24. Job 26:7

25. Michael Behe, *Darwin's Black Box*, © 1996 by Michael Behe, Simon & Schuster, New York, NY and Phillip Johnson, *Darwin On Trial*, © 1993 by Phillip Johnson, Intervarsity Press, Downers Grove, IL

26. William M. Ramsay, *The Bearing of Recent Discovery on the Trustworthiness of the New Testament*, Baker Book House, Grand Rapids, 1953, as quoted in: Josh McDowell, *Evidence That Demands A Verdict*, Volume 1, © 1979 by Campus Crusade for Christ, Here's Life Publishers, San Bernadino, page 71.

27. Lee Strobel, *The Case For Christ, A Journalist's Personal Investigation of the Evidence for Jesus*, © 1998 by Lee Strobel, Zondervan Publishing House, Grand Rapids, MI, pages 60-63.

28. Josh McDowell, *Evidence That Demands a Verdict*, Volume 1, © 1979 by Campus Crusade for Christ, Here Life Publishers,

Inc., San Bernadino, CA, page 50.

29. Frederic G. Kenyon, *The Bible and Archeology*, 1940, Harper and Row, New York, as quoted in: Josh McDowell, Evidence That Demands A Verdict, Volume 1, © 1979 by Campus Crusade for Christ, Here's Life Publishers, San Bernadino, page 41.

30. Lee Strobel, *The Case For Christ, A Journalist's Personal Investigation of the Evidence for Jesus*, © 1998 by Lee Strobel, Zondervan Publishing House, Grand Rapids, MI, pages 64-65.

31. Josh McDowell, *Evidence That Demands a Verdict*, Volume 1, © 1979 by Campus Crusade for Christ, Here Life Publishers, Inc., San Bernadino, CA, page 43.

32. Josephus, *Antiquities of the Jews*, 18.3.3

33. *Babylonian Talmud*, Sanhedrin 43A

34. *Eusebius' Ecclesiastical History*, (1.13.6-9), C.F. Cruise, trans. © 1998 by Hendrickson Publishers, Inc., page 30.

35. Josh McDowell, *Evidence That Demands a Verdict*, Volume 1, © 1979 by Campus Crusade for Christ, Here Life Publishers, Inc., San Bernadino, CA, page 84.

36. Lee Strobel, *The Case For Christ, A Journalist's Personal Investigation of the Evidence for Jesus*, © 1998 by Lee Strobel, Zondervan Publishing House, Grand Rapids, MI, pages 84-85.

37. F.F. Bruce, *The New Testament Documents: Are They Reliable?*, © 1960 Intervarsity Press, Downers Grove, IL, page 31.

38. Matthew 21:15-16, Mark 10:46-52, Luke 1:30-33, Revelation 22:16, 2 Timothy 2:8-9

39. Matthew 1:1, Mark 1:1, Luke 9:20-22, John 1:35-41, Romans 1:1-4, 1 Peter 1:3, Jude 1:21

40. Matthew 14:28-33, Mark 16:19, Luke 24:1-6, Romans 1:7, Jude 1:21, 1 Peter 1:3-5, James 1:1, Revelation 22:20-21

41. Mark 1:1, Luke 1:31-35, John 1:49-51, Romans 1:1-4, 1 Peter 1:3-5, Matthew 14:28-33

42. James 2:1, Jude 1:3-4

43. John 20:28, John 1:1-14, 1 John 5:20, Romans 5:9, Colossians 1:15-20, Philippians 2:5-11

44. 1 Corinthians 15:3-8, 1 Peter 3:18, John 1:29, Matthew 26:26-29, Mark 2:9-12, Luke 24:35-47, Jude 1:21-25

45. Matthew 3:11, Mark 1:6-9, John 14:26, Luke 11:13, Acts 2, Romans 5:2, Jude 1:19-20, 1 Peter 1:12 and 4:14, James 4:4-5

46. Hebrews 8:1-13, 1 Corinthians 14:24-25, Matthew 26:28, Mark 14:24-25

47. Matthew 5:17, Acts 3:16-18, John 5:39-47, Romans 1:1-4, 1 Peter 1:6-12, Mark 14:46-49

48. Revelation 1:4-8, Matthew 26:63-64, Mark 14:61-64, Acts 1:9-11, 2 Peter 3:1-18, 1 Thessalonians 1:15-17, James 5:7-8, Jude 1:1-25

49. 1 Peter 1:18-22, Revelation 11:15, 1 Corinthians 15:22-28, Luke 1:30-33

50. Ephesians 2:8-9, Romans 3:21-31

51. James 2:17

52. Acts 15:1-21

53. *Eusebius' Ecclesiastical History*, (1.13.6-9), C.F. Cruise, trans. © 1998 by Hendrickson Publishers, Inc., page 30.

54. Samuel Hugh Moffett, *A History of Christianity in Asia, Volume I: Beginnings to 1500*, © 1998 by Samuel Hugh Moffett, Orbis Books, Maryknoll, NY, pages 46-56.

55. John 13:18-30 and Mark 10:32-34

56. John 12:20-36, Mark 8:31 and 10:32-34

57. John 13:31-38

58. Mark 8:31

59. John 14:15-27

60. Matthew 21:12-19

61. Matthew 24:1-2 and 15-24 and Luke 21:20-24

62. F.F. Bruce, *The New Testament Documents: Are They Reliable?* © 1960 Intervarsity Press, Downers Grove, IL, page 12.

63. Mark 13:1-36

64. Mark 13: 22-27

65. Daniel 7:13-14

66. Joel 3:1-2 (Joel 2:28-29 in Christian translations)

67. Ezekiel 37:14 and Job 33:4

68. Joel 3:1 (Joel 2:28 in Christian translations)

69. Jeremiah 31:33

70. Ezekiel 36:26-27

71. John 16:1-15, John 6:62-63, and 2 Corinthians 3:6-18

72. Billy Graham, *How To Be Born Again*, © 1989 by Billy Graham, Word Books, Dallas, TX and Billy Graham, *The Holy Spirit*, © 1978 by Billy Graham, Word Books, Waco, TX

73. Judges 3:10-11, Judges 6:34-7:22, 1 Samuel 10:1-11 and 2 Samuel 23:1-5

74. Psalm 32:1-5, Psalm 38:18, and Psalm 51:1-11

75. Exodus 31:2-3, Numbers 11:16-17, Numbers 24:2, 2 Chronicles 15:1, 2 Chronicles 20:14, 2 Chronicles 24:20, Judges 3:9-10, Judges 6:34, Judges 11:29, Judges 15:10-14, 1 Samuel 10:1-9 and 1 Samuel 16:13

76. 1 Samuel 16:14

77. Ezekiel 37:1-28

78. Deuteronomy 5:26 and 6:5 (in some translations: 5:26 is 5:29)

79. Leviticus 19:18

80. Marvin W. Cowan, *Mormon Claims Answered*, © 1989 by Marvin W. Cowan, Utah Christian Publication, Salt Lake City, UT, pages 57-61.

81. 1 Nephi 18:25

82. *Encyclopedia Britannica*, June 26, 2000 Web-site reference for South America, (http://www.britannica.com/bcom/eb/article/3/0,5716,117563+8+109561,00.html), © 1999-2000 Britannica.com Inc.

83. Ed Decker and Dave Hunt, *The God Makers*, © 1997 by Ed Decker and Dave Hunt, Harvest House Publishers, Eugene, OR, pages 111-116.

84. Marvin W. Cowan, *Mormon Claims Answered*, © 1989 by Marvin W. Cowan, Utah Christian Publication, Salt Lake City, UT, pages 54-58.

85. Anthony Hoekema, *Mormonism*, © 1963 by William Eerdman's Publishing Co., Grand Rapids, MI, pages 36-43.

86. 1 and 2 Nephi contain seventeen chapters from the KJV translation of Isaiah: 1 Nephi 20-21 is Isaiah 48-49, 2 Nephi 7-8 is Isaiah 50-51, and 2 Nephi 12-24 is Isaiah 2-14.